No Easy Choices

GW00775745

They that go down to the sea in ships, that do business in great waters; These see the works of the Lord, and His wonders in the deep.

For he commandeth, and raiseth the stormy wind, which lifteth up the waves thereof.

— Psalms 107, 23 – 25

NO EASY CHOICES

A Personal Account of Life

on the

Carrier HMS Illustrious 1940 – 43

Albert H. Jones
ex POSM Royal Navy

and

Michael H. Jones BA

A Square One Publication

First published in 1994 by
Square One Publications
Saga House, Sansome Place, Worcester, WR1 1UA

© Albert H. Jones and Michael H. Jones 1994

ISBN: 1 872017 85 1

British Library Cataloguing in Publication Data
is available for this book

Typeset in Times Roman 11 on 12 by Avon Dataset, Bidford-on-Avon,
Warwickshire B50 4JH
Printed in England by Antony Rowe Ltd, Chippenham, England

Dedication

To Eric, Joe, Frank, and Wallace and to all my shipmates from Illustrious who are no longer with us.

Acknowledgements

We wish to express our sincere gratitude and appreciation to all those who gave us help and encouragement in the writing of this book.

In particular we would like to thank Jim Newton, a shipmate from Illustrious, stoker, and classmate from Guz training division. His help in contacting publishers and guiding us around London was invaluable, not to mention his memories of the old ship which helped to fill in the gaps.

We would also like to extend thanks to other members of the Old Illustrious Association like Arthur Hobson, Tom O'Loughlin, and Bill Lawson whose anecdotes helped to inspire us; and of course Ethel Needham who along with her late husband Wallace, an ex-Jack Dusty made the Old Illustrious Association a reality by their perseverance.

A sincere thanks to Jack Williams, founder and historian of the Algerine's Association – minesweepers – whose advice was of great assistance in looking for a publisher.

Finally, to Inge for her patience, enthusiasm, understanding, and proofreading.

Last but not least we want to thank Mary Wilkinson of Square One Publications whose most favourable review of our book was instrumental in deciding to go ahead with publication.

Contents

Foreword

In World War Two, Albert Jones served as a stoker aboard two Royal Navy ships from April 1940 to June 1946. Both vessels were of completely different types in terms of their size and roles. The first was a mighty aircraft carrier of some 23,000 tons and a crew of about 1,400 men. The other was a deep-sea minesweeper of only 1,000 tons and carrying a little less than 100 men.

The carrier HMS Illustrious was built as a new breed of fighting ship. Soon she distinguished herself by proving that a few aircraft armed with bombs and torpedoes and manned by determined, courageous pilots could make the traditional once thought invinceable battleship obsolete.

Something similar may be said of HMS Rosario which too belonged to a new breed of fighting ships. She was a member of a new class of small vessels called Algerines which were designed to combat the growing underwater menace of sophisticated sea mines. Unlike the carrier, she did not individually achieve fame and glory but collectively, these small ships, 110 in all, earned respect, admiration, and the reputation for being efficient and daring. These ships took part in most of the major landings such as North Africa, Sicily, Anzio, Normandy, and the South of France and were present in all theatres of operations including the Pacific.

By war's end, these ships were still urgently needed for the enormous task of clearing the shipping lanes of untold thousands of mines laid by the enemy and Allies alike. A very dangerous and nerve-wracking undertaking for those taking part but a job that had to be done nevertheless, and taking another six years to complete.

Both ships had some things in common and survived the war. One made history and added a new concept of warfare. The other with her sister ships proved that new and more sophisticated mines could only be beaten by modern technology instead of using the old method of having vessels which were considered expendable and needlessly losing many brave men.

This then is Albert Jones's story of how it was.

Introduction

It is now over fifty years since the beginning of the Second World War. What I experienced during the war was a mixture of all sorts. Some was good and some was bad, much of it was quite out of the ordinary because we lived in an extraordinary time in history, the likes of which we will never see again.

Whenever I have told people about my life back then, they have often commented that I should write a book about it. Until recently, the idea had not really interested me seriously.

As the bewildering pace of change has unfolded on the international scene in Europe with the collapse of the Soviet Union, the Eastern Block countries have been struggling with their new independance and trying to rebuild their shattered economies. With this and the end of the Cold War, I have changed my mind about the idea of writing my story. Everything we see in Europe is a result either directly or indirectly of the last great conflict.

The most disturbing change to me was the speed of German reunification. There was almost no protest or concern whatsoever from the forces of occupation who themselves fought to bring the rule of tyranny to an end in Nazi-Germany. Since reunification we are seeing scenes on our televisions about Germany, where large numbers of youths carrying flags with the Swastika and Iron Cross are openly displaying their Nazi beliefs and their hatred by violence. This brings back bitter memories of scenes reminiscent of pre-war Germany. Many people try to play this down by saying they are isolated incidents, because they refuse to face the truth that this is a resurgence of National Socialism which could eventually lead to the unthinkable possibility of another world war in this nuclear age where there can be no winners, only losers. We must not allow another conflict as global as the last one to occur again. Therefore, if for no other reason than focussing people's attention on this stark reality, writing this book will be well worth all the effort.

Albert Jones
Portage la Prairie
Canada

January 1994

Chapter One

The Decision to Join Up

In ordinary life, people have to make decisions of one sort or another every day. These choices may be what to have for lunch or supper or they may be business decisions where money and power may be gained or lost. Seldom are we required to make a choice that could put our life on the line by signing something that could turn out to be our own death warrant. However, in the years 1939 – 40, countless thousands of people did exactly that when they flocked to the colours for military service.

In July 1939, just prior to the outbreak of hostilities, the choice was made simpler for some by a partial military service call up. This call up was for six months army training for men age 20 – 21.

For others, the choice was not so simple. There were those like myself who were caught at a crossroads. Being not quite 20 years old, there was still enough time to enlist voluntarily in the branch of service preferred. In the event of war, I still had the slim hope that my choice would bring me through with the minimum of wounds or scars. Soon, my decision would turn into a dilemma which only time and events would prove correct.

The Munich Crisis of 1938 where Hitler's demands for control of the Sudetenland in Czechoslovakia had been appeased by the British and French governments had passed, but darkening war clouds still hung. Everyone felt it was only a question of time.

The Great Depression still lingered and unemployment eroded at the self respect and dignity of all those without jobs and their families. I worked as a weaver in the Lancashire cotton mills making ladder-web tape used in Venetian blinds in warmer climates. The mills suffered badly trying to compete with fierce competition from abroad and especially Japan. As a result, my work became a series of layoffs with only a week or two here and there.

Gradually, my situation became intolerable, particularly when they put me on a loom (weaving machine) which was so old and lumbersome it wouldn't work properly for more than a few minutes at a time without breaking down. It was a sheer monster. The reason this old relic had been resurrected and pressed into service was that the government had placed a large order for .303 machine gun ammunition belts. This was another sign that the 'Peace In Our Time' that Sir Neville Chamberlain spoke of when he returned from Munich was soon to come to an end.

After many days of wrestling with this monstrosity of a loom, I asked the foreman if he could put me on another machine as this one was useless, but it all fell on deaf ears. I made up my mind to take the next day off though I could ill afford the loss of pay, to go to the Royal Navy recruiting office downtown near Albert Square in Picadilly, Manchester. Strangely enough, the office was just around the corner from the First Great War cenotaph.

The date by now was mid-July, 1939, only a matter of weeks before the outbreak of WW II. Before going inside, I looked long and hard at the glamorous posters of sailors sitting on the barrels of the guns of a battleship. Other pictures were of happy, smiling sailors visiting exotic ports of call surrounded by girls with the slogan 'Join the Navy and see the world'. My first impression was how smart looking the men and uniforms appeared, after all this was the British Navy, the most powerful and respected in the world. Like everyone else, I confidently felt that no enemy including Germany would ever get past Britain's pride and joy and reach our shores. Resolutely but with butterflies in my stomach I then went inside and told the petty officer at the front desk that I would like to enlist.

One big question remained, it was still peacetime and to join one had to sign up for twelve years. If accepted there would be no backing out but would it have to be for the full twelve years or just the war?

The Navy had very high entrance requirements I was told. Only the best and fittest would be accepted. You had to be British born and not wear eyeglasses except in certain circumstances. Why not? They had plenty of eager volunteers on a waiting list and plenty of reservists so they could afford to have high standards.

Now that I had made the decision to join up, I had another

unexpected choice to make. What branch would I enter? Able seaman sounded attractive and you only had to do seven years active service and then five on the reserve and get paid for it. Looking back, it seemed that there was an unexplainable force at work within me. Perhaps it was fate guiding my decisions because I chose to be a stoker in the engineering branch, which was a straight twelve year engagement.

After passing the required physical, eyesight, and academic tests, they told me to go home and wait until called. There was no signing or any hard and fast commitment yet. I didn't take an oath of allegiance but the Navy doesn't take an oath anyway because of its past history of press-ganging men into service. This method of augmenting manpower in the King's navy of old was the cause of some resentment to say the least.

Little did I realize that soon I would have to make what I considered to be the most crucial decision of my life. I am now certain that this would have a great influence on my future as to whether I actually had one. The fact that I survived the war proved to me that the best course of action is to stick to one's guns and let fate do the rest regardless of the odds.

I arrived back home that afternoon with mixed emotions about what I had done. I felt proud but yet a bit apprehensive about my life ahead which was still as yet unknown. Looking at my parents' faces, I saw a sadness that I will never forget in my dear old Dad. He was by now in his eighties and I, being his only son of a second, late marriage, was everything he lived for. Joining the Navy meant that I would completely disappear from his life forever. My mother was a little younger and she seemed to stand up to the news better but was no less heartbroken and shed many a tear. After questions as to why I should enlist when still only nineteen, my defence was that I would have to go anyway on the next military call up. At least this way I had some choice of service still left open to me.

I remember a close pal, Jack Williams, who was a few months older than myself. He went in the first batch of conscripts that July, supposedly for only six months army service. That group of men didn't return until after the war ended six years later. Many like Jack were killed in France with the British Expeditionary Force (BEF) or suffered similar fates elsewhere.

The next day I went back to work at the mill as usual somewhat refreshed and with a renewed determination to make my decrepit old machine work well enough so that I wouldn't go over the edge in frustration and do something I would regret like chucking my job or worse, getting fired after sabotaging it. To go back on the dole again was unthinkable; besides, I wouldn't be entitled to any, not having enough stamps to get benefits. The requirement was to work six months in order to receive money for six months. Ironically, the amount you got on the dole was the same as a stoker's starting wage in the Navy, seventeen shillings and sixpence (17s 6 d.) per week. The only other alternative was an even more meagre welfare allowance called the Means Test on which one could barely exist. With these thoughts I struggled on. At least I was consoled by the thought that the Navy would soon call me and the firm was paying me a flat rate of two pounds a week until I could get the loom to work properly.

The very first thing I actually did that morning when I arrived at work was tell another close friend and workmate Eric Taylor what I had done the previous day. When told, Eric's face lit up in a big smile and he acted a little envious because we often talked about joining the Navy. He never gave me any indication of what his immediate plans were but to my astonishment, a week later he went and did exactly the same as me and joined the RN.

Eric was a well built lad, blond-haired and blue-eyed a contrast to my smaller, darker, and more boyish features yet he was nearly two years younger than I. Eric had no need to worry about being conscripted at that time. He could have sat back and probably earned bigger wages on essential war work. Besides, he was the main breadwinner of his family because he had no Dad, just an elder sister and younger brother. Compared to my loom, his machine ran smooth and fast and gave very little trouble. Nevertheless, just like in my case, Eric's mother was heartbroken too.

I'm sure Winston Churchill took us into account when he spoke of blood, toil, sweat, and tears in one of his speeches. We were just a few of the many more yet to come from uncountable mothers and fathers all over. At least we came back.

The crisis in Europe came to a head on September 1, 1939 when Germany's unprovoked attack on Poland resulted in a forty-eight hour ultimatum from Britain and France. The whole world watched and waited for the outcome of this ultimatum which expired at 11 am, Sunday, September 3. That morning I sat with my whole family by the radio in the front living room of our rented house on the corner of Ayres Road, Old Trafford, Manchester as we listened to Prime Minister Sir Neville Chamberlain tell us that no word had been received from Germany and that a state of war now existed between Britain and Germany because of the Anglo-Polish alliance which guaranteed Poland's security. A general mobilization of the forces and conscription would begin almost immediately.

Shortly after my twentieth birthday on the nineteenth of that month, another batch of men age twenty to twenty-one were required to register for military service at the local unemployment exchange (employment office). This was the moment of truth where I really had to decide whether to go where they sent me, possibly the army, or tell them I had previously enlisted in the Navy. I was only on the waiting list to be called and the man at the office must have checked my story because I never heard from them any more.

The next day, I decided that I should act fast. I went down to the naval recruiting office with the intention of asking if I could volunteer just for the war now that hostilities had begun. After all, I would be taking the same risks as if I had gone in for twelve years. What would be the difference? Unfortunately, the first thing that I saw in the doorway when I arrived was a sign chalked on a blackboard in big letters that read 'No HO's Required'. HO stood for Hostilities Only. This was somewhat of a shock but it didn't deter me from going in and asking.

The curt answer I got was that if I didn't want to join for twelve years on their terms, I could go and take my chances on the call up instead. This would probably have meant going in the army. Reluctantly, I said that I would stick with a twelve year engagement and wait until they called me. Even now that war had begun, the Navy was still being picky but it would only last for a while.

Too late for me but soon the Navy would need large numbers of men who couldn't be obtained through their regular, peacetime recruiting methods. This was especially apparent with events like what happened on September 17 when HMS Courageous, an aircraft carrier was torpedoed and sunk in the English Channel with 514 men killed. Soon after on October 14, the battleship HMS Royal Oak was sunk at her anchorage in Scapa Flow by a U-boat with a loss of 833 men. These huge

5

Albert Jones with parents Mary and William, Old Trafford
Manchester, just after joining Illustrious – May 1940

losses of regular, peacetime sailors would have to be replaced,
mostly through conscription.

Eric and I continued to work at the mill for a few more weeks
and I did manage to persevere with my loom so that it was
working well enough to produce. Finally, at the beginning of

November I received a notice instructing me to report to the recruiting office with the bare necessities on the morning of November 8, 1939. From there with other recruits we would be sent by train to Plymouth to report to the Royal Naval barracks at Devonport for naval training. Exactly one week later, my friend was given the same instructions as myself and as it turned out, we were to share the same life and dangers for the next three and a half years until we were separated.

Chapter Two

Life in the Training Division

After a sad goodbye to my Mum, Dad, and family, I took the double-decker bus from Old Trafford to St. Peter's Square from which I walked to the recruiting office a short distance away, arriving just before 8 am as this great, industrial city was coming back to life. People began to go about their usual morning routine and one could hardly tell there was a war on except for a few building protected by sandbags.

Already at the office, a small group of lads my own age were waiting. Oddly enough, I didn't know any of them yet, but little did I know that some of them would become shipmates. Soon after, all our names were checked off a list by the staff and after signing some documents, we were each handed a florin (two shilling piece). Traditionally, acceptance of the King's shilling was the final step in joining up. No oath of allegiance was taken as the Navy doesn't take one. Another point about the two shillings was that the Navy never paid money in odd numbers, always to the nearest two shillings. I was now officially in the Royal Navy and wouldn't be able to get out in less than twelve years unless deemed unfit for further service through war wounds or extreme extenuating circumstances of a compassionate nature or getting killed.

After all the initial paraphernalia was completed, we were taken on foot to London Road Railway Station, now called Picadilly Station, escorted by a PO (petty officer) and one or two killicks (leading hands). These sailors were to be our escorts all the way to Plymouth. At the station, we waited until tickets were arranged and then boarded a third class coach on the midday train. The trip takes about eleven hours but I don't recall being given anything to eat or even the customary bag lunch the Navy provides on long trips. As we were under escort, we were not allowed onto the platform at any stops to buy a snack in case anyone didn't get back on for a variety of reasons. In those days of class distinction, third class passengers were not provided with a buffet car and so we were to endure a long, tiresome, and hungry trip.

At prearranged stations along the way, more lads destined to become sailors were picked up and our group swelled to two or three dozen including the escorts.

Late that night we arrived at the Plymouth station very tired, hungry, and rather stiff. We were told to muster on the platform and then were escorted through the barriers into the main station. From there we waited quite a while until the transport arrived. Some of us were quite cold as we stood and waited on that cold, damp, November night. Finally, after nearly an hour we were told to go outside where a couple of dark blue lorries with RN in big white letters stood. The tailgates were dropped and the heavy canvas flaps thrown up. We were ordered to climb in.

Down Plymouth's dimly lit streets we rumbled. Sitting rather uncomfortably and feeling cramped we hardly spoke and felt apprehensive as we wondered what would be next. Eventually we came to a bumpy stop and heard voices followed by the clanging of a big iron gate being opened. The lorry moved ahead a few yards, then stopped again. It appeared that we were now inside the Royal Naval Barracks in Devonport. The momentary halt was to allow the officer of the watch at the guardhouse to report us in officially in the same manner one would do as if going aboard ship. We moved off again over the lumpy cobblestone roads of this centuries old base until coming to a final stop a few moments later. We were told to jump out and directed to go down some dimly lit steps which led into the basement level of what appeared to be a storeroom. It was exactly that, a place where we were to be kitted out.

We were each given a hammock with the rope and nettles and a blanket.* They told us to fix the nettles to the hammock and sling it up to one of the overhead hooks attached to steel beams, just like aboard ship. We were all quite mystified with these instructions as none of us had ever slept in a hammock before. They then gave us rough directions on how to fasten the nettles to the hammock and put the thin palliasse inside. No pillow was

---

*Naval terminology for hammock rope and nettles is clews and lashings.

9

included, for this I rolled my clothes up. I did the best I could and like everyone else, I copied the person next to me. The time by now must have been 1:30 am so the staff were as tired as we were and it had been a very long day. All anyone wanted was to get some proper 'kip' (sleep) before the inevitable wakey-wakey bugle call. Reveille would come all too soon and there would be no sleeping in, in here. I hoisted myself into my hammock by the overhead bar and settled down to sleep on my back like a banana. This was the end of day one in the Royal Navy.

It only seemed as though I had closed my eyes for a few minutes when I was awakened by the sound of a bugle blowing and a voice shouting over the PA system, 'Wakey, wakey! Lash up and stow!' All the lights came on and someone was in the room making sure we were awake and making an attempt to get up. I had no idea what time it was. I didn't have a watch. I couldn't afford such a luxury. Our disturber of sweet dreams appeared to be the barrack room duty PO.

We tumbled out of our hammocks and did the best we could with our limited knowledge to lash and stow them in racks along the wall. The time was just past 7:00 am and it was still dark outside.

After a quick wash we were herded to one of the mess halls where we queued on some stone steps at the rear entrance. Every few seconds we were pushed aside as regular sailors made their way in saying "make way for a leading hand". Meanwhile we stood around shivering outside with only our thin civilian clothes on that damp November morning.

After a while they let us in and we were led to a table near the end where a rough and ready breakfast greeted us, a plate of something not too memorable, tea in a big metal urn and course, brown sugar. At least it was hot and warmed us up a bit.

Taking us back to the kitting up room, the rest of the morning was used by everyone being issued with a sailor's kit, bag, hammock, and gas mask.

The afternoon began with another rough and ready but wholesome meal eaten in the corner of the mess hall. From there, escorted to a barrack room we set about to mark our belongings with small types which were a part of our new kit. Larger items like our bag and hammock had to be done with special bigger letters which did not belong to us. It was here my first problem began.

The type letters caused confusion as everyone was looking around for those required to stamp their name. When I reached the point where I needed one particular letter, I found a lad by the name of Melling was using it. I decided to stand aside and wait until he was done after informing him that I needed it next. When he finished, to my dismay he deliberately gave it to one of his pals. I complained but he told me to go 'eff' myself. I'm not aggressive by nature but I quickly realized that here in this new life one had to stand up for oneself. Although a bit smaller than him, I grabbed him and attempted to throw the first punch which he blocked. A big scuffle ensued and was only ended when the others separated us before the PO returned. Had this not happened, we both would have been in trouble (rattle). At least I had asserted myself and had no problem with anybody after that. Melling became a good friend and the type letter I had wanted wasn't long in coming.

That night onwards, we slept in one of the regular barrack rooms now that we had all our kit and our hammock. The next few days were spent with medical and dental checks. At sea, good teeth were considered very important, especially in those days of strict peacetime requirements and most ships not carrying a dentist. Those recruits needing treatment were done right away myself included. I was given a couple of fillings and although the Navy dentist was not as gentle as a civilian would like, these lasted and stood me in good stead for many years after.

A visit was also made to the paymaster's office for those wishing to make allotments home to next of kin out of their pay. To my mother I gave eight shillings a week. Allotments to next of kin were never paid for by the Navy with the exception of marriage allowances which was thirty five shillings a week. We were also informed a kit upkeep allowance of 1s. 6p. would be included in our pay for each week but from there on, any item to be replaced whether lost, stolen, or worn out was our own responsibility and come out of our pockets unless your ship was sunk or damaged through enemy action. Only in events like those or similar circumstances would the Pusser's stores replace your gear meaning uniform kit not tiddley suit or other personal stuff and definitely not money, jewellery, etc.

Finally, as a conclusion to all this preparation, everyone have to have an identity disk (dogtag). This was a round piece of asbestos, (not metal) about one and a half inches roughly in diameter and a substance which wouldn't burn with our name, rank, and service number punched on it while we waited.

This procedure being completed by the end of the week was prior to going down the River Tamar a couple of miles to the disciplinary camp at Trevol Rifle Range for two months. However as it wasn't until about Monday they sent us we had the weekend relatively free in barracks except for Sunday Divisions (parade) and church. One might say our last bit of freedom before, putting the screws to us and knocking us into shape. Nevertheless it afforded the opportunity to have a look around the depot and also go into the Town.

Guz barracks, HMS Drake was one of three main naval bases in England. The other two were HMS Nelson at Portsmouth and HMS Pembroke at Chatham. Drake and Nelson were names of very famous admirals who defeated fleets which outnumbered them in guns and ships. Drake defeated the Spanish Armada in the English Channel in 1588. Nelson defeated the combined French and Spanish Fleets at Cape Trafalgar in 1805 thus gaining undisputed supremacy for the British Navy on the high seas for a great many years afterwards.

These bases were referred to by sea-going lads as stone frigates because although they retained all the aspects of shipboard life, they of course went nowhere. One can only imagine what it was like there at this very early stage of the war when the Navy was mobilizing to a war footing. Thousands of men, reservists in all categories were reporting for duty and waiting to be drafted aboard ships that were being brought out of the mothball fleet. The organization involved must have been a formidable task indeed for those in charge. With so many men returning there can be little doubt as to why the authorities could not be bothered with raw, untrained recruits for hostilities only. Just we few who were considered regulars were enough then and were soon kitted up and gotten out of the way in less than a week to make room for the next bunch coming.

Devonport barracks and its large dockyard facilities provide the mainstay of life for both Devonport and Plymouth. The connection of these towns with the Navy goes back centuries to the time of Sir Francis Drake who was finishing his game of bowls on Plymouth Hoe when the Spanish Armada was sighted. Just a short distance from the Hoe lies the very old part of town called the Barbican. Once a very rough area along the waterfront, this was the place where the Mayflower set sail with the Pilgrim Fathers to the New World. The jetty from which she left today flies both the Union Jack and the Stars and Stripes. The dockyard itself lies on the River Tamar which forms part of the border between the counties of Devon and Cornwall. The river mouth opens up into Plymouth Sound which provides an ideal deep-water anchorage for capital ships. In some places the mouth has a depth of over four hundred feet which makes this a very important base along with the fact that it is near to the major shipping lanes in the Channel and Western Approaches.

My first and lasting impression of Guz has never changed, a most depressing place. The buildings and walls were tall and grey made of solid blocks of Portland Stone. Granite which is the same material used in the maximum security prison Dartmoor. To enter, one had to pass through big iron gates or a small, adjacent stone archway where a sentry was on duty. One passed the guardroom where the ever vigilant Officer of the Watch and his staff (which included a PO from the Master-at-Arms office referred to as the 'Crushers') would check everyone in and out.* Anyone failing to give a 'Pusser' (by the book) salute, whether they could see the officer or not would be inviting trouble in the form of being quickly hauled inside for a reprimand or worse. Wisely, nobody took chances.

Further on down the cobblestone road, one would begin to see barrack room blocks which all looked alike, two stories high and made of the same ugly Portland stone. On more than one occasion in the past these cold, drab, and ill lit buildings had been condemned. Inside the barrack rooms there were a few dark coloured leather sofas, armchairs, and wooden tables all of which had seen better days. At each end was a large coal burning fireplace. Both of them put together were quite inadequate to heat such a vast area approximately the size of a gymnasium. Each block consisted of two rooms one on top of the other and named after a byegone admiral, eg. Raleigh, Boscawen from the old British Navy. Hundreds slept side by side in hammocks at night about eighteen inches apart as per pusser regulations for the entire length of the room. Each had hooks to sling four or five rows across its width. Even this kind of accommodation eventually became so overcrowded at times

_____

*Today the Officer of the Watch is only a Chief Petty Officer.

as the war dragged on that one could only be sure of getting a sleeping billet if you slung your hammock no later than four o'clock in the afternoon. Otherwise it was tough luck, sleep ashore, on the floor or wherever.

Such were the conditions for Britain's fighting Navy. Lads were coming and going from sea in this place which was unaffectionately nicknamed by the lower deck 'Jago's Mansions'.

Strangely enough, as the war at sea got worse and casualties mounted, there developed those type of individuals who seemed to favour this bleak existence to life aboard ship where at least more comradeship prevailed. The average matelot preferred to take his chances at sea unlike these 'barrack stanchions' as they were always called who rumour had it, engaged in some very dubious carryings on in order to get out of undesirable drafts for service afloat etc. or even the opposite a cushy number ashore.* Unable of course to corroborate the authenticity of these detestable practices, it was widely believed that such things like the rum ration and bribery were involved besides quite an ingenious piece of trickery fashioned out of a block of good old Pussers hard. In remembering all this one can only think of some other poor bugger who would end up with the draft which may have serious consequences perhaps even costing him his life.

These not so comfortable surroundings at the depot were soon to look good compared to the conditions at Trevol Disciplinary Camp that we would have to put up with in the next few days.

Like shipboard routine, the barracks had its Saturday morning cleanup, where everything was scrubbed and polished by those detailed off to help the messdeck dodgers. The rest simply vanished out of sight. I also disappeared with them. Sunday morning, all hands attended compulsory Divisions and inspection held in the drill hall. From there we were marched to a church service close by which was provided in the two major denominations. For me, this first Sunday in the barrack church was one I never forgot as we said the Naval prayer, 'For Those

---

*These carryings on might include using a block of 'Pusser's Hard' (laundry soap) to forge a stamp which would make your papers read "unfit for sea".

14

Trevol Rifle Range Disciplinary Training Camp, Torpoint, Cornwall, now HMS Raleigh. Beresford Class after two months.
(Author middle row, second from left)

In Peril On The Sea'. Most appropriate considering what lay ahead.

Monday morning, we new entries were mustered together and all those who were stokers, twenty-two of us by now, were put into a group called Beresford Class. From now on we would all stay together in the training division for the next four months. Those from the other branches such as seamen, wireless telegraphists (sparkers), signallers (bunting tossers), and the rest would go to their respective training camps. For example, seamen went to the gunnery training school, HMS Defiance across the Tamar from the barracks.

As I recall, we spent the rest of the day finishing our new entry procedure in preparation for shipping out to our new home the next day.

The following morning we were told to pack our bag and hammock and muster down at the jetty where a Naval launch came alongside. We loaded our gear and hopped aboard for the short ride to Trevol. When we landed, the camp was not far so we carried our gear on foot for a short walk.

Trevol Rifle Range was a makeshift camp with nissen huts instead of the permanent stone buildings found in most Navy establishments. It was fairly small in as much as there were only two classes here, all stokers. We were to be knocked into shape by disciplinary training in the form of rifle and bayonet drill, shooting, and marching. This was to last eight weeks and what a time it was. Conditions here were terrible, much worse than Jago's Mansions. At least you could get a proper bath in the barracks. Here we didn't have a bath or even a shower. After several days we were taken out into a field where there stood a small building. Inside was our 'bath', a big tiled trough about nine inches deep. The water reeked with the smell of disinfectant. Using these facilities in small groups, we had to bathe as best we could but groaning about this most undignified method.

For our rifle training we were each issued a .303 Lee Enfield and bayonet which, when not in use were stored in racks in a separate building.* These were only for training purposes. They weren't issued as a part of your kit as the army does. The rifle was used in learning to march in columns of four, square bashing, and all the various movements. We were also taken to a firing range where the bulk of us including myself were rather lacking in accuracy. Word even went around that one of our bullets went astray and killed a farmer's cow. Our instructors were not pleased. One thing I did learn that I always remember, a Lee Enfield without a bayonet weighs eight pounds, seven ounces.

The rest of our routine included the usual physical training, running, jumping and exercising which for me wasn't hard as I didn't smoke. Though not very big I was quite fit despite Depression years living. Before joining, I had been an ardent cyclist having even cycled from Manchester to Blackpool and

---

*The reason for this sort of training was in the event of being picked for landing or boarding parties.

back in a day for an outing, a distance of one hundred miles. Our class instructor was a PO Heath, seaman branch. He wasn't too bad a chap really although he could bawl as good as any drill sergeant. From him we got good advice. One particular piece I have never forgotten and always practice. He told us 'look after your clothes and you'll have more money in your pocket to spend'. In this throwaway society we now live in, one would do well to heed this and make things last longer, sound advice and environmentally friendly. Also, do not lend money.

About a week after I got to Trevol my old pal Eric arrived with his class. I certainly felt glad to see him again and didn't feel quite as much alone now with all the others being complete strangers. Close quarters living in Navy life, one soon sorted out who was who for an oppo.

We all came from working class backgrounds, no toffee noses or upper class types here. There was Paddy Flynn from Southern Ireland, a quiet and likeable lad who sadly didn't live long. Being from a neutral country, he need not have fought for England but chose instead to join the RN. He served on the carrier Illustrious with me but was wounded in the bombing attack later killed when the hospital ship he was on was rumoured to have been sunk.

Our group was a real cross-section of the British Isles. There was Taffy Davis and Harry Thomas from Wales, Jim Newton from Liverpool, Rimmer and Hay from the West Country, and Sid Nuttall, Kenny Baker, Harry Buckley, Collier, and Akroyd, all from around the Midlands. After the training was over, many of these lads from both classes were to become my shipmates but a few like Buckley, Collier, and Akroyd who went to other ships got sunk on a destroyer, even before I went to Illustrious. At least I heard that they survived though Buckley was unfit for further sea service and given a shore job.

This part of the war, labelled the 'Phoney War' by historians and many writers, was not phoney as far as the Navy was concerned. It was the real thing.

Our spirits were buoyed up when told we would get ten days Christmas leave plus travelling time which meant an extra day. In those uncertain times every day counted. At least we could now look forward to the date when we could get away from this mud hole and enjoy some home comforts and a bit of freedom, if only for a little while.

It was at Trevol we received our first pay. In home waters pay came every fortnight and abroad, every month. In order to get paid everyone was mustered in alphabetical order being all stokers, also there were less men here than in barracks* or aboard ship. The Paymaster (Pay Bob) carrying his tray of cash, the Duty Officer, Crusher, and accountant with his pay ledger all appeared. Everyone was brought to attention and then stood at ease. Names were called out with rank and serial number. You then had to respond when your name was called with a 'Sir' and step in front of the table, repeat your name and rank and then salute. According to a specific method, you took your cap off with your left hand from the right side and the assumed position thereon was both hands holding the cap straight out in front. The said amount was then placed on top of the cap by the officer. You then took the money off with the reverse procedure. Money in left hand, replace the cap with the right hand from the left side. Take one step back, salute smartly, then turn and march away. My pay came to a grand total of one pound, two shillings. I really felt well off.

This regimented mode of payment seemed designed to impress discipline and subservience to those in authority, in accordance with the class distinction we were accustomed to in those days.

Just before Christmas, the camp was divided into two leave periods. Scottish people usually prefer to celebrate the New Year so they were among the second batch. Eric and I were amongst the early group. This was our very first leave. We travelled home together proud to be wearing the Navy uniform, our new 'Tiddley suit' (no. 1's) bought out of our own pockets. This was a special dress uniform made to order from a naval tailor. The Navy doesn't issue no. 1's as part of your dress uniform, no. 2 would suffice but wasn't as 'tiddley' looking.

My leave was very memorable; seeing home and family again and made me realize how much they all meant to me. It was extremely hard to say goodbye this time not knowing what would lie ahead after the training division.

Reaching Plymouth station again and the prospect of spending another month in that primitive camp was a dreary thought indeed, and made me feel homesick.

---

*Usually, men mustered according to branch and rank.

Trevol, situated at Torpoint, was a miserable and most uncomfortable place made worse by winter weather.* The fact that England has a nasty habit of raining all the time made everything damp and muddy. After washing your clothes, nothing seemed to dry properly and those nissen huts were both draughty and poorly heated. One could easily catch a cold. We did hear that someone had died there from the conditions, catching pneumonia, but never knew who it was.

Toward the end of January 1940, Beresford was finally sent back to barracks and Eric's class followed a week later. I was almost glad to be in Jago's Mansions which was slightly but only slightly a bit more comfortable. That night I just soaked myself in one of the big old bath tubs. Maybe they didn't have showers but it sure beat a disinfectant trough.

The next two months we would spend in the Stoker's Mechanical Training Establishment and more square bashing.

January 1940 and WW2 was only just five months old. Our ruthless enemy, the Germans were apparently not treating this time as a 'phoney war' but taking every advantage of our unpreparedness by infiltrating and setting up their Fifth Columns in the countries soon to be overrun. Even in Britain we had one notable traitor, William Joyce known better by his nickname coined by the Daily Express, Lord Haw-Haw.*

A well known fascist in peacetime, he offered his services to the Nazis when war broke out by broadcasting to Britain and giving precise details of things that were supposed to be secret.

German U-boats were harrassing and sinking merchant ships and had already scored successes against our own warships. The first major British victory had just been won however at the Battle of the River Plate just outside Montevideo, Uraguay, where the elusive pocket battleship Graf Spee had been hunted by three gallant warships, the cruisers Ajax, Achilles, and Exeter. After a fierce battle the Graf Spee had taken refuge for seventy-two hours in the neutral port of Montevideo. After much political intrigue she was compelled to leave by international law. Believing that powerful units of the Royal Navy

---

*Trevol, named HMS Raleigh after Sir Walter Raleigh the explorer and reputed to have invented smoking, is now the largest training base in the country for the Royal Navy.
*William Joyce was sentenced to death at the Old Bailey in 1946.

were waiting, her Captain decided to scuttle her, and then committed suicide. Hitler was furious at the outcome but this was a morale booster for the British public.

Back in the prison-like atmosphere of the depot, I found it somewhat of a relief to go ashore. Guz and Plymouth never did appeal to me very much, being strictly Navy towns for centuries. Even the boozers were often run by ex-matelots so one couldn't escape the Pusser flavour by just going for a pint. To get away for a few hours made me feel a little better except for having to salute passing officers every few minutes and watching out for shore patrols who kept everybody on their toes. One popular stop for many sailor's was Aggie Weston's, officially known as the sailors rest. Though not my cup of tea, it had originally been founded by the lady whom it is named after to provide some kind of accommodation for those who had returned from long voyages. Later on during the war it was bombed and destroyed during the 'Plymouth Blitz'.

The second and final stage of training began on Monday with classroom instruction on the workings of ship's boilers and machinery pumps etc. At this phase we were now issued with a Stoker's Manual to study and for later advancement in rank to Stoker First Class.

The square bashing on the proper parade ground was a pain in the neck. Oddly enough, not having the rifle and bayonet any more to drill with, I somehow lost some of my coordination which resulted in getting personal attention from the drill instructor. He pulled me out of the ranks and was showing me how to change direction to the right or left on the march or do about turns. I couldn't seem to time my turns with his orders so I always ended up being out of step. This resulted in some very choice language such as: 'You stupid bastard. Don't you know your right from your left?' To which I would reply sheepishly 'Yes Sir'. 'Well then, let's effing well see you do it right this time', he would say. So it went whenever we drilled. There were others too who marched with two left or right feet and the same arms to match which didn't improve our PO's frame of mind.

Just as before, exactly a week after we arrived back in the barracks, Eric's bunch followed on to do their training with us. We all knew each other fairly well by now. Another lad I should mention who became a close oppo of ours was Frank Lord. He came from Blackburn, Lancashire, a very poor neighbourhood which the majestic name of his address, Coronation Street, belied the surrounding poverty there. Frank was tall and slim and had a small turned up nose. He was always cheerful and had a good sense of humour but far from a pushover. Then there was Sid Nuttall who we mentioned briefly before. Sid was of medium height and a bit plump. A little older than the rest he always looked smart even in his overalls being very particular, and when dressed to go ashore with his ready wit made him rather debonair. Sid was very streetwise and also not one to be messed about. Unlike most poor working class people, he knew how to drive a car and so managed later on to get a soft number as the Captain's driver. Sid was always the friendly type but quite independent and had his own ideas of what he wanted to do. Both served for a long time on the Illustrious with me.

As our training progressed, we all had been put into our respective parts of watches for Duty Watch Aboard and shore leave. This involved having a small folding card with your name, rank, serial number, part of watch, and ship. Part of watch was designed as either first or second part of port or starboad. Duty Watch Aboard in barracks was for Fire and Repair parties in the event of an air raid called Passive Defence. On this duty we had to muster at certain times for fire drills etc. Duty Watch could also involve being on a spud peeling party detailed for PO's PPP, Petty Officers Potato Peeling Party or CPO's PPP, Chief Petty Officer's.

One forenoon in January, an outstanding event I always remember happened. The voice on the tannoy ordered all hands to muster down at the pier head clearing out the whole barrack blocks. When I got there I saw hundreds all asking the same questions about what was happening. As usual it was a dreary and overcast day but everyone strained out looking towards the mouth of the Tamar. The buzz went round that one of the heroes from the Battle of the River Plate, HMS Exeter was about to enter harbour. As she slowly came into view an officer amongst the crowd climbed upon something like a bollard and directed everyone to get ready to give the ship three hearty cheers as she passed in the finest traditions of the Navy. Just as expected from a toffee nose. The officer then said 'Don't shout 'ooray, say hurrah'. Nothing changed.

The ship bore the scars of the battle in the form of badly mauled superstructures and turrets from Graf Spee's 11-inch shells. Exeter had received the worst damage with all but one of her 8-inch turrets out of action and the bridge and Director

Control Tower had been smashed by direct hits.* All this showed the signs of the savage war at sea which was intensifying. Little did I realize that just a year from now I would be going through almost the same thing as my ship was cheered in after being crippled by German dive-bombing attacks. Some Phoney War! Seeing that battle-scarred ship brought the grim realities closer to home where I now began to think what kind of a ship I was going to be drafted to when my training was completed. My future looked very uncertain from this point onwards but I did console myself with the thought that at least everybody else was in the same boat as me although it didn't actually help very much.

Another constant reminder of naval discipline was visible whenever I passed the Provo (barrack prison). The sight of it provided a sort of mental deterrent to all those Jack Stropps (troublemakers), those reporting back late from leave, insubordination, and anything that constituted prejudice to good order and Naval discipline. By the rumours that we heard about it only the foolish and the foolhardy would ever want to go in there.

The second part of our training also included the obvious, swimming. This too wasn't a problem for me because I had been a regular attender at the local baths before joining up and learned to swim fairly early in life as it was part of my school curriculum. I was really glad as it seemed to make up a bit for my parade-ground performances.

Those unfortunates who couldn't swim got no sympathy from Clubs, the PTI's (Physical Training Instructors). First we each had to show whether we could actually swim or not by doing a couple of lengths up and down the pool changing to different strokes like treading water and resting types such as the breast stroke. The reason for this made sense in case your ship got sunk and you were forced to swim for it; in these times, a very distinct possibility. Needless to say, this was only useful if one was even lucky enough to reach the water in time after getting out from the deep bowels of the ship such as boiler and engine rooms and other machinery spaces where you could be caught like a rat in a trap, unable to escape. A stoker's chances

*HMS Exeter was overwhelmed and sunk by Jap warships in the Java Sea March 1 1942 along with the cruisers HMAS Perth, USS Houston, and the Dutch De Ruyter and Java.

I'm afraid were often very slim indeed. The poor sods who showed they couldn't swim properly or not at all received poolside instruction from the Clubs who would be ready to assist with his boat hook but not always to let them get out when they tried to splash their way to the side. From there on they would be given personal attention until they were able to swim adequately.

Those of us who Clubs considered good enough to take another test were told that next time we came to bring a duck suit. This was a heavy, half-white in colour, canvas two piece sailor's outfit consisting of a jumper and trousers. They were issued to peacetime sailors as a tropical working rig called no. 4's and no. 5's I believe. This could also be worn for shore leave abroad if one didn't have a tiddley no. 6 which was a comfortable, white outfit of soft material with a blue trim around the cuffs and bottom of the jumper and was for use in warm climates. Regarding those ducks they were heavy and stiff as a board and I never did see anybody wearing them either for work or ashore except a glimpse of those in the provo.

Wearing one of these suits to swim up and down the length of the pool a couple of times was the final test to simulate having to abandon ship wearing all your clothes. We all dived in and straight away I could feel myself being dragged down by the weight so I struggled doing all sorts of strokes to keep going. I tried my very best to stop my feet touching the bottom because Clubs was watching out for anybody who made attempts to cheat a little bit. Warnings of dire consequences were bawled out like; 'Keep your effing feet off the bottom. If this was the so-and-so oggin you'd go under and drown. Keep going!' Somehow I managed to get to the other end and back with a struggle to keep my head above water, more than glad to get this lot over and done with feeling nearly 'arry flakers'.

By now our training was getting close to finishing and Easter was just around the corner where we hoped to be given another ten days leave about the end of March. In spite of everything we'd been through we could look forward at least to going home again and having a good time before our inevitable draft to a seagoing ship.

Eric and I as close oppos and 'townies' once more travelled back to Manchester together. What we found was a civilian population having to alter its lifestyle to wartime conditions. Food rationing had been introduced January 8 1940. Just before we left everyone was issued with ration coupons which we picked up with our leave passes. At home, like everybody else we were entitled to the weekly ration of 4oz ham, 8oz bacon, 4oz butter, and 12oz sugar.* This was just the beginning of rationing which was enforced for the purpose of equality so that the more well off couldn't hoard food and leave very little for the poorer people. This was to be a war where everybody suffered, rich or poor.

It felt great to be in good old Manchester again rainy though it was. How people could be so cheerful in such a dreary climate I'll never know but Northerners for the most part have a good sense of humour and we were determined to make the most of our leave and have fun with lots of pubs and nightlife. That is until 11 pm; time gentlemen please.

Seeing Mother and Dad again and now able to give a pound or two for my keep with money leftover to spend made things a lot easier. I know they were very proud of me in uniform but could tell they worried about what might happen when I went to sea. By now, my sisters had left the soap factory where I had worked. Flo was now working in a cotton mill which was making .303 machine gun belts and did the monotonous job of checking every slot in the belts with a dummy bullet to ensure a proper fit in each pocket so as to prevent jamming. Unlike Flo who was still living at home, my other sister Olive was married to a railway bricklayer who repaired bridges. He was later called up for the army and went into the Royal Engineers (sappers).

Working in the factory my sisters brought home all the daily news about who had been called up and who had volunteered for the services. The younger men were now disappearing at a faster rate. This included many of my own friends from other mills and those I used to play billiards and snooker with. I even saw Jack on this leave which unfortunately was the last time.

This was the period of the so-called 'Phoney War'. So far, there had been no air raids as Hitler was still busy mopping up his conquests in Eastern Europe. The dark stain of Nazism had not spread to the West yet but England's turn was coming soon.

Preparations for what was coming could be seen. Air raid precautions were taken by barrage balloon sites being set up in

---

*March 11 1940, meat was rationed at the value of 1s 10d per week, per person over the age of six.

parks and any available open spaces in order to force enemy planes to maintain higher altitudes. This turned out to be of little value as a deterrent because the enemy used them almost for target practice.

By now, every single person in Britain had been issued with a gas mask and were required to carry them at all times although people tended to disregard the seriousness of this rule as no raids had yet occurred and some even used their gas mask cases to carry thing other than their mask.

Blackout regulations were in force and ARP wardens made their nightly rounds to assist the police in enforcing compliance.

These measures were taken far too lightheartedly at this early stage as a result of the 'Phoney War' but soon this would all quickly change into stark reality.

While on leave, I met another childhood friend. He wasn't as close as Eric but we grew up together in the same street called Brookside. His name was Leo. Oh how some of those places with their high sounding names made me just wonder who thought of them. Ours was poor enough but I recall others looked much poorer still.

Leo was a soldier and marginally older than myself. He and his sister Lilly had had an extremely hard life even by normal standards of those poverty filled days of pre-war Britain. Their father hadn't worked for years and was very strict. Needless to say their financial situation was a meagre existence at best, living on the Means Test subsistence allowance most of the time. It hardly kept the family in the bare necessities of life.

After leaving school at 14, Leo got a job in an iron foundry to earn his keep and help support his family. Only the rich and well off sent their children to secondary schools. Not surprisingly, soon as he was old enough he joined the Territorial Army (known as Terriers), the British reserve army which Canadians and Americans would call the Militia or National Guard. People often laughed and said they were just 'Saturday Night Soldiers'. These same people who scoffed at them were shortly going to appreciate the true value of those young men when they quickly filled the ranks to form a large portion of the BEF Leo had been mobilized during the 1938 Munich Crisis and then stood down after it was over. Now he was in for the duration proper, a private in the Eighth Manchester Ardwick Regiment, Eighth Ardwicks for short. I never did meet him again but know from my sisters that he survived the war.

25

Why did such people as Leo and countless others from underprivileged backgrounds serve their country so patriotically and courageously? It certainly wasn't to defend their demeaning and wretched lifestyle.

There was one other aspect of life that had undergone some changes. Many thousands of children and their mothers had been evacuated from the cities to 'safe' areas. Most of these children were from the impoverished urban areas although my young nephew Fred was not one of them and his mother, Florrie was working on essential war work as were many more. At the start of the war, a fair number of children were shipped out to Canada and America by parents who could afford it and had some influence but this was stopped after one of the ships tragically got sunk by a German submarine.

It was on this leave that Eric and I experienced a sense of pride also felt by ordinary people towards the Royal Navy, traditionally looked upon as England's first line of defence. Certain customs existed that expressed this feeling such as when you walked down the street, occasionally girls would come behind and touch your sailor's collar which they said would bring them good luck. Of course obviously some did this for ulterior motives too and get attention. As the old saying goes, all the nice girls love a sailor.

The time came very quickly for us to go back to Guz and goodbyes were getting harder and harder to do. Fortunately I was still fancy free and didn't have any girlfriends to worry about so perhaps it was made a little easier. Mum and Dad were visibly upset as we said a tearful farewell from the house. My sisters came to the railway station to see me off. The scene there was of families saying sad goodbyes to sons, husbands, and brothers in all the services. Although this kind of thing was repeated millions of times in the years to come, nobody ever got used to it. I made my mind up that in future it would be said at the front door of the house to make it easier to get on the train as it just became too hard to bear.

Meeting up with Eric again made me start to feel better even though I could hear the whistle blowing that signalled the train's departure. Each stop along the way we picked up more and more servicemen until the train was so crowded we were packed like sardines. When we eventually arrived at Crewe which was a major junction, we met up with other Navy lads that we knew and commiserated with one another which, in a strange way, cheered us up a bit. This is how it was all the way to Guz, our destination where cheerfulness took a turn for the worse at the sight of Naval patrols called the (Gestapo) and the big, ugly, grey barracks.*

Training completed, we all waited and wondered what kind of a draft we would get. This was not long in coming and we were glad not to be hanging around Guz for much longer. For one thing, it didn't have the perks that towns further away had. Sailors here were a dime a dozen and we had no people going out of their way to talk to us or girls coming up and touching our collars for luck. We were almost ignored. Consequently, most of us except the 'teddy oggies' were downright chokka block of the place.

---

*The Gestapo which was the name of the dreaded German (Nazi) secret police was also the nickname of the Patrol Service Branch (Naval Police), Master at Arms (Jaunty, Crusher) etc. Particularly it applied to those in authority who used to search the barrack rooms for anyone thought to be trying to dodge work details or malingering. It also included the Shore Patrols.

Chapter Three

The Carrier – HMS Illustrious

The time soon arrived for a draft. It was mid-April when one day about noon, someone came in the mess with a big bunch of slips of papers called 'Draft Chits'. These were put on the table with the daily incoming mail. Immediately everyone was crowding around checking them out to see who had got one. Eric and I spotted ours right away. This long slip of paper contained: our name, rank, serial number, and the expected job number of whatever you were being sent to for security reasons. Many including Eric and myself had the same, No. 732. Strangely enough, as the day wore on we discovered that scores of others of all ranks and departments had identical draft numbers to ours but nobody had any idea what type of ship it was. Also, the same instructions were given. Pack your bag and hammock and report at 0800 the next morning outside the main drafting office ready to entrain from Mill Bay Station adjacent to the barracks, destination unknown.

We duly reported as ordered the following morning and were handed the usual customary bag lunch of a 'teddy oggie' and some other meagre morsel which was supposed to sustain us no matter how long the journey. No extra food or drink was forthcoming along the way unless one was in the position of authority to use an excuse for obtaining perks by nipping off the train to grab something without getting a bollocking. The rest just had to drip and suffer the pangs of hunger and thirst.

When we all mustered on Mill Bay Station platform we numbered somewhere around five hundred strong. Kit bags and hammocks were piled everywhere until they got loaded into the baggage cars. This was one hell of a big draft and the buzzes were flying in all directions that it must be a battlewagon or something like it but as so often happens it was proven wrong. The big one which kept everybody really guessing at first was our final destination. Speculation about the direction we might be going was running rampant. There were some who thought we could be heading for Scapa Flow, that bleak, forbidding deep water anchorage for capital ships up in the Orkney Islands north of Scotland which as far as the lower deck was concerned was only good for sheep and goats.

So it went on until at last we were herded onto the train by those in charge. Crushers, jaunties, and the like were scurrying around making sure everyone was accounted for and on board.

Eric and myself with a few others we knew from the training division tried to stay together more for moral support than anything else. At this point, all this began to seem a bit of an adventure and would do at least until the novelty wore off for us green recruits. Deep down one could sense that things were starting to take on serious overtones as to what might lie ahead. No matter what kind of ship we were being sent to, the war was now heating up with the invasion of Norway on April 9 and we could be sure that the Navy was not sending us on any pleasure cruise.

The train whistle blew and then it started to slowly move off packed chokka block full of His Majesty's blue jackets and a sprinkling of Royal Marines known affectionately by all as the 'Royals' The Marines were traditionally seagoing soldiers with a dual purpose as a buffer between officers and lower deck ratings in case of mutiny.

Leaving Guz and the prison like atmosphere of the barracks, I felt no regrets nor perhaps did very many who were on that train with the exception of the few who lived near there. Little did we know there would be more than a few among us who would never return again to Guz to get another draft chit.

As the train rolled along and the hours passed, all the station names that we read seemed to indicate even to those of us that had a poor knowledge of geography that we were heading north and it was going to be a long journey. It was still daylight when we arrived at our destination, Barrow-in-Furness. We all got off and were lined up in columns of four. Preceded by our baggage which was loaded onto lorries, we marched the short distance into the Vickers-Armstrong's Shipbuilding Yard. Here we found out what Job No. 732 was, a brand new aircraft carrier towering high out of the water like a cross between leviathan and a skyscraper. This was HMS Illustrious.

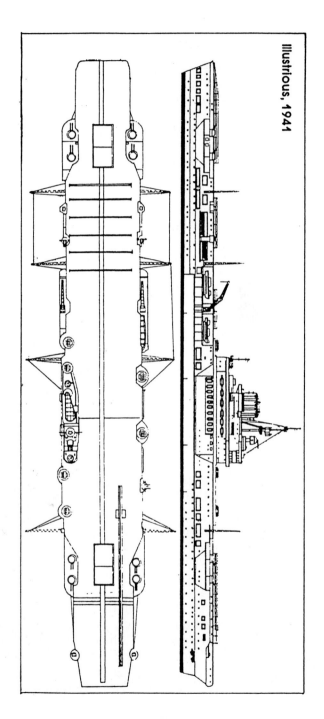

Illustrious, 1941

Captain Denis Boyd DSC RN, Commanding Officer
HMS Illustrious 1940 – 41.
Later he became Rear-Admiral and Fifth Sea Lord

Illustrious was to be my new home for the next three years
and even longer for Eric. At 28,000 tons and 740 feet. long, she
would eventually have a complement of up to 1500 men. She
was the first of a new class of carriers and had been ordered by
the Admiralty in 1937. Somewhat revolutionary in design, she
had an armoured flight deck 3 inches thick and hangar sides 4½
inches. This armoured design was meant to provide maximum
protection from surface guns and air attack. The idea was to
prove its worth later on in her career although at the time it was
feared that all this extra weight would make her top heavy. So
much armour plate was used that her completion was delayed
through a shortage. Despite her size and displacement the
boilers could drive her three steam turbines to a speed of 32
knots. This combination of speed and armour plus being able to
carry over thirty aircraft and having the new secret weapon,

radar with a range of sixty miles, she was one of the most powerful units in the Royal Navy at that time. Later on, she would set the stage for future carrier operations and her actions would change the face of naval warfare forever.

Upon reaching the quayside we halted and were lined up facing the ship. Before boarding we had a few minutes in which we gazed in awe at this mighty new breed of man-of-war as most of us had never expected to be drafted to a ship such as this.

We then filed up the gangway by departments. As stokers we were shown the way to our messdeck by a killick or somebody having no idea where to go. On a vessel of this size one could almost get lost in the maze of bulkheads and passageways.

The stoker's messes consisted of an upper on the waterline and a lower messdeck just below aft of the capstan flat where the anchor chains were hauled in. Mine was on the upper messdeck, starboard side. Unfortunately I didn't know anybody in this mess and Eric had been assigned to one of the lower messes. The whole arrangement was designed to mix older men with the new inexperienced sailors. Regardless of this separation, we were all still in close proximity to one another.

Because we had just completed a long train journey, the first thing most of us looked for was the 'heads' (toilets). These conveniences which were for'ard of the capstan flat did not allow for total privacy but only cubicles which were three or four feet high. Nevertheless, this place did make for good conversation and from time to time some of the best buzzes originated here.

When it came to victualling the Andrew (Navy) had two different systems. For small ships from destroyers down it was called canteen messing. This meant that the members of each mess had to prepare their own food from each month's victualling allowance which came in the form of mostly tinned goods. From there it was sent to the galley to be cooked and collected at meal time. Each day's menu was the responsibility of the delegated mess caterer.

On larger vessels upwards, the system was called general messing where everything was provided from the ship's galleys and collected by cooks of the day from each mess and brought back. This was the system we had on HMS Illustrious.

We had our first meal although on big ships, food was plain and nothing to write home about. Typically it might be 'bangers and mash', 'boiled spuds', 'toad in the hole', 'straight rush', etc. There was nothing fancy like steaks or pork chops. For dessert we might have figgy duffs, a type of pudding. One other delicacy worth mentioning was the famous Pusser's peas. These were dehydrated and required soaking overnight to make them edible. The common saying was that if they ever ran out of small arms ammunition, they could use Pusser's Peas for bullets.* Our group was the first big draft to Illustrious. We were the commissioning crew and it was our job to get the ship ready and then sail her down to Plymouth to pick up the rest. After that we would take Illustrious on her working up trials and prepare to operate aircraft.

Apparently the Navy was wasting no time. We had received our drafts Monday which was April 15. The ship then officially commissioned on the 16th. She was signed over to the Royal Navy from her builders by Capt. Denis Boyd and the White Ensign was hoisted for the first time. We were all present at this ceremony which took place only a very short while after we came aboard.

Our day was completed by picking out a locker for ourselves, stowing gear, and choosing a spot to sling our hammocks and settling down for the night. Tomorrow would seriously start shipboard routine.

The following day everybody was given parts of ship for harbour working parties and steaming watches. Mine was the centre engine room at sea and different jobs like boiler cleaning party etc. in harbour. We also took the opportunity to familiarize ourselves and look around the ship for a personal inspection of bulkheads, welding, and rivets. In case we got shelled or torpedoed we were concerned how well these would hold up and what our chances of survival might be. Comments like 'I hope these effing rivets don't start popping out if we get hit or this effing welding doesn't give way otherwise we won't stand an effing chance living on the waterline' were rife among many of the stokers. We knew that the armour belt didn't protect the for'ard stoker's mess decks.

Aboard ship and now out of the training division all those 20 years of age or older were allowed the daily grog ration of one

---

*One other thing we often got to eat worth mentioning was H & TS — Herrings in Tomato Sauce. This we would be given for breakfast but few could stomach it so early in the morning. A cup of tea and a fag would suffice.

tot (two ounces) per day for those who wanted it. In lieu of, one could receive threpence a day extra pay but I never knew anyone who did as rum was worth its weight in gold as a morale builder and the favours that could be gotten through 'sippers' and 'gulpers' which officially were not allowed. From then on I drew my tot being old enough but Eric was still under age.

On big ships, the issue of rum was done in a very Pusser manner. At 11:00 hours every day a voice would pipe over the PA 'Up Spirits'. These were magic words to everyone of the lower deck and literally brought the ship's company back to life. Anybody available from each mess would immediately grab a fanny (container) and dash off to the galley flat where the big rum tub was placed. This was embellished with brass letters that were polished every day and read 'The King God Bless Him'. Nearby would be the duty officer, a crusher, somebody from the victualling office with a ledger (jack dusty), and an able seaman. Rum on bigger ships for those below the rank of petty officer was watered down to the ratio of two parts water and one part rum or in short two and one. Therefore the amount of neaters brought up from the spirit locker was added to the appropiate amount of water in the tub and mixed with a paddle. Each mess would then have measured out by the AB, (tanky) precisely triple the amount of liquid for every man entitled. On returning to the mess a row of cups would be set out and meticulously scrutinized by those around the table to ensure fairness. No short measure would in any way be tolerated by anyone to safeguard the interest of the men on watch. The effect of the grog was almost instantaneous. The lads would become more lively and talkative and our plain type of food when served up for dinner seemed to take on an extra appetizing flavour. Not exactly the Ritz but after a tot of Pusser's Rum, one could eat just about anything.

We spent a few days in Barrow and then on April 24, Illustrious picked up an escort at Lightning Knoll Buoy and headed out for Liverpool.* Back in January she had been in the

---

*Illustrious was the first carrier to be built by Vickers Shipbuilding at Barrow which traditionally specialized in submarines. Fifty-two years later on April 30 1992, HMS Vanguard, the first of Britain's new Trident nuclear subs was christened in the same yard. Like Illustrious she is a new breed of fighting ship, revolutionary in design and more powerful than anything before her.

Cammell Lairds Dockyards to have her guns fitted. Even at that early stage Illustrious and Adolph Hitler seemed destined to lock horns. On that earlier trip she had been routed to take the inshore channel. Around the same time, Hitler's new secret weapon, the magnetic mine had been taking its deadly toll of shipping which including the battleship HMS Nelson and cruiser HMS Belfast which suffered considerable damage. Every effort was being made by the Navy, in particular the minesweepers to bring this menace under control.

Fate which so often seemed to lend a hand to this great ship, timely intervened. One of the trawler sweepers Thomas Leeds, working the area just prior to Illustrious proceeding up that inshore channel had miraculously exploded a magnetic mine with her skid and was seriously damaged. She then steamed like hell at full speed for the beach and sank in shallow water at a landing stage for a ferry steamer. The results of all this was that the alarm was raised and the carrier altered course. Later on, a minefield with another 23 mines was found in the inshore channel. Little doubt Thomas Leeds, a small trawler had been instrumental in saving a very valuable and much needed aircraft carrier. Had this twist of fate not providentially occurred, perhaps some history may have turned out differently, especially in the Mediterranean War. Il Duce, the Italian dictator Mussolini may have been spared some embarrassing moments after his fleet suffered a crippling blow at Taranto.

Time was now pressing to get Illustrious into active service. What that meant for us only those old boys in London with the scrambled egg on their caps knew. They had plans in the making one could be sure but the situation in Europe was becoming increasingly volatile. By this time Denmark had fallen to the German onslaught and British, French, and Norwegian forces were making a valiant effort to save Norway. The 'Phoney War' was over for certain.

On the way to Liverpool, Illustrious saved time by trying out some of her gear; steering gear, compasses, echo sounders etc. At Liverpool we were put into Gladstone dry dock, one of the few in the UK big enough to take us. Here we had underwater work done by having bilge keels installed and the bottom repainted. We also had the temporary cast iron propellers exchanged for huge, bronze screws. On occasion I would be one of the unfortunates detailed off for the miserable task to chip, scrape, and file clean the barnacles from those monstrous great blades with a hammer and chisel. Up top there were inspections of our electronics equipment and other vital mechanisms. While there in dock, advantage was taken to clean boilers, a necessary but distasteful job to us stokers. Being a sprog I was among chiefy's chosen ones. This entailed having to crawl through an oval shape manhole into one of the lower water drums or the top steam drum after the furnaces have had sufficient time to cool down. You then had to use a wire scrub brush to remove foreign particles and scale that had accumulated, especially around the fire holes and water tubes. All this was done lying mostly on your back or in some other cramped position with barely enough room to move. Eventually one would emerge for stand easy a couple of hours later or dinner etc. black as a chimney sweep. Many ribald comments were forthcoming from mess mates but no sympathy. This was a stoker's job and had to be done.

Despite all this work we managed to get shore leave. Liverpool being only thirty odd miles from Manchester, it was a golden opportunity to go home. We never knew when we would get another chance. Mother and Dad were overjoyed and very surprised to see me show up so unexpectedly even though it was only for the day. When I told them my ship was a new aircraft carrier they feigned to be impressed. Regardless of what it was, they now knew I was at sea and in danger. It would be all the more worrying for them listening to the war news which wasn't very good and realizing the Navy was really the front line defence.

How much danger I was actually in we could hardly imagine at this time. The Admiralty had plans to send the Illustrious to help in Norway. A brand new ship with a mostly green and untried crew without any aircraft, it would have been suicidal. This disastrous plan was only avoided by Captain Boyd having the courage to put his career on the line and confronting their Lordships with the sheer futility of this undertaking. Had we gone we may have suffered the same fate as HMS Glorious, another carrier who was sent to Davy Jones' Locker while taking part in the Norweigan campaign.

Captain Denis Boyd, our skipper had always been a proponent of Naval aviation. In 1911 he had applied to join the new Air Department of the Navy but didn't succeed being only one applicant out of nineteen to a branch that would accept just three. His Captain had been against him joining what he felt was something simply ridiculous. Naval Aviation was a very new thing and accepted by few of the old school. Boyd was given the command of a torpedo boat at the start of the First World War but finished the war on submarines after completing a torpedo training course at the depot HMS Vernon in Portsmouth.

In 1934, as Director of the Tactical Division he had lobbied a great deal towards getting the Fleet Air Arm into the hands of the Navy and not the RAF. At this post he was concerned with the planning of the Illustrious class carriers. Not surprising he was given command the first of its class.

Captain Boyd was very impressed with his new appointment unlike anything he had commanded before. The name Illustrious even seemed like she was destined for glory. He did notice however, that the ship's crest of three brazen trumpets inherited from a captured French man-of-war L'Illustre at the time of Nelson was lacking a motto. He consulted his brother who was a classical scholar and asked him if he could find something that related to God and War otherwise the trumpets suggested just making a lot of noise. After all, in these dark times we needed the Almighty God on our side with the way the war was going.

His brother found a verse from the Bible, 1 Corinthians 14:8 'For if the trumpet giveth an uncertain sound, who shall prepare himself to the battle'. The motto for Illustrious was then adopted from the Latin words 'Vox Non Incerta' meaning 'No Uncertain Sound'.

Liverpool was in those days a bustling port city with shipping from all parts of the world. As to be expected, with so many sailors from both the Royal Navy and Merchant Marine this could get a bit rough at times in places. The situation was such including the black out that the Bobbies on the beat used to patrol in pairs along the main street pubs and dock areas. For 'Jolly Jack' well known arteries like Lime Street meant an 'effing good run ashore'; lots of boozers and 'Judies' (women). There was no use worrying about tomorrow, there wasn't any but the inevitable sailing orders. Like the rest, Eric and I enjoyed ourselves as much as possible in 'Scouse Land'. We liked Liverpool regardless because we were Northerners too.

Eventually we sailed and headed for the South of England. I was sorry to leave 'the Pool' knowing how close we were to my home. I wondered if or when I would ever get another opportunity again such as this. Literally speaking a lot of water would flow under the bridge before Illustrious might return here but only a precious few like Eric and myself would be lucky enough to be still aboard out of the original ship's company.

Along the way we did some more sea trials testing her armament, arrester-gear, and doing full power trials. At this crucial period, everything had to be speeded up and no time wasted. Her full power trials which should have taken at least a day were done in only a few hours. Illustrious was desperately needed more than ever now.

On May 10 Hitler's Wehrmacht had invaded the Low Countries; Holland, Belgium, and Luxemburg. Against the onslaught of the Panzer divisions, these countries fell in less than a week. That same date our Prime Minister, Neville Chamberlain resigned and Winston Churchill, the First Sea Lord took over and formed a coalition government. Now that we had a strong leader at the helm and the Navy still yet intact at least was some consolation.

The situation continued to worsen. France too was about to fall and the British Expeditionary Force of three quarters of a million men was in dire peril of either capture or complete annihilation. It had hoped that the BEF along with the five million man strong French army would stop the flow of Germany's conquests and save France. The Maginot Line on France's border with Germany was impenetrable but we had not reckoned on the German army circumventing it by invading France through the neutral Low Countries. Our First World War style planning was no longer effective and we would have to learn the hard way. Adding all this together along with the enemy's propaganda and Fifth Column movement of Quislings and sympathizers in France, their will to resist was lost.

On May 26 1940, Illustrious anchored in Spithead, off Portsmouth, the same day that the evacuation of Dunkirk had begun.

From there we returned to Plymouth where we picked up the rest of our crew and flew on our aircraft. Our pilots were a mixture of raw recruits and experienced men who had already taken part in the fighting in Norway.

While there I saw a grim reminder of what was happening at Dunkirk and France itself. One evening on shore leave amid all the confusion of this evacuation the old French battleship Paris berthed alongside one of the jetties with her pitiful cargo. To say she was crammed would be an understatement. She was absolutely loaded everywhere above decks and probably below too with French soldiers and whoever else she had managed to bring with her. These men looked weary and haggard as though they had just scrambled aboard wearing anything they might have had at the time. Some still with their equipment and others practically nothing which all told the sad story. Basically they had escaped with only their lives. Britain was now fighting alone.

Illustrious spent a short time in Plymouth making final preparations and provisioning before heading out for Bermuda in the middle of June.

We hit heavy weather as soon as we entered the Bay of Biscay. As we sailed further on into the Western Atlantic it became even worse. The seas ran so high that the foc's'le cable-deck was continuously awash as Illustrious dipped through the troughs and then rode the swells. The ship was tossed about like a cork and at times the waves nearly came over the flightdeck. All around the ship gear was smashed. Scuttles and deadlights which are meant to seal the portholes to darken ship and for heavy weather were smashed in. The shipwrights had a very busy time shoring up the damaged scuttles made of light new alloy which didn't withstand the pressure like the old tried and tested ones. In addition, a thirty foot cutter was washed overboard, searchlight platforms were punched in and the ship's anti-magnetic mine degaussing belt was torn to shreds. The weather took on such a fury that our destroyer escort was ordered to turn back and we ploughed on alone. This was my first taste of the awesome power of the cruel sea and its effects very soon began to take its toll on me also.

My steaming watch at sea was in the centre engine room and we were in three watches of four hours on at a time. As this was more or less an initiation so to speak of being at sea in a full blown gale, I felt at the time I wasn't much of a real sailor. What with the pitch and roll of the ship and the hot, sickly smell of lubricating oil, I was throwing up every few minutes all over the place. Somehow I managed the effort to keep going below and finishing my watches as being seasick was hardly good enough an excuse to get out of doing your job. Needless to say one's own pride had to be considered too.

Even off watch I would just lie down in some obscure corner

39

heaving up my insides caring little about anything other than how wretched I felt. Nobody gave me any sympathy though. All the older hands would say 'you just have to effing well get used to it. You shouldn't have joined the Andrew'. I continued to suffer throughout the rest of the storm but tenaciously hung on thinking at times if I might die of seasickness.

Years afterwards I have reflected on all this talk about the mysteries surrounding the Bermuda Triangle. The area in question is a part of the Atlantic where countless numbers of ships and aircraft have literally disappeared over the ages without even a trace. Stories and speculation have ran rampant as to what may be the cause of this including phenomena ranging from aliens, ghost ships, the lost city of Atlantis to more practical explanations which could be electrical and magnetic storms or other natural causes. Whatever it is, Illustrious lived to tell about it and I can't ever remember experiencing storms as bad as that since. Perhaps too the Almighty in his own way was using the power of the sea at its worst as a sign of things to come for all of us.

Chapter Four

Lower Deck Life on a Carrier

Shipboard living conditions for ratings below the rank of PO was rough and ready to put it mildly. Living cheek by jowl left no room for modesty or privacy. This was a man's world, completely without women yet women and sex were the predominant topic of conversation. In a perverse sort of way they were a morale booster in that they kept us in touch with home and reality. The Navy also had its own vocabulary for describing things and people which included constant swearing as the norm. The air of the messdecks was always blue but it wasn't necessarily from the smoke of 'Ticklers' (Navy Cut tobacco) which filled the atmosphere all the time.

The lower stoker's messdeck which was below the waterline obviously had no portholes. The upper messdeck which I was in was just above the water so at least while in harbour, we had portholes we could open for fresh air during the day. At night however, it was another story when we had to darken ship and all scuttles and deadlights had to be closed. For air circulation we had only our forced air ventilation through small louvres on the deck-head ducts. We had no air conditioning such as sailors of today enjoy along with their ice cream and Coca-Cola machines. This was wartime and in the hot climate of the Med. or the tropics of the Red Sea, Indian Ocean and the like, a crowded messdeck was stifling. No matter, we all needed to sleep somehow so we just sweated it out until it was time to go on watch. The saying that prevailed amongst the lads on warships both big and small was that 'Those that build and design these ships don't have to effing sail 'em.'

Regardless, the Navy had strict high standards of hygiene and cleanliness. Messes had to be cleaned and scrubbed out every morning and everything put away. Hammocks had to be properly lashed up and stowed and no gear was to be left lying around. After dinner and supper, dishes and utensils must be cleaned and stashed away. Before night rounds, messdecks were swept and tidied up by 21:00 hours when the duty officer and PO would do the night inspections of the crew's quarters. Before coming onto the messdeck, the Bosun's whistle would be piped and the PO would order 'Attention for messdeck rounds'. Everyone would immediately obey, stop talking and smoking, and turn off the wireless. The inspection would only be a quick look around unless anything outstanding was noticed and then the order 'Carry on' would be given.

One hour later at 22:00 hours sharp, the order would be piped over the PA, again preceded by the Bosun's whistle 'Pipe down. Lights out. Turn in'. This was immediately complied with not just out of duty but for consideration of our messmates who may have had the middle or morning watches and would need their sleep.

'Saturday morning routine', a naval term for the big, thorough clean up in the forenoon was a peacetime custom carried over into wartime when circumstances permitted.* This involved an extra clean over and above the usual where even mess gear and cutlery had to be polished and the battleship linoleum on the steel deck would be scrubbed by hand. This Pusser's routine was carried out more strictly on big ships than in the small ship Navy where living conditions were more cramped (hard layers) and things were a little less Pusser. The smaller a ship got, the less Pusser it usually was taking into consideration the wartime conditions and the job they had to do. No matter what ship, life was hard and uncomfortable in as much as wherever one wanted to go it was either up a ladder or down a ladder. One had to be physically fit which also produced the philosophy when climbing a ladder of 'one hand for the Navy and one hand for yourself'. In other words, look out for your own safety.

Leisure time for ratings such as myself had few diversions. Mostly it was eat, sleep, go on watch, do your dhobiying (laundry) and then have a bath by chucking buckets of water

---

*Also known as 'Captain's rounds' and led by the skipper followed by the heads of departments. The procession would be preceded by a marine bugler. As each mess was inspected, only a killick was allowed to be present. All others had to be out of sight.

over yourself. Strangely enough, this would in itself be a sort of pastime. Men would be standing there starkers, dhobiying their clothes, some with cigarettes hanging out of their mouths and talking, laughing, or telling dirty jokes.

Keeping clean was done with meticulous care. Nobody would allow themselves to get in such a state where they might be described as crabby. Keeping clean was one of the unwritten laws of the lower deck and nobody needed to be told by their messmates. Another part of this code of ethics was that one did not touch another man's belongings on a seagoing ship. Sadly, this code did not apply to the Royal Navy Barracks where nothing was safe and kitbags were known to be slashed open.

There were a few things that you could occupy yourself with in your spare time. The most important being writing letters home to wives, girlfriends, or family which was in itself good for morale although one had to keep in mind that all outgoing mail was censored. Envelopes were never sealed. Incoming mail which came at infrequent intervals was eagerly awaited and was always a major topic of discussion as to what was happening at home. This was extremely important for morale, all ranks included.

All messdecks had decks of cards, cribbage boards, chess sets, and other similar games which were always being used by someone. Men often had to devise their own forms of entertainment by talking intimately about their lives to each other which in normal times would probably not be confided to anyone by these same men.

Being on an aircraft carrier had at least one advantage. When not at action stations, in bad weather, or not flying on and off, one could go up to the flight deck and have a brisk stroll on an area the size of a long and very wide street with no traffic. Small ships did not have this sort of luxury.

Illustrious had one other feature of recreation not available on most ships. She sported a rec. room just below the flight deck which provided ample space but was sparsely furnished with tables and chairs. There was also a space where the NAAFi manager would sell a few soft drinks, not much of anything at certain times.* His main store was down in the galley flat.

---

*This small canteen was known as the Goffer Bar, named after Goffers, the lemonade soft drink sold there.

43

Anyway, this rec. room was good for the odd time when a Tombola game was organized by an entertainment committee. Tombola or Housey-Housey as the army calls it is what we now call Bingo. This would be organized with the permission of Jimmy when conditions allowed and could only be played when the ship was outside the three mile limit. This was always welcomed as an opportunity to make extra money to supplement our very small pay and provide some excitement. As we had a big complement, the stakes in our estimation were quite high. Threepence (three pennies) a ticket was the cost and there were prizes of maybe a few pounds for a house, less for a line.

Apart from Tombola games, the rec. room wasn't a place I frequented too much. The company of my messmates meant more to me as was the case with most of the lads.

It was on one of those few occasions when I went to the rec. room, just as we were starting to sail for Bermuda that I got an unexpected surprise. Just as I was going in I saw a face that I never thought I would see on any ship. It was my older brother's friend from civvy street who I also knew well, a chap called Joe. He was just as surprised as I was, both of us saying at the same time 'What are you doing here?' He had joined the Navy as an HO which was what I had wanted to do originally. The Navy was now in need of men to supplement its losses.

Joseph Patrick Fitzpatrick or 'Fitz' as he was nicknamed was a short, stocky, and very tough individual, especially when he was ashore and had been drinking. Otherwise he was easygoing and got along well with everyone on the messdeck. Joe was a chap who had been around and had seen the world. Older than us new recruits he had served in the army for seven years and did five on the reserve. During that time he served overseas which usually meant India or the Middle East. When the war came, his reserve time had just ended and he decided to join rather than wait to be called back. He might have felt like I did, that his chances of surviving could be somewhat better in the Navy. Both of us were dead wrong in our thinking for who would want to be trapped and die a thousand agonies in some ship's stokehold or other compartments where stokers were sent.

Joe did his basic training in Royal Arthur, one of the famous Butlin's holiday camps on the coast that had been commandeered as a training establishment by the RN. Needless to say, Joe's experience in square bashing, rifle and bayonet drill soon

44

made him outstanding to the instructor where he almost became his assistant on the parade ground.

It wasn't long before Joe showed his other talent as a barber after joining Illustrious in Plymouth. Joe would come over to our house before the war to cut my hair to make a little money when he went through his share of unemployment so I already knew he was a good barber. Having a large clientele consisting mostly of stokers, he just used to cut hairs when he needed extra money to go ashore. Sometimes when I would ask him when he would be cutting hairs, his reply would be 'I ain't broke yet'.

When I met him again for the first time after forty years at a reunion for Old Illustrians, he seemed to have mellowed quite a bit. I asked him how he had to get permission to cut hairs and he replied that he had to cut Capt. Boyd's hair first as a free sample to see how good he was. God only knows what the skipper would have done if he had made a mess of it. I guess he would have been in the 'rattle' instead of being the barber.

Joe was a bit of a 'rum rat' too but he wasn't the only one. We all liked our grog including me but there were those who would do anything for it.

There were other 'celebrities' I should mention. In particular we had a couple of old three badgers (stripeys), men who earned their good conduct stripes which are received after three, eight and thirteen years service.* These guys were actually pensioners who came back as Royal Fleet Reservists and were almost in their middle forties or even a little bit older. Men like these usually got a job as a 'messdeck dodger' or 'captain of the heads' – keeping the messdecks and passageways swept or cleaning the toilet. Sometimes they would also do messman's duties for Chiefs and PO's.

One of these three stripers was called Charlie Giddy, a real cheerful character though a bit crusty at times and short and stocky in appearance. Charlie lived on the lower messdeck with Eric. On the upper messdeck with me was another chap like Charlie called Di Yanto, a real Welshman. A character who was also known to be a bit crusty, he could be located by his laugh which sounded more like a squeeky chuckle. Both men were more like the Daddies of the messdeck with the younger men

---

*Ratings would get threepence a day extra for each good conduct stripe earned.

often coming to them for advice and asking them about their experience in the old Navy. Charlie and Yanto were both held in a position of respect and both were old 'rum rats'.

Then there was big, hefty Bungy Williams, a two badge killick who had arms as big as my legs. Bungy was a good swimmer and an enthusiastic water polo player. While in Bermuda he talked me into playing since I was known to be a reasonably good swimmer but I soon found out that water polo was a pretty rough game, especially against guys as big as him. Bungy would swim right over you or grab you and hold your head under water with one arm. This was the first and last time I played.

Big Bungy was also on the upper messdeck at first but at my individual mess which was the men that shared one table and could number at least a dozen there was another Bungy Williams, 'little Bungy'. He used to pal out with a Northern Irishman called Mick Beatty and both of these were very close friends because of what they had in common. Both had been in just over two years and they really thought they were old timers wearing their now light blue collars dhobied more times than necessary to take the dark blue out and make them look 'more salty'. To top things off they both had served on the battler HMS Warspite for a short spell and so were comparing things to life aboard her. They would always be saying it was the 'Spite' this and the 'Spite' that. They really fancied themselves as a couple of 'Jack Me Hearties'.

With us on Illustrious as well were many members of my class and Eric's from the training division, Sid Nuttall, Jim Newton, Frank Lord, and Harry Thomas to name a few. There was one other fellow amongst the stokers that I should mention. I can't recall his name but he was a two badger and his twelve years was nearly up. This did not please him as the war was on and he couldn't get out so he would be 'dripping' all over the messdeck about the 'effing Navy'. He was a rum rat for sure and whenever he couldn't get ashore he would be mixing and concocting his own home brew or jungle juice as we called it which could contain anything from Brasso or boot polish to vanilla extract which he obtained by devious means from the galley. He often looked very odd at times with slurred speech but he wasn't too bad to get along with as long as you didn't take his homosexual antics too seriously. That sort of thing went on too behind the scenes, not necessarily by him though. There were individuals who were referred to by regular sailors as 'arse bandits'. One had to be on the lookout for these types who wanted to point out the ship's 'golden rivet' to any unsuspecting person, especially sprogs.

Water was one of the most important commodities on any ship. As we had a complement of 1,400 men and as time progressed, even more, the need to keep everybody supplied with fresh water for drinking, washing and cooking was a priority which kept our four evaporators, two port and two starboard going all the time. Yet despite the great need for the ship's company for distilled water, they were only secondary when considering the need for feed water for the ship's massive boilers. Three boiler rooms with two boilers each to supply the steam required for our three engine rooms which could generate 110,000 shaft horsepower took an enormous supply of water.

Distilled water meant completely salt free, literally dead and tasteless because it contained no nutrients. The 'vaps' were a killick's job so I never looked after them on Illustrious but I did on the minesweeper later on and for two years after the war while on the carrier HMS Unicorn which was in the reserve fleet at Plymouth after serving during the war as a seagoing aircraft maintenance carrier. On Unicorn, the method of testing the water was similar to that on Illustrious. The water was checked constantly by going though a salinometer with a graph on it and samples were taken in a test tube with silver nitrate being added to test its salt content. If the water in the tube turned cloudy, it would be pumped into the bilges to avoid contaminating the feed water tanks as this would cause corrosion in the boilers.

With all the different machinery on such a large, new ship which had to be kept steaming and ready for any emergency now preparing to go into action, our complement of stokers including killicks was considerable. Take for instance there were three engine rooms with a killick and there would be three watches per day, two vaps with a 'Hookie' in each one at three watches, six dynamos with a killick each in three watches, a killick in the control room in three watches, plus three watches on the steering gear and CO_2 room where they made the ice (for the wardroom). Finally, there were other jobs on the steam catapults and hydraulic lifts making a total of at least fifty killicks including other miscellaneous jobs. For every leading hand there was approximately two second and first class stokers making a grand total of at least 150, all living on our two messdecks. The organization of all this was done by Regulating Chief Stoker, nicknamed 'Reggy'. Reggy was fairly popular because eveybody tried to be nice to him so they might get a 'soft number'. Some even tried to 'flannel' him up at times but it didn't work. Reggy was the senior Chief Stoker and had been in a long time so he knew all the ropes and dodges.

Going on the night watches one had to draw the supply of Carnation milk, brown sugar, and the ration of 'ky'. After Pusser's Rum, Pusser's Ky was the most famous drink in the Andrew. It was actually cocoa and meant to keep one awake which it did, half the time by just trying to make it. Ky was rationed out according to how many was on the watch and was in rock solid blocks which couldn't be scraped, broken, or chipped no matter what you did. The only way it could be dissolved was to put it on the 'Ky Drain'. This was a little steam pipe that was improvised usually by the ERA's (Engine Room Articifer) by being fitted on one of the larger pipes controlled by a little valve. The Ky would be put inside a fanny partly filled with water and gradually allowed to boil up until it dissolved completely and requiring just an occasional stir. This was a long process but it produced a thick rough tasting chocolate drink which, when added with sugar and milk succeeded in keeping you awake. Hardly the Cadbury blend but at least it was hot and wet.

With so many men being thrown together from all walks of life and locations – Jocks, Taffs, Paddies, Geordies, Scousers, Janners, Cocknies, and even a Springbok (South African), you would think there would be chaos and many disagreements. However, the opposite was true. Gradually we were all welded into a team that before long our Captain would inform us that he was proud of. Among our regular duties there were drills and practices like closing up at action stations, fire and repair parties, and damage control exercises. For the Fleet Air Arm there was flying on and off, crash on deck, and gunnery practices. Everyone was kept constantly busy. We didn't know what was in store for us but it seemed quite obvious that those in the 'nuthouse' had some definite plans and it wouldn't be very long before we would find out. A sample was very soon forthcoming. Despite this and the fact that it was wartime, we were considered a happy ship and it would prove that we were an efficient one. This was later to be a major contribution to saving many of our lives and the ship itself.

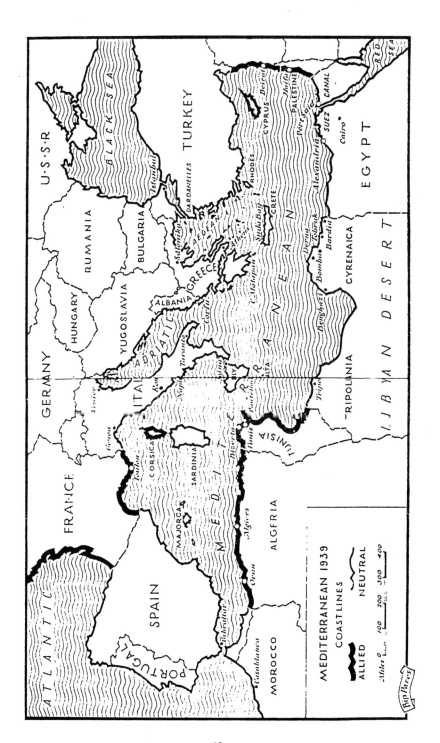

MEDITERRANEAN 1939

COASTLINES

━━━ ALLIED

┄┄┄ NEUTRAL

Miles 0   100   200   300   400

BIP PARES

U.S.S.R.

BLACK SEA

TURKEY

Istanbul

DARDANELLES

AEGEAN

RHODES

CYPRUS

Beirut

Haifa

Jaffa

PALESTINE

Port Said

SUEZ CANAL

RED SEA

Alexandria

Cairo

EGYPT

CRETE

Middle Bay

Derna

Tobruk

Bardia

Bomba

Benghazi

CYRENAICA

L I B Y A N   D E S E R T

RUMANIA

BULGARIA

HUNGARY

YUGOSLAVIA

GREECE

ALBANIA

Salonika

Corfu

C. Matapan

ADRIATIC

ITALY

Taranto

Rome

Naples

Taranto

Bari

MALTA

TRIPOLITANIA

Tripoli

GERMANY

FRANCE

Toulon

CORSICA

SARDINIA

M E D I T E R R A N E A N

Tunis

Bizerta

Pantelleria

TUNISIA

Tunis

ALGERIA

Algiers

Oran

MAJORCA

SPAIN

Gibraltar

Casablanca

MOROCCO

PORTUGAL

A T L A N T I C

49

Chapter Five

Out to the Med.

Illustrious sailed into Bermuda in early July 1940 somewhat battered after the North Atlantic storm she had encountered on the crossing. She immediately pulled into the dockyard to fix her damaged gear throughout the ship. Unfortunately this delay caused the flying training for our air group to be shortened but it did afford the ship's company some extra time ashore. Bermuda is a tropical sunspot with white sandy beaches and turquoise water. This beautiful climate made a pleasant change from the dull, damp, and depressing weather that England has. For me personally it was a chance to get over my seasickness and I enjoyed myself getting a first taste of what I considered to be 'foreign service' and seeing the sights of Hamilton, the capital. Bermuda has a slower pace of life and a narrow gauge railway with open cars which travel along the coast which is most definitely scenic. I also got my first sample of the toffee-nosed colonials who inhabit these places throughout the Empire with certain places being off limits to ratings or enlisted men but not officers. Class distinction extended far beyond the shores of Britain I was to find out.

One other thing in particular happened which I found unsettling while in Bermuda. The day we arrived on July 4, Lord Haw-Haw announced on the radio that HMS Illustrious had been torpedoed by a U-boat. He even gave the name of the U-boat commander as Lieutenant Endras who today is known as one of the U-boat aces. When the BBC denied the sinking of Illustrious, Haw-Haw replied 'It was not claimed that she sunk, but that she was hit by torpedo. HMS Illustrious is at present carrying out repairs in Bermuda Bay.'[1,2]The frightening part of this report to us was that the Germans knew where we were and when the news reached the British press, the families of those serving on Illustrious were alarmed and the Admiralty received a flood of calls including one from Captain Boyd's wife. She was relieved however when told by the authorities that they knew nothing about it.

The remaining time in Bermuda was spent steaming about giving the pilots of our Fulmars and Swordfish practice on deck landings and other flying training. By the time we were finished at Bermuda, the Illustrious and her crew were a well trained and efficient team.*

I was a little sorry to leave so soon. It had been somewhat of a change but at least we didn't encounter another big storm on the way back across the 'pond'. We even managed one of those rare occasions for a Tombola game. This turned out to offer a particular surprise for me even though I didn't actually win a line or a house. Having several hundred playing all crowded into the rec. room, some buying obviously more than one ticket to increase their chances of winning meant that there would be a big mess to clean up afterwards if all the tickets were thrown away. It was decided by the committee to avoid all the work by having each man put his tickets in a barrel from which, when all the games were finished, there would be a final draw of one ticket only as the winner. The prize would be 7s 6p. After the last game and before everyone had left the draw was made. Everybody was silent as the committee member placed the barrel on the table and mixed up all the tickets. All eyes anxiously watching and wondering, someone from the committee was asked to put their hand in and pick one. With your name and rank on the ticket the name was read out. Who else but yours truly, A. H. Jones, Stoker 2nd Class. Shocked, I jumped up and shouted 'here'. Voices then shouted obscene things from all across the room, 'By 'eck, effing money-bags', and 'How 'bout a rubber'. I didn't care, I thought I was really rich now!

July 23 1940, Illustrious returned to the UK and sailed into the Clyde. Captain Boyd was summoned to the Admiralty right away and briefed on the situation in the Mediterranean by the

---

*Although well trained, the crew was still green and untried but our baptism of fire would come soon and our training would prove its worth.

First Sea Lord, Admiral Sir Dudley Pound. He was then told to sail Illustrious through the Strait of Gibraltar into the Med.

On August 19, Rear-Admiral Lumley Lyster arrived on board and hoisted his flag as Rear-Admiral, Aircraft Carriers, Mediterranean.

Three days later, in company with the battleship Valiant, the anti-aircraft cruisers Coventry and Calcutta and escorting a large convoy, we set sail for Gibraltar.

Being that this was going to be foreign service for real, everyone received various inoculations along the way. These shots included Yellow Fever, TAB, and a number of other deadly diseases one could pick up as these places don't have the same standards of hygiene that we have in the West. One of these shots in particular was very painful in its after effects. The needle itself wasn't that bad although some would faint at the thought of getting it. The worst part was what it did to your arm afterwards which would become all red and inflamed with a big swelling. This was so painful that all those that had it which might be most of the ship's company would be walking around protecting their arm and swearing at anybody who went anywhere near it. Getting in your hamock also became a real chore and you would feel ill for best side of a week. Regardless, this was no excuse for not going down on watch and you just had to put up with it and suffer, but not necessarily in silence.

The trip from Scapa Flow to Gib. was uneventful in as much as I don't remember any scares although we had to take the usual precautions. U-boats roamed the Atlantic at will. When we approached Gib. I saw for the first time the famous Rock which has long been regarded as a symbol of strength in the Empire. This huge rock made Gibraltar a formidable fortress as it guarded the Western entrance to the Mediterranean a thousand miles from Britain and a vital part of a chain of bases that extended around the globe. The Rock of Gibraltar was a network of military facilities, many of them built right into the protection of the Rock with a myriad of tunnels and gun emplacements. It also had other inhabitants too, apes so they say. An old saying developed that when the apes left it would also be time for the British to leave. I never did see any of those creatures.

Going ashore I was thinking of all those exotic delights that the old sailors used to talk about in foreign parts. This didn't come anywhere near my expectations. What I found was one main street that was overcrowded and a few bars, one might call them dives, with the girls wanting you to buy them drinks and then take your money, what little money we had.

Every night at six o'clock, the border between Spain and the Rock was closed and therefore all the Spanish people who lived in La Linea had to go back. This included many of the girls. These measures were for security reasons as Spain was barely neutral. Hitler was trying to convince Franco and his Fascists to come in on the side of the Axis as payment for the German help in the Spanish Civil War 1936–39. Fortunately for us, Spain chose to remain neutral as they were already war weary. Nevertheless, Germany still had its share of spies in Spain trying to pick up information about Allied convoy and warship movements.

Shipping and troops coming and going meant tight security which brings to mind my run ashore there. Wending my way through the crowded street, something struck me as rather odd and almost funny until I found out why. I noticed taxi and car drivers half hanging out of the side windows, banging like hell on the doors, and at the same time shouting and yelling for people to get out of the way. Apparently all the horns had been taken out or disconnected so as to thwart any would be enterprising enemy agents from passing on coded signals to others and find its way across the border.

After a one day stay, we left the Rock on August 30. I wasn't really sorry to leave it as it was basically a garrison town with not much to do although we weren't there as tourists anyway. Our main business at hand was just around the corner heading for the Med. Most of the lads like myself did take advantage of buying the fairly cheap and plentiful fruits that the local vendors sold just outside the dockyard. Grapes, bananas, apples, and oranges etc. were things that were rationed or virtually unobtainable to most people in England by this time. The Pusser's menu didn't include these luxuries either. Most of the time for dessert we would have heavy as lead 'Figgy Duffs'.

Illustrious, Valiant, and our two escorting cruisers sailed from Gib. along with Force H which was the Western Mediterranean task force based at Gib. and included the famous carrier Ark Royal. This operation was code-named 'HATS' which stood for Hands Across The Sea and involved ferrying much needed supplies to Malta and Alexandria, the Eastern Fleet Task Force base. Not only did merchant ships take supplies but we too were crammed full of every conceivable war supply from ammo to petrol. Even the vast area of the hangar was utilized as a storage facility. With all the extra gas and explosives plus our own we were like a floating bomb which if hit would have catastrophic results, and this was a very real possibility as we would soon have to run the heavily defended gauntlet of the Pantelleria Straits.

As I have mentioned, we were steaming in company with the 'Ark'. This carrier was built shortly before us and the forerunner to the Illustrious class design. The Ark was to become our nemesis in terms of always getting the glory despite having a fairly short career compared to ours and actually less battle honours. The old Ark became legendary after her part in hunting the Bismark which retrieved England's honour after the loss of HMS Hood, the pride of the Royal Navy, nevertheless we accomplished similar feats such as the almost suicidal attack on the Italian fleet at Taranto and later on surviving Stuka dive-bomber attacks. Even today, documentary films seem to omit this crucial phase of the war in the Mediterranean in which Illustrious played such a vital role yet there are films of the other carriers including the Ark Royal.

At an Illustrious reunion we spoke to an old shipmate who had been in the Fleet Air Arm and he related a story which illustrates the sort of rivalry which existed between our ship and the Ark. Being a new ship with new equipment and a newly trained air group, someone came up with the idea that we could get our aircraft on deck and ready for flying faster than the crew of Ark Royal and to prove it, a race was organized to see who could range an aircraft the quickest. Everything went according to plan. The plane was put on the lift and taken up to the flight deck where the handlers pushed it to its parking spot with as much speed as they could muster. Unfortunately, when the officer yelled 'Brake', someone noticed that there was no pilot in the plane to pull the handbrake. The aircraft kept right on going and over the side into the 'oggin'. This no doubt resulted in the men of Ark Royal's air group feeling very smug about their win and some rather awkward explaining to be done about the loss of one of His Majesty's kites. Being a stoker, I wasn't in a position to verify this but one can imagine the sort of goings on with inter-ship rivalries.

The situation in the Med. east of Gib. was reaching a critical stage, with Mussolini, the Italian dictator seizing what he thought was a golden opportunity to cash in on the spoils of the Axis conquests by declaring war on Britain and France on June 10 1940. Thinking after the evacuation of Dunkirk, it was only a matter of time before Britain would fall too. France was about to surrender, the British army was in dissarray having lost most of its equipment in France, and the greatly outnumbered Royal Air Force was preparing for the onslaught of the entire Luftwaffe. Except for what help the Commonwealth could give, Britain was totally alone as a defender of the free world. All of Europe was under Axis domination which included the Soviets who were carving out their share of Eastern Europe.

This left the Mediterranean in a very precarious position. The pompous and arrogant Il Duce saw himself as another Caesar and he referred to the Med. as an 'Italian Lake'. In North Africa, the Italian army was massing for the attack on Egypt which began on September 13 against General Wavell's outnumbered army known originally as 'Wavell's Thirty Thousand'. Italy's air force, the Regia Aeronautica, though not very aggressive, still had the advantage of numbers and was a constant threat to the British Fleet which had for air defence only the old aircraft carrier Eagle, a converted battleship of WW I vintage. Eagle had been doing her best since May providing air cover for the whole fleet in the Eastern Med. and doing other operations. Against the fast, powerful and more modern Italian battlefleet, Admiral Cunningham tried to bring his adversaries into battle against his smaller number of capital ships which were slower and less modern. The chance to even up the odds was not forthcoming until the arrival of much needed reinforcements in the form of the fast, new carrier Illustrious with her radar which would become the eyes and ears of the fleet for a range of 60 miles and would give a real advantage. Once spotted, the Italian aircraft which were harrassing the fleet could be quickly intercepted by her Fairey Fulmars although not being high performance like the Spitfires, they provided effective Combat Air Patrols which the Italians were surprised to find waiting for them whenever the fleet was attacked. Adding this with the firepower of Valiant and her mighty fifteen inch guns and the two fast anti-aircraft cruisers, the fleet was strengthened.

Up until this time, Admiral Cunningham's work was compounded by the lack of support from the powerful French Navy which was mostly still intact but lying idle in French North Africa and even in our own base at Alexandria. Their ships were taking orders from the Vichy government, collaborating with the enemy and were refusing to fight alongside the British, their former ally. The main fear was that these crews may be replaced with German sailors which would then be used against us and this could not be allowed to happen at any cost. As a result, on July 3, the ships of Force H under Admiral J. F. Somerville consisting of the battlecruiser Hood, battleships Valiant and Resolution, and the carrier Ark Royal opened fire on the French squadron in Mers-El-Kebir after negotiations broke down and the French Admiral refused to join us. One French battleship was sunk and two severely damaged. In Alexandria, the French Naval Squadron was disarmed by more peaceful means through talks and our ships were once again able to put to sea to fight the Italians instead of possibly the French. Perhaps if those French ships had been more loyal to the cause to fight on and liberate their country by helping us instead of the enemy, things would have been much easier for us in the Med. and many good men and fine ships would have been spared. As it was, the British Navy was stretched dangerously thin all around the world.

Despite being so short handed, the Navy did have some success before our arrival at bringing the Italian fleet to battle. Mostly it was a matter of chasing the Italian Navy around which was usually faster. One notable exception occurred on July 19 1940 and came to be known as the Battle of Cape Spada where the Australian cruiser HMAS Sydney and five destroyers operating off Crete ran into two little cruisers, the Bartolomeo Colleoni and the Bande Nere. The little ships immediately tried to steam away and were confident that their trial speeds of 37 knots would enable them to outrun the Sydney. Very shortly however, they were shocked to see the Aussies keeping up with them and lobbing six inch shells. The speeds of Italian ships are often overestimated because their high trial speeds are obtained without the extra weight of fuel, stores, and ammo. The Colleoni's speed was no greater than the 'Digger's' thirty knots and she was soon a blazing wreck which was finished off by a spread of torpedoes from the destroyers. Sydney was responsible along with the five destroyers for the first sinking of a major Italian warship.* The other cruiser which had been with the Colleoni did manage to escape but not until she too had been damaged.

The battle involving the Sydney occurred exactly ten days after the famous action off Calabria which on July 9 took place after an Ittie fleet consisting of two battleships, twelve cruisers, and a number of destroyers was spotted returning to it base at Taranto after covering a convoy to Benghazi. The Itties were first reported by a British sub. and as the fleet moved in to intercept them, their position was accurately relayed by a reconnaissance aircraft flying out of Malta. Engaging the Italians were the Warspite, Malaya, and Royal Sovereign, the carrier Eagle; the cruisers Orion, Neptune, Sydney, Gloucester, and Liverpool, and seventeen destroyers. After dodging attacks by torpedo bombers from Eagle and the consistently accurate firing of Warspite's 15-inch guns, the Itties showed that they had very little stomach for a fight and they quickly disengaged under the cover of a heavy smoke-screen. As the action took place near Calabria which is the 'toe' in the Italian 'boot', their fleet was soon able to call upon the Regia Aeronautica which covered them with hundreds of aircraft and showed that the numbers that Eagle was able to put into the air were insufficient to provide adequate cover for Cunningham's fleet. The results of the battle were damage to the Gloucester by a bomb hit to her bridge which killed her Captain and seventeen other men. The Ittie battleship Giulio Cesare and cruiser Bolzano were damaged by fire from Warspite but the effects were more far reaching. As Admiral Cunningham said in his book *A Sailor's Odyssey*: 'Never again did they willingly face up to the fire of British battleships, though on several subsequent occasions they were in a position to give battle with great preponderance in force'.[3] The chance to engage Italy's battlefleet was denied to the Med. fleet after this time though they still posed a great

---

*HMAS Sydney later went out to the Far East where she became famous for engaging the German Q-ship Kormoran on November 19 1941. Tragically, Sydney sank with all hands and her fate would not have been known had it not been for Kormoran's survivors who last saw her drifting away ablaze. Kormoran went down too and the majority of her crew reached Australia where they were put in POW camps.

threat to Allied shipping. The arrival of Illustrious and her consorts would be instrumental in changing this.

All politics aside, the opinion of the lower deck regarding the overall situation confronting us was that the French had folded up and let us down stinking, also that Italy's 'Musso' had stabbed us in the back and we were now on our own. Rumblings coming from the Far East from the third member of the Tripartite Pact, the Land of the Rising Sun or simply the Japs showed that their intentions were not quite clear yet but precautions such as trying to strengthen the defences of Singapore, Hong Kong, and other key points were being taken with what could be spared. It looked like it was going to be a bloody long war.

Back at sea, my steaming watch was still centre engine room with Mick the Irish killick and a fifth class tiffy who over the years, I have forgotten his name and of course the Chief Tiff, E.R.A. Downs, a really Pusser 'pensh'.

At first Chief Downs was a real miserable so and so. No unnecessary joking or laughing and he tried to keep everyone busy even when at cruising speed and the pace was slower. However at a later date, the three of us decided to work out a plan to tame him. We 'sent him to Coventry' meaning none of us would speak to him from one end of the watch to the other day in and day out except to tell him what was necessary and obey his orders. Eventually this silent treatment began to take its toll and wore him down where we began to notice he became more sociable and tried to make conversation. After one or two off watch consultations, the three of us decided we would give him a chance to redeem himself. He was as good as gold after that and we all got on well. It goes to show that living cheek by jowl on a warship or probably any ship for that matter, life was hard enough without anybody making things more unendearing than it already was.

Further on into the Med. we sailed with Force H, Valiant, and the two C Class cruisers. Illustrious then started to show what she could do so she and the newly modernized Valiant were valuable assets to Cunningham's fleet with the new Radio Direction Finding units or Radar which gave us a clear edge. Some Ittie planes picked us up but we already had them spotted. Illustrious swung into the wind and the command to launch aircraft was given. Within minutes our Fulmars had three Wops in the 'drink'. Then we had some more practice for our planes when our Swordfish dropped 250 pounders on Cagliari in Sardinia before we finally parted company with our compatriots. Our four ships steamed on alone to run the gauntlet.

Going through the narrow straits of Pantelleria was timed for the dark hours to avoid detection but no chances were taken as we closed up at action stations in the evening and stayed at a third degree of readiness all night before we were safely across. Having the graveyard (middle) watch, I stretched out on the hard deck at my action station, No. 3 Fire and Repair Party, damage control in the keyboard flat aft.* Here was an armoured bulkhead that separated us from the wardroom flat and the officers' quarters on the other side, something that would save my life and I would be grateful for in the not too distant future.

The night passed uneventful although it was said that we passed close enough to the Italian shore batteries our lookouts could see the glow of cigarettes being smoked by the Ittie sentries. Those of us who had to stay below decks or in any of the machinery rooms when anything was happening could only hope and pray that everything would be alright and had to rely on our PA system for any information that may be broadcast. This morale builder was taken over by our ship's padre, Rev. Henry Lloyd whose running commentaries whenever we went to action stations were a source of strength and reassurance to everybody. No matter how bad things got, his voice was always calm and informative and I'm sure that anyone who served on Illustrious in those days would remember it well.

When daylight broke after steaming full speed all through the night to put as much distance as possible, it was discovered that we had steamed right through a minefield because mooring wires had to be removed from the starboard paravanes. This seemed even more miraculous than the minefield that Illus-

---

*The keyboard flat was the place where a Royal Marine sentry was on duty 24 hours a day standing at a desk and in front was a colour coded and numbered keyboard with keys to all compartments of the ship. Above the board was a clock. This colour coded system was invented by an officer on Illustrious and was so efficient that it was later adopted throughout the fleet.

trious avoided at Liverpool in January. We must have been living a charmed life.

We met up with the main battlefleet and the carrier Eagle and proceded to our main base at Alexandria, Egypt and on the way our Swordfish flew sorties with the old Eagle's aircraft against airfields in Rhodes which had been a constant threat to the fleet. We were making our presence known with a vengeance as a sign to the enemy of things to come.

As we approached Alex, everybody on the lower deck was now talking about some shore leave and all the exotic delights we had heard about from the older matelots, particularly the famous brothels of Sister Street. What a bunch of hags! No real disrespect really for the ladies of that red light district but that's what it really turned out to be when I went past it briefly.

For my part, Alex was a dump but as a naval base in wartime it was of immense strategic importance. It was about 200 miles from Port Said, the Mediterranean entrance to the Suez Canal, a man-made strip of water literally cut out of the desert to provide a shorter route to the Far East. At a hundred miles long it had Port Suez as the other entrance at the Red Sea end. The canal was a lifeline which had to be defended at all costs as it was also our back door in and out when later supply convoys couldn't fight their way from Gib. without staggering losses.

Having said that, going ashore for the lads of the lower deck was a chance to get away from the ships for just a few hours. I say hours specifically because of the reason that ships were always at notice for steam in case of emergency to be ready for sea according to the situation. It could be one hour, two hours, four hours, or six hours; no one could be sure as fleet orders and signals were constantly being sent and changed. Everybody went ashore to just let off steam. No 'Harry Grippo's' here either.

The Gyppos or Wogs as we called them were poor as church mice except for the shopkeepers in the city part in Muhammed Ali square (fairly modern) and the adjoining side streets. The rest scratched out an existence in squalid surroundings by begging or carrying shoe shine boxes around trying to harass sailors into getting their boots polished. If we told them to 'Veer' or 'bugger off' one ran the risk of getting a black streak of shoe polish smeared across your nice white No. 6's and then the bloody Gyppo would quickly run off into a side street with Jack in hot pursuit screaming oaths and obscenities. You could never catch them as the wogs all looked the same to us in their long 'night shirts'.

As for the shopkeepers, their main purpose was to try to fleece Jolly Jack for as much money as possible by demanding outrageous prices for everything. We soon got wise to this trick and haggled and bartered just as hard until eventually this became part of our fun and entertainment during a run ashore.

Fortunately we had the Fleet Club where we could drink a few beers and buy something to eat. The food was nothing glamorous, just the usual Naval 'scran' but you knew it was safe to eat being done under Pusser supervision even though they employed Egyptian staff to do the menial tasks. I never ate anywhere outside the club because of the notorious unhygienic reputation of these places.

The beer was called Stella and it had a flavour of onions which I believe was an ingredient in the brewing. Even though it was called onion beer we could still drink it without it bringing tears to our eyes as we couldn't be too fussy. There was no other choice available and the lower deck didn't rate hard liquor which was in abundance wherever the officers went. At least you could still get drunk there.

The big highlight was the Tombola games at the club whenever they were put on. Each ticket cost one Piastre or 'Acker' of Gyppo money worth tuppence halfpenny (2½d). This was almost a comedy at times with all the grunts, groans, and remarks coming from someone out of the hundreds playing whenever a number was called out especially when one was near to winning a line or a house. Many of the common expletives of the day could be heard as some lucky individual claimed his prize which may be fairly high, possibly twenty or thirty pounds. To the average matelot this was several months' pay.

All of this at least helped the lads to forget for a little while what might be waiting for them when they went back to sea.

To wrap up this short sample of a run ashore in this miserable, unexotic port in the Near East, suffice to say many others had much wilder runs ashore to the 'bag shanties' of Sister Street and the like but paid the price later with a trip to see 'Bones' in the sick bay. No wonder the common saying of 'roll on my twelve' was beginning to take on more meaning to me now as I had a long, long way to go.

Chapter Six

From Alex to Taranto

Friday, September 13, 1940, the Italian army which had been massing in Libya for some time invaded Egypt which was defended by General Wavell's beleaguered Thirty Thousand, the forerunner to the famous Eighth Army, the 'Desert Rats'.

After only a very short stay in Alex, Illustrious put to sea to do her stuff which was to harass the enemy wherever we could find them. We started out by attacking Benghazi on the 17th which was a main supply base for the Ittie army. Our two squadrons of Stringbags (the nickname for the Swordfish which were antiquated biplanes), no. 815 and 819 dropped mines in the harbour and sank two merchant ships and a destroyer. The old Stringbags which were flimsy, fabric covered flying machines could barely reach 120 mph when they were fully loaded with bombs or a torpedo but they were to really prove their worth in sterling service. I never envied the pilots and crew flying those crates. When we went on the flight deck to watch them take off they seemed to disappear over the bows and we often thought they had gone into the 'oggin'. They would then reappear struggling to gain altitude with a big 'tin fish' hanging underneath. You could almost imagine those wings were literally flapping like a bird.

Landing these kites back on seemed to us to be just as hazardous. The ship would turn into the wind and steam full belt which created a heck of a breeze on the deck which you could barely stand up in. 'Bats' would be there with his ping-pong paddles waving the planes around and telling them when and how to land. Those pilots would have had damn good eyesight to see such tiny signals and nerves of steel to land on an airstrip which would look like a matchbox from up there. Doing this sort of caper in the dark after attacking ports in Libya or airfields in the Dodecanese seemed almost suicidal. The Royal Navy's Fleet Air Arm though using poor quality aircraft more than made up for this inadequacy by skill and daring. Of all the world's navies, our naval air arm was the only one that did night flying with any success and the real proof of this would be soon forthcoming.

Back in September 1938 when the Munich Crisis captured the world's attention and Europe was brought to the brink of war, the Mediterranean fleet under the command of Admiral Sir Dudley Pound was alerted to the fact that Mussolini might side with his pal, Adolph.

Admiral Lumley Lyster who was then Captain of the converted carrier HMS Glorious at Alexandria, put together a plan with the help of some of his officers which would involve an air strike on the Italian battlefleet in its own ports. The next day, the plan was brought before Admiral Pound who had suggested it in the first place. What they came up with was an air strike using planes armed with mainly torpedoes and then bombers for secondary targets against the principal Italian naval base which was Taranto on the heel of Italy. Owing to the heavy anti-aircraft defences at Taranto, the raid would have to be done at night.

Admiral Pound approved the plan but the crisis passed and Germany was appeased. The plan was mothballed and its inventor, the Admiral went to London to become the First Sea Lord of the Admiralty.

With the arrival of the fast, new carrier to the Eastern Med. Fleet in September 1940, this plan was reactivated. Mr Churchill was anxious to see some very strong action taken against the Italian fleet in case the Germans decided to take matters into their own hands.

When Illustrious reached Alexandria, Admiral Lyster went aboard Admiral Cunningham's flagship HMS Warspite to discuss the tactical situation and the resurrection of the plan to attack Taranto. The raid was to be called Operation Judgement and to be executed by thirty Swordfish in two flights of fifteen each flying from Illustrious and Eagle. The date was set for October 21 to coincide with the anniversary of Admiral Horatio Nelson's Battle of Trafalgar in which a smaller British fleet defeated the combined French and Spanish Navies.

From here on, night flying was intensified in preparation and we were constantly going to sea. This meant plenty of watchkeeping, closing up at action stations and not too much shore leave. In some ways there was a little bit of consolation, small though it might be. A lot of the lads including myself were getting a bit ambitious about trying to pass from Second Class to First Class Stoker which meant another shilling a day in our pay and a star over the top of the propellor on our uniform.

In order to pass as a Stoker First Class, one had to flog up on the Stoker's Manual to find out and memorize how the steam cylindrical boiler worked to produce steam to the main turbines. Also how the fuel pumps worked to spray the oil fuel into the furnace and so on was learned. You then had to go before the Engineer Officer for an oral test which usually made for a nerve wracking experience for us sprogs. This procedure had to be done in a Pusser like manner by first putting in a request through the Chief Stoker to see the divisional officer. This gained us a little more time for the last minute cramming for the test.

Over the next month, Illustrious's aircraft when not brushing up on their techniques for the raid, continued to bomb and strafe enemy installations and ships. The Italians retaliated by trying to bomb us but our radar always gave us advance warning and we would be already closed up at action stations. The Ittie bombers would be greeted by a barrage of anti-aircraft fire and our fighters which had already been scrambled. The Italian bombing was usually high level and no great threat because the bombs often fell wide but the risk was always there that they might score a hit. Bombs weren't the only threat as they would use aerial torpedo attacks as well but the keen eyesight of our lookouts and skilled handling by the bridge crew always enabled us to dodge them. The Itties had one squadron calling themselves the 'Green Mice' which was based in Rhodes and always seemed to make Illustrious their specific target. We seemed to have acquired a reputation. All this carryings on to us matelots below decks and in machinery spaces was still scarey as we never knew if the enemy was going to get a lucky hit on us. If it wasn't for our 'sin bosun' Rev. Lloyd and his running commentaries over the tannoy, we wouldn't have known anything other than the buzzes that went round. We weren't told very much except what was absolutely necessary. Only those back aft seemed to know what was going on because they were told, we weren't. Those on the upper deck could see what was happening for themselves.

During our operations with the fleet that autumn of 1940, we did manage one or two runs ashore in the place known in the vernacular of naval slang as the 'Matelot's Paradise' – Malta. The Grand Harbour and capitol is called Valetta and made up of small communities separated by canals. The quickest way to cross these waterways was to take a local taxi, a small rowboat called a Dghaisa.* This boat would look something like the gondolas of Venice, only smaller, with Jose, the Maltese 'Dghaisa Man' pushing and wiggling the oar around rather than the standard rowing stroke. However he always got us to the other side OK but the trick was to have the right change. Jose never had any. The usual fee was threepence.

The main place all the lower deck headed for was Strait Street or Stretta Strada in Maltese, commonly known as 'the Gut'. This was a long sloping street with wide steps leading all the way to the bottom and each side was made up of dives where you could drink and dance with the local girls if you bought them drinks. Each bar had a very colourful, cabaret type of name such as the Egyptian Queen or the Moulin Rouge, to name a couple. Outside each of these cabarets would be a fast talking Maltese trying to entice sailors by saying 'Come in Jack, have a good time. Lots of nice girls' and things of that sort. We knew that none of these girls were raving beauties but they were just trying to earn a living too as Malta's economy depended heavily on the Royal Navy. We just took this in our stride for the most part but there could be some rough goings on as Jolly Jack got progressively more 'stroppy' on the Malta Blue (beer). Needless to say the shore patrols were never really far away so things rarely went too out of line.

After our night's entertainment it wasn't hard to find a nice clean bed for 1s 6d even though it was only a folding camp bed. Jose was pretty good. He always used to wake us up on time to get back to our ship. If someone had a bad hangover and happened to be 'spuing' all over the place, Jose made allowances for that too. As a rule we got a good night's sleep, those who were allowed all night leave if you were age 20 or over and your ship was not under sailing orders. Jose was very well experienced at accommodating the British fleet. Over hundreds of years a rapport had been established and this was

_____

*Another type of local taxi was a small horse drawn carriage similar to the Egyptian gharry.

to pay dividends with Malta now being under seige by Italy since June and they knew that their very survival would depend on the Navy bringing the convoys through.

Malta, stuck right in the middle of the Med. 1000 miles either way from Gib. and Alex and only sixty miles south of Sicily, she stood as a thorn in Mussolini's side that he could never take out even with the help of his pal Adolph.

The island never gave in even though it was close to starvation at times and we had to temporarily abandon it as our main naval base being considered undefendable right from the start. Convoys tried again and again over the next three years to get supplies through at tremendous cost to the Royal Navy and Merchant Marine.

In the early days, Malta had virtually no fighter cover except one day when crates were found containing four outdated Gloster Gladiators. These planes were quickly put together and manned by the RAF who flew them into the fray. They even had names for them. After the first one was shot down, the remaining three were christened Faith, Hope, and Charity. I believe one did survive but I am not sure which one. This almost seems to be a case of providence lending a hand as Malta dates back to Biblical times and even today is still strongly Catholic.

In 1942, King George VI conferred the honour of presenting Malta with the newly created George Cross. The highest civilian award for outstanding courage and roughly equivalent to the Victoria Cross.

One day a stranger began to appear in our midst. I don't know exactly when he came aboard but on my occasional duties where I had to go back aft into 'officer country' I noticed a very tall, rather slim, and smart looking naval officer with two and a half rings on his tunic sleeve and a lone star above them. He seemed to have close cropped hair that wasn't the usual style of Royal Navy officers and his uniform was slightly different too. I didn't see him very often at first because we lived for'ard but gradually we became accustomed to seeing him all over in the hangar, on the flight deck etc. This was Lt. Cdr. Opie, United States Navy. This to us seemed rather odd as America was still neutral and for him to be aboard a warship of a belligerent nation sounded like something very top secret was going on because he was obviously liasing between the two navies and observing naval air tactics. Needless to say, probably only a few people in the Pentagon and the White House including

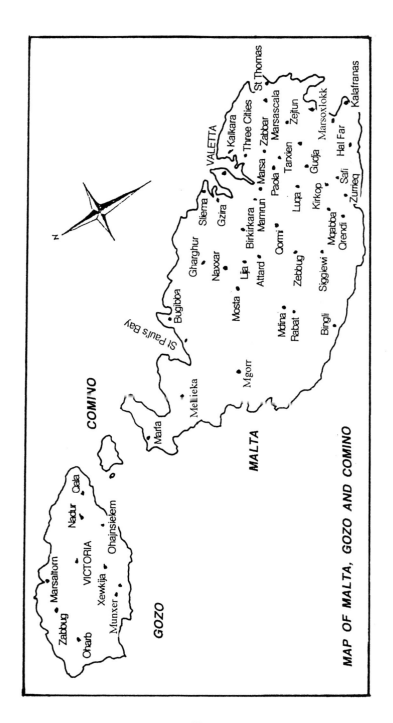

MAP OF MALTA, GOZO AND COMINO

President Roosevelt himself may have known that he was here, particularly as this was Britain's latest and most modern aircraft carrier. At least it looked like the United States was sympathetic to the point of unofficially helping us even though the time when they would enter the conflict as our ally was still fourteen months away. With the planned raid on Taranto looming up, the USN would no doubt learn some useful tips on carrier warfare from Cdr. Opie's reports. For Illustrious, this would be the beginning of a long and close association with America and her Navy and for Eric and myself a special relationship that would last for the rest of our lives, as in later years we would both make a new life on that side of the Atlantic. Mine would be in Canada and Eric would be as an American citizen. This part of my story will be told in greater detail later on.

Incidently, on the September 19 I had just reached that magical age of manhood, 21, and had been in the Navy not quite a year. The reason for mentioning this is that in those days the coming of age meant several things in peacetime England. Firstly it meant becoming an adult and getting a key to the door of the house as well as a celebration such as a party if one could afford it. A young fellow would complete his seven year apprenticeship in a trade at the age of 21 and would be classed as a qualified tradesman in his profession which would entitle him for tradesman's pay. The bad thing about this during those terrible Depression years was that he didn't look forward to it as the firm usually fired him at this point and threw him out of work and on to the dreaded dole.

At this particular time my reason was a little bit different least to say I celebrated it by having the middle watch in the centre engine room on a carrier at war. This was the last place I ever thought I would end up spending such a significant day in my life. I couldn't complain though as there were so many men in worse places like POW camps and such. There were also countless others who wouldn't even live to see their twenty-first birthday. I had much to be thankful for.

However the point in question was that I didn't want anyone to know because the custom in the 'Andrew' was that everybody would be giving me sippers and gulpers of 'Nelson's Blood' and not being much of a drinker at that time although I did like my Tot, I know what could happen if I drank all the rum which probably would have been offered to me. I had seen the results of other birthdays where men would literally fall off the mess stools and collapse on the deck to remain unconscious for 24 hours or more. This Pusser's grog could be deadly stuff when taken in excess. I remember one incident later on where a fleet order was posted up on the notice board relating a tragedy which occurred on some other (name long forgotten) ship where a pair of identical twins, strangely enough on the same ship which is unexplainable, came of age. They were given so much rum that they had to be taken to the sick bay to have their stomachs pumped out but it was too late. We were all warned not to give sippers but it still continued. The rum was to prove a valuable morale builder without which we might have lost the war and the rum ration was still continued right up until July 31 1970, a date now known in the Navy as 'Black Day'. The reason for the demise of this well loved routine was that the higher ups regarded the daily drawing of a tot as not synonymous with a modern, technologically advanced fighting force.*

While at sea a few days before the planned attack on Taranto, the ship caught fire of all places, in the hangar. The cause of this mishap occurred while fitting a long range fuel tank on one of the Swordfish to enable the old biplanes to have enough petrol to make it back to the carrier if they were lucky enough to survive the heavy flak that was expected. It was sheer bad luck, a freak accident that caused the fire. One of the FAA men was crouched in the cockpit securing the tanks when he stood up for a moment for a brief stretch from his cramped workspace. As he did so, he slipped on the greasy floor and a screwdriver fell out of his hand on to a pair of exposed battery terminals. The resulting spark caused an explosion by igniting the Av gas fumes which were heavy in the air. Within moments a couple of planes were engulfed in flames and before it could be put out, two more were damaged. The rest of the aircraft, having been sprayed by our salt-water hoses were all rendered unserviceable. Some were near wrecks and it meant that the raid now had to be postponed for ten days until October 31 and until the damaged planes could be repaired or replaced.

Throughout this emergency which to say the least endangered the whole ship itself had it been allowed to spread but was brought quickly under control by the attendant fire parties, I

---

*In 1982, the rum ration was reinstated on a number of occasions during the Falklands War.

can't remember specifically where I was although I was probably on watch. The fire wasn't bad enough to require my fire and repair party but this proves just how vulnerable an aircraft carrier really is, more than a regular warship with all the Av gas and the deadly vapours they give off.

Again, very few of us on the lower deck knew what was really going on because we never heard much talk about it although usually there were a lot of buzzes going around when anything big was coming off. The planned raid and the postponements were not known to us until the day it actually happened. When we were finally told, a mood of tense excitement seemed to go around the ship like an electric current.

Before I say too much at this point about the attack there was yet another delay and a couple of incidents which would alter the plans somewhat.

Somebody noticed that on the night of October 31 there would be no moon so this would require flares to provide light to mark the targets. Our flare-droppers had not had enough practise and so the date was moved back to a very historic and appropriate date, one that nobody could ever forget, November 11, Armistice Day.*

The fire in the hangar caused serious damage to our aircraft but as they were badly needed and replacements hard to get, our aircraft mechanics and crews worked long hours to make them airworthy again. Regardless, we detached from the fleet along with Eagle to make air strikes in the Dodecanese and the island of Leros, stirring up a bit of a hornet's nest. We then raced back to rejoin the main battlefleet off Crete.

As the fleet was steaming back towards Alex, the cruiser, HMS Newcastle with a crew of 750 was steaming only a few miles astern of us when she signalled that she had ben hit by a 'tinfish', blowing her bows right off almost to the bridge. It was as though a third of the ship had been torn right off and she later had to be towed stern first by the cruiser Orion back to Alex. There must have been many casualties. In the meantime action stations sounded and enemy aircraft from the hornet's

---

*Strangely enough, November 11, 1940 was the date that the famous American Jeep first rolled off the assembly lines as Lee Lacocca, President of Chrysler reminded everyone on one of his commercials. Who would doubt that this great little vehicle would have an illustrious career too.

70

nest in Rhodes that we had stirred up were approaching. We put up an intense barrage as we definitely couldn't afford to get hit now and were making emergency turns to avoid tinfish coming at us. This meant increasing speed and one could tell by the vibration of the ship as our engines gave everything they had to get us out of harm's way. I'm not afraid to admit that I experienced some very tense moments and made damn sure that there was air in my lifebelt. The Itties were no ball of fire but they could give us a hell of a good scare and didn't give up trying, not to mention they had just bashed up one of our modern cruisers and killed and wounded many fine lads, God Bless 'em. Although this didn't actually delay the attack, for all I know the poor old Newcastle may have been one of our escorting cruisers to share in the glory of Taranto. Nevertheless, Cunningham's fleet was now one cruiser short and the situation was rapidly deteriorating.

On Monday, October 28, 27 Divisions of Mussolini's 'Legions' poured over into Greece from Albania and the Med. Fleet was now stretched even thinner. With the situation in Greece and the continued advances of the enemy in North Africa, the destruction of the Italian Fleet at Taranto became even more imperative.

An operation called Plan Mb8 was put into effect to send convoys to Malta, Greece, and Suda Bay Crete. Operation Judgement, the attack on Taranto would fit into this plan which would begin on November 4 but just as Mb8 was about to begin, one more snag came up. The old Eagle was suffering from defects which were the result of being heavily bombed back in July. The defect was in her petrol system and it could no longer be patched up temporarily. Nothing short of major repairs in dock would suffice and it looked like Illustrious was going to do the job on its own.

The attack was supposed to involve thirty aircraft from the two carriers so in order to make up the numbers, five Swordfish and eight crew were transferred to us from Eagle which would put the striking force at 24 aircraft in two waves of twelve aircraft each.

In early September 1940, a new RAF unit was formed called No. 431 General Reconnaissance Flight and was based in Malta under the command of a Squadron Leader Ernest Alfred Whitely. 431 Flight was charged with the task of maintaining surveillance over Sicily and Italy as far north as Naples and keeping tabs on Musso's Supermarina as far south as Tunis and in the Ionian Sea. Flying three Marylands which had been built by the Glenn Martin Aircraft Company of Baltimore USA for the French Air Force but with the collapse of our French ally, these planes were taken over by the RAF, 431 Flight also kept an eye on shipping in and out of Taranto in the weeks and days prior to the attack.

Squadron Leader Whitely immediately recognized the importance of Taranto and was flabbergasted when the RN told him that they planned to attack it with a relatively small number of old, obselete, Swordfish. Previously Whitely had suggested to the Air Officer Commanding (AOC) Malta that a force of medium bombers numbering about 50 should bomb the harbour, but as the Battle of Britain was now being fought and the RAF had no planes to spare, the suggestion was met with very little enthusiasm. For the Navy to make the attack, he felt, was near suicidal and would only succeed in scaring away the Ittie fleet. Operation Judgement seemed more than ever to be a mission impossible from many points of view.

The 'recce's' by 431 Flight succeeded in obtaining valuable information about Taranto which would help make the attack a success and ultimately save lives.

Illustrious had an RNVR Lieutenant aboard named David Pollock. Unlike most lower deck sailors, Pollock's station in life seemed to place him among the ranks of the more afluent. He was a graduate of Trinity College, Cambridge and became a partner in a law firm. Before the war he was also an enthusiastic amateur sailor and so had joined the Royal Naval Volunteer Reserve. He was called up in September 1939 but because he was doing important war work, did not go into the Navy until June 1940 when he did his training at HMS King Alfred. Now as a 'Subby', RNVR, he received his first draft in August to Illustrious.

As the Intelligence Officer and Assistance Staff Officer to Admiral Lyster, he took a five day course with the RAF Photographic Interpretation Unit in Cairo. One day Pollock was looking over photos of Taranto taken by 431 Flight and was carefully plotting the gun emplacements and anti-torpedo nets. While doing this he noticed white specks which he first thought were blemishes on the prints but after some thought and closer examination he realized that they were barrage balloon which, up to this time were not known about. Pollock knew he must show his discovery to his superiors as this information would be vitally important to the attack plans which would now have to be changed. To back up his theory he would need to have the photos in his possession for a short time but there was only one set of prints which were not allowed to be removed from the RAF facility. Fortunately he found an opportunity where the photos could be 'borrowed' and then returned unnoticed 24 hours later. Within a short time, Pollock was returning to Illustrious aboard a waiting Swordfish.

Back aboard the ship he found that Admiral Lyster had gone ashore but instead, Captain Boyd examined the photos and agreed with Pollock's observation. Boyd then made arrangements for Pollock to go aboard the Warspite to show the Commander-in-Chief. On the Spite, Pollock spoke to Rear-Admiral Willis who was Cunningham's Chief of Staff and he was impressed at the discovery. Pollock was instructed to arrange for RAF confirmation of the balloons to be sent to the C-in-C and while in Cairo again he returned the photos unnoticed but not before he had the Illustious's photographer make copies of the prints.

Pollock's discovery no doubt resulted in saving numerous lives by alerting the aircrews to an unseen and unexpected hazard. This is typical of the best laid plans of mice and men having to deal with last minute obstacles which could threaten the entire operation. Above everything else we would need the element of surprise on our side, otherwise it could prove fatal to the aircrews and possibly the ships of the strike force. The plans had to be in the minutest detail.

There was one last unexpected surprise which was encountered just before the attack. Unlike all the other surprises and incidents which threatened to jeopardize the operation often by sheer bad luck, this more than compensated all the difficulties. A matter of hours before the attack, on the afternoon of November 11, an RAF Sunderland flying boat keeping a watch on Taranto in order to make sure that the Supermarina didn't put to sea at a most inopportune time signalled that a sixth battler had entered harbour. We had hoped for just five Ittie battlers but unbelievably all the chickens had come to roost in the same coup. It seemed that fate was finally being kind to us after so many mishaps and disappointments. This seemed like a good omen for all of us.

November 11, 1940, I had the middle watch but before I went

down I spent a few minutes getting some fresh air on the upper deck near the gash chute, the place where rubbish and mess slops is jettisonned from the ship during dark hours. The night was clear and moonlit and the sea seemed relatively calm. As you looked at the bow waves, the phosphorous seemed to sparkle. We were steaming at a pretty good clip in company with the Third Cruiser Squadron consisting of Gloucester, Berwick, Glasgow, and York and four destroyers at the flying off point, about 170 miles from Taranto in the Ionian Sea.

Since detaching from the main battlefleet and now knowing that we were going on a big operation which was entirely different from any of the others we had been on, buzzes were flying around all over the place. The entire ship from stem to stern and everyone from the lower deck right up to the senior officers seemed to be wound up like a clock spring and yet calm in the typical British fashion as they went around performing their respective duties. There was no mistaking that atmosphere of apprehension and fear that lay underneath as this was a classic case of the old Roman legends of Christians putting their head in the lion's mouth as they entered the arena.

Before I went on watch, Captain Boyd had already turned Illustrious into the wind and the strike force had flown off. Everybody was closed up at action stations and it was there that we listened to Rev. Lloyd giving his usual commentary of the tannoy as each aircraft took off.

At 23:35, I went down on watch which was now in the control room having had my steaming watch changed a short time before from the centre engine room. This relatively small but very important compartment was strategically located amidships and linked all the main machinery spaces by a wall full of dials and gauges eg. steam pressure gauges, vacuum gauges, oil pressure etc. which duplicated everything. Sitting at a desk at the front of all this was an engineer officer. This officer could be anything from a Lieutenant to a Warrant Officer in charge of what was essentially a command centre for the ship's machinery. This place was responsible to Commander (E) John Tamplin and the senior Engineer Officer. Oddly enough, I never hardly saw Commander (E) come down to this confined space with its small hatchway and steep ladder, possibly because of his portly figure when compared to the lean and mean frames of the rest of us. Maybe it's just coincidence but if I recall correctly, Tamplin's office was right next to the

74

officers' wardroom pantry which was on the other side of the armoured bulkhead from the keyboard flat, port side.

In the corner to the left of all the gauges in the control room was a telephone switchboard panel with all the paraphernalia of an ordinary telephone exchange. Whenever anybody phoned up from the machinery spaces and other parts of the ship including the bridge and Tamplin's office, a buzzer would go and a little light would flash. The operator would be a stoker like myself although I was a messenger, I was also required to do this as a relief from time to time.

Besides myself as a runner, the other stoker at the switchboard, and an engineer officer, we had a killick and a Chief. The killick was standing at a desk making entries into a logbook and Chiefie would be sent to check on things or perform various other tasks and report back to the officer. This Chief Stoker, Harry Arrowsmith or Arrow for short was also my Chief in this place when swinging round the buoy in harbour at auxiliary. This meant we had shut down from main engines to standby machinery as we always had to be ready for emergencies and keep at least one boiler with steam in it for flashing up purposes and for keeping up our fresh water supply in the vaps, lighting, fire main pressure etc.

Having an officer around meant that everything was always done Pusser but now with Operation Judgement in progress and everybody tense and on the alert, the atmosphere was deadly serious with suspense. As the minutes and the hours slowly ticked by we were all kept busy as the ship steamed to reach position 'Y' for Yorker, near the Greek Island of Cephalonia where we would rendezvous with the returning planes. At 01:00 hours, we reached the rendezvous position after steaming a zig-zag course to avoid possible enemy subs and then we turned into the wind to provide the necessary lift across the flight deck for any of the returning planes. Now all we could do was wait and hope we weren't discovered.

Everyone aboard was worried about the ship's safety as were now sitting ducks and Ittie airfields were only a short distance away. For all we knew the Ittie fleet might even decide to come after us. Being members of the lower deck, the main focus of our worry was for ourselves really but I'm sure each one of us felt concerned as well for the crews of those 21 flimsy aircraft and the predicament they could be in as this was generally viewed as a near suicidal mission.

I say only 21 aircraft because we were unable to put all 24 into the air as planned due to engine failures from contaminated gasoline. Even at the last we nearly went down to 19 as two of the Swordfish taxiing to their take-off position had a collision. One was undamaged and the other manned by Lts. Clifford and Going had the fabric torn on a wing and was not going to be sent until Lt. Going told Boyd and Lyster that the damage was superficial and could be repaired in a very short time. In the face of such determination to take part in the attack, Admiral Lyster replied 'Well, you're flying the bloody aircraft. All right, off you go.'

One more thing is worthy of a special mention too. The old bootnecks, the Royal Marines were represented by a pilot, Captain Oliver Patch from HMS Eagle. It is even said that somebody gave him a pair of Marine's marching boots to tie to the bombs as a symbolic gesture of the Royals kicking Mussolini up the arse.

As the night wore on steaming up and down the rendezvous point waiting for the returning planes, this ideal moonlit night now seemed dangerous moonlight for us. Ships silhouetted against a bright night sky at sea presented good targets if spotted by an alert and watchful enemy so this became an added worry as we needed to be clear of the area before dawn broke.

We anxiously fretted the time away in an electrifying atmosphere of suspense in which over five thousand men's lives hung in the balance regardless of the outcome of Judgement.

Finally, after what seemed like an eternity to the frayed nerves of the whole crew, radio silence was broken and a single two word signal was received on the bridge from the commander of the second strike, Lt-Cdr. Hale. It read simply, 'Attack Completed'. There had been a prolonged wait for this message because the aircraft carrying the first strike commander, Williamson who was supposed to send it, was shot down and taken prisoner. Right now, he and his observer Scarlett-Streatfield were now having gulpers of rum on an Ittie destroyer, the same one that shot him down. Depending on your point of view this could be considered either lucky or unlucky but nevertheless they would spend the rest of the war in a prisoner of war camp, first in Italy and later in a German Oflag. The Italian hospitality was only temporary.

As for the rest of the strike, we wondered if the same fate awaited them. Our first indication came a couple of hours into the middle watch when Lt. Schierbeck, Royal Canadian Naval Volunteer Reserve (RCNVR), the radar officer noticed the returning planes on his set and then shortly afterwards the dim navigation lights flickered on two aircraft.

Down in the control room and all across the ship, all ears were glued to the loud hailer over which the Padre was making one of his most famous commentaries which we all appreciated especially in these nerve wracking times. As each plane appeared and then landed on, Padre counted them one by one until we were down to the last two who never returned. Nineteen came back and it was later confirmed whose planes didn't. Williamson of course was taken prisoner. The other plane with Lt.s Bayly and Slaughter was destroyed. Both men were killed and only Bayly's body was recovered to be buried with full military honours at Taranto and later moved to the Imperial War Graves cemetery at Bari. The losses were considered a small price to pay for such a victory considering the odds but Illustrious was to pay the real price in the weeks to come.

Although we of the lower deck did not know it, a second attack the following night had been scheduled. Captain Boyd worried quite a bit about the extra risks involved in this idea firstly because he didn't know if the aircrews would be up to it. They were all quite cheerful and fairly willing but as they had had very little sleep, they were beginning to show the strain they were under. As one aircrew member put it, 'What – again. My God. They only asked the Light Brigade to do it once'. This quote refers to that famous charge by 600 cavalrymen into the Valley of Death surrounded by Russian artillery in broad daylight during the Crimean War.

The other thing that Boyd worried about was that the Italians would be ready for them this time and to attack again might mean annihilation not only for the airmen but the task force which sent them. Furthermore the weather was deteriorating and there were low cloud banks.

Late afternoon it seemed that Admiral Cunningham had been having similar thoughts and so he signalled Admiral Lyster and told him to use his own 'judgement', literally speaking. By six o'clock in the evening, the weather had deteriorated to the point where Cunningham called off the

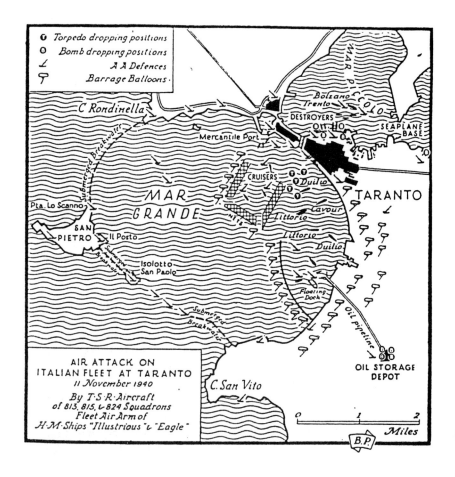

Torpedo dropping positions
Bomb dropping positions
A.A. Defences
Barrage Balloons.

C. Rondinella

MAR PICCOLO

Bolzano
Trento
DESTROYERS
OIL H.Q.

SEAPLANE
BASE

Mercantile Port

CRUISERS

Duilio

Cavour

MAR
GRANDE

Littorio

Pta. Lo Scanno

Littorio

SAN
PIETRO

Il Porto

Duilio

TARANTO

Isolotto
San Paolo

Floating
Dock

Submerged
Breakwater

Oil pipeline

AIR ATTACK ON
ITALIAN FLEET AT TARANTO
11 November 1940
By T·S·R·Aircraft
of 813, 815, & 824 Squadrons
Fleet Air Arm of
H·M·Ships "Illustrious" & "Eagle"

C. San Vito

OIL STORAGE
DEPOT

0   1   2

Miles

B.P.

operation altogether. Illustrious then changed course to rejoin the fleet and head back for Alex to the relief of everybody including me. We had been fortunate. It wouldn't have been wise to tempt fate a second time.

When the aerial reconnaissance photos from 431 Flight were examined, they showed the extent of the damage we had inflicted on the Supermarina and proved that a second attack wouldn't have been necessary anyway. The first attack had obtained two torpedo hits on the battleship Littorio and one on the battler Conti Di Cavour. The second strike made another hit on Littorio and on the Doria class battleship Caio Duilio. The planes carrying bombs had wrecked the seaplane base and hit the cruiser Trento. Two more Trento class cruisers were leaking oil from damaged fuel tanks and the destroyer Libeccio was hit by a bomb which failed to explode. The Conti Di Cavour sank in shallow water and she was later raised but never saw service again. Caio Duilio had to be beached in shallow water where she sank and was out of service for eight months. Littorio's bows were awash and she too was towed to shallow water as a precaution and she took six months to repair.

Over fifty years have now passed and I still feel, having been part in an action that is almost unparalleled in British history, that it hasn't yet been fully told by historians and was possibly less appreciated at the time by those in the high command when our country's future and very existence was in jeopardy. As a lowly stoker and a small cog in a big wheel during this momentous operation which almost never happened, with so many mishaps and unforseen happenings, we gave Mr Churchill something that he wanted more than anything else, a naval victory and a piece of good news that he could give to his people. With so many defeats and retreats such as Dunkirk and the fall of France in this fateful year of 1940, the morale of the British people has been starting to sag.

Having said this, the biggest and most obvious heroes were those who actually flew those old crates we call Swordfish and earned the nation's gratitude in full measure for the risks they took. The gratitude they received fell far short of what they deserved when it was announced what awards were presented (see Appendix 2). Only the Squadron Commanders received the Distinguished Service Order (DSO) and their observers along with Capt. Patch the Royal Marine and his observer Lt. Goodwin received the Distinguished Service Cross (DSC). That was all. When it was announced over the tannoy that the awards had been put up on the ship's notice boad, everybody crowded around it to see who got what. When we saw it, to a man we were absolutely shocked and disgusted not for ourselves but for the aircrews. What they had done was worthy of some Victorian Crosses instead of these totally inadequate awards. After all, they had altered the balance of naval power which would benefit the convoys who would now be able to supply Malta and Greece but they went up against terrible odds to do it. Even though we were irate we couldn't alter decisions that had been made in the 'nuthouse'. Perhaps this was the same line of thinking used when Admiral Nelson ran up his famous signal — England Expects That Every Man Will Do His Duty; just don't expect anything in return.

When the New Year Honours List of 1941 came out, it announced that Capt. Boyd and Capt. Bridge of Eagle were awarded the CBE and Admiral Lyster, the CB.

The rest of the aircrew didn't get any awards for about six months by which time our ship had paid a terrible price for that victory by being divebombed by Stuka dive bombers (this had brought the Germans into the Med. for we had well and truly stirred up a hornet's nest) and a third of those crews were dead never to enjoy the satisfaction of getting an award which was only small at best.

The real crunch came when no awards or any recognition was given to the Illustrious or her gallant escorts or any member of their crews to my knowledge. Many men made this operation possible and at least a few of them should have shared in the glory.

Other than a few still photographs, no documentary or film has ever been seen about this almost impossible mission and its far reaching results and consequences.

Perhaps the only suitable tribute to the men of Operation Judgement came from Winston Churchill himself when he addressed the House of Commons on November 13, 1940.

The result affects decisively the balance of naval power in
the Mediterranean and also carries with it reactions upon
the naval situation in every quarter of the globe. I feel sure
the House will regard these results as highly satisfactory

RAF reconnaisance photo of Taranto harbour after
the raid of 11 November, 1940

and as reflecting the greatest credit upon the Admiralty
and upon Admiral Cunningham, the Commander-in-Chief
in the Mediterranean, and above all on our pilots of the
Fleet Air Arm . . .[4]

Today, this operation is regarded as the Fleet Air Arm's
Trafalgar of the air and is celebrated throughout the globe in
every FAA establishment ashore and afloat on November 11. It
is known as Taranto night.

Chapter Seven

'For Those in Peril . . .'

In the weeks following the successful attack on Taranto, Illustrious continued to operate with the Med. Fleet. Our air group provided cover for Wavell's army in North Africa and for the fleet; especially on the Malta convoys which were essential in order to keep Malta supplied with ammunition, food, and all the other items necessary to keep her alive now that she had been under siege for over six months.

It was around this time that reconnaissance planes from Illustrious began to notice a build up of aircraft in Sicily around Catania and Comiso. Numbering in the hundreds they were observed to be not Italian planes but Junkers and Heinkels; in other words, German.

These aircraft were in fact a part of the Luftwaffe's Fliegerkorps X or Tenth Air Corps under the command of a General Geissler. Made up of 150 Heinkels and Junkers 88's, 150 Stukas, and 50 Messerschmitts, Fliegerkorps X had just been transferred from Norway, Denmark, and the Low Countries to Sicily because Hitler now realized that Musso was losing control of the Med. The Ittie army was also getting beaten back by strong Greek resistance and in North Africa by Wavell's army.

Fliegerkorps X was renowned as one of the best anti-shipping units anywhere and they had earned a reputation during the Norwegian campaign where the Royal Navy had suffered terrible losses and where Illustrious was nearly sent.

After the Italian Navy's losses at Taranto had been calculated, it showed that the Royal Navy would have to be dealt with by stronger forces than the Itties could muster.

Fliegerkorps X was given the job and ordered specifically by Hitler himself to destroy two main targets. One was Malta. The other was Illustrious which had to be sunk at all costs.

The ramifications of Taranto were now to reach unprecedented proportions in every aspect of the Mediterranean War and us to start with.

January 10, 1941 found Illustrious taking part in an operation code-named 'Excess'. The object was to escort a convoy of four merchantmen to the Eastern Med. Three of the ships carried supplies needed by the Greeks and the fourth carried a cargo of four thousand tons of ammunition for Malta. All four would be escorted from the west by Force H from Gib. and then handed over to Cunningham's fleet at the Pantelleria Channel.

While all this was taking place, Cunningham also took the opportunity to escort two more merchant ships to Malta from Alex with oil fuel and petrol and dispatch an oiler to Suda Bay. A convoy would then be escorted out of Malta and the cruisers Southampton and Gloucester would drop off troops at Malta and continue to pick up the four east-bound merchantmen in the Pantelleria Strait.

Complicated this operation certainly was because it involved almost all the Eastern Med. Fleet as well as major units of Admiral Somerville's Force H. 'Excess' was an appropriate name for this operation in which Illustrious was to play a key role providing air cover and early warning radar to the fleet.

Operation Excess started off without a hitch. The four merchant ships passed into the hands of the two cruisers safely on the 9th except for a Ittie air attack which was beaten off by aircraft from Ark Royal.

On January 10 at 04:30, Illustrious in company with Warspite, Valiant, and seven destroyers were northwest of Malta on their way to meet the convoy. Two enemy destroyers were sighted by the cruiser Bonaventure which was west of us at 07:30. Almost immediately afterwards, gun flashes were sighted and we increased speed to join in the engagement. By 08:00 we were still at least five miles away but the two destroyers were being fired upon by the Bonaventure and Hereward at close range.* One of the enemy was crippled and burning and soon

---

†The Ittie destroyer was the Vega.

blew up[†] but the other escaped. The battle-fleet then returned to the convoy.

At this time, my part of the ship was still as a messenger in the main control room and had had the middle (graveyard) watch. Nevertheless, when Dawn Action Stations sounded, flaked out as I felt after crashing for a couple of hours on a narrow mess stool using my gas mask case as a pillow, I staggered along the passageways half asleep until I reached the keyboard flat aft on the starboard side, No. 3 Fire and Repair Party. It wasn't a very comforting thought knowing that here we were right on top of one of the 4.5 in magazines. We knew something was up though we didn't know exactly what as Jolly Jack was not always told everything, especially those between decks. As it turned out, two of our vessels were slogging it out with a pair of Ittie destroyers.

I secured from dawn action stations and had just enough time to dash down to the mess again and have a quick wash and a cup of tea. I didn't bother with a fag as I didn't smoke − yet; at least not for a few hours. 07:55, I was going down the narrow hatch once more into the control room little knowing that this was the beginning of the worst day of my life and one which I would never forget.

I relieved the other stoker whose name time has erased and took my station near Mick the Irish killick. For a while, things seemed more or less normal until the tannoy sounded and all hands were piped to close up at defense stations which was a lower degree of readiness than action stations. Something must have been cooking for sure. Somehow, we then found out that the destroyer HMS Gallant had struck a mine that blew her bows off right up to the bridge. This seemed to bode that things would not be well for any of us today and nothing like we had encountered before. It must have been terrible aboard the old Gallant when you think of all the men, many like myself killed and wounded.* I wondered how much longer our good luck could last. Up to this point our's was apparently good. I didn't find out until researching this book how miraculous it was that

---

*Hereward was eventually lost at Crete on May 29, 1941 after being torpedoed by Italian aircraft.
*Gallant was towed into Malta stern first by Mohawk escorted by Gloucester, Southampton, and Bonaventure. She was never repaired.

we didn't suffer the same fate as the Gallant for the minefield where she was hit had been passed through by us and the rest of the battle-fleet only a short time before. This was the third time our ship had escaped a terrible fate due to an unknown minefield, especially scary for those in the engine room branch whose job demanded they be below the waterline.

Things again calmed down temporarily but we stayed at defence stations and the rest of the watch gave me the impression of a calm before a storm. What a storm it turned out to be shortly after my forenoon watch ended.

As the watch drew to a close after running messages here and there, which wasn't such a bad job as you weren't stuck in a claustraphobic compartment all the time, I relished the thought of my tot of 'bubbly' and we were all in a relatively good mood.

End of watch, I climbed the single ladder to the main deck and went for'ard to my mess which was deserted because everybody was closed up at action stations at second degree of readiness. Action stations can be categorized into about three levels. The lowest degree would be defense stations which was done every dawn and sunset, the two most vulnerable times for a sneak attack. This was simply to prevent us from being caught with our pants down literally speaking but involved some flexibility by allowing men to come and go as needed. After defense stations came third and second degree of readiness where the possibility of attack was more likely and the only movement permitted was change of watch or other necessities. Then of course we had first degree of readiness which meant everybody closed up for action which would be imminent and all watertight doors and bulkheads would be closed.

Anyway, there I was on the mess all alone just like my tot of 2 and 1 rum which was sitting at the end of the table. This was one of the many aspects of the lower deck code of conduct where a man's tot is saved for him and left untouched no matter what, equally shared. Also my dinner was left in the hot oven for me, such as it was, but still the same as everybody else had had.

I gulped back my 'bubbly' right away, enjoying every drop. After it started to take effect, I momentarily forgot everything that might be happening up top and just felt ravenously hungry. No matter how unappetizing, you can eat almost anything after your tot of 'Nelson's blood' as it was in this case.

I had just about finished my meal and it was getting towards half past noon. I was wondering if things would quieten enough for me to get my head down when all of a sudden I heard a click like somebody was going to make an announcement over the loudhailer. Then it came, the bugler sounding off those dreaded notes to be followed by 'All hands close up at action stations at the double'. I could sense the urgency; that this would be somehow different from all the other times by the awful wailing of that klaxon horn.

Instinctively I grabbed my gas mask and lifebelt and just flew out of the mess. Men from other messes were doing the same thing. Stokers customarily wore their boots without laces so they could be kicked off more quickly if they had to abandon ship, but we clip-clopped along the passageways and messdecks as fast as our legs could carry us.

Within a minute or two I arrived at my action station in the keyboard flat next to one of the armoured bulkheads which lay between us and the wardroom flat. The port and starboard armoured doors had been closed and dogged sealing off the after part of the ship. Thank God for those doors.

Our party all reported in and were checked off by the Chief and PO in charge. My friend Eric was at his respective station which I have forgotten but I know I didn't see him again until the next day when we mustered for a roll call to see who was missing. I specifically remember the Royal Marine sentry standing at his desk and the clock above him which was still ticking away − for now.

We all waited tensely, wondering as all the guns had started to open fire and inwardly I was fearful and speculating on my chances if we were hit and went down. Just in case I gave a few furtive looks up the ladder nearby as this would lead onto the upper deck.

Apparently what was happening although I didn't know at the time was that we were being attacked by a pair of Ittie Savoia torpedo bombers coming at low level. Capt. Boyd turned the ship around to avoid the torpedoes which were coming straight at us and they passed harmlessly astern of the Valiant. In hot pursuit of the two Ittie attackers were the last two airborne Fulmars of our combat air patrol. They were decoyed away to a lower altitude. At the same time a half dozen rearmed and refueled Fulmars were getting ready to go on patrol.

We had been lured into a trap. All morning we had been

shadowed by single Italian aircraft who had to be driven off by our six Fulmars that had been launched around 10:00 hours. Two of the Itties had been shot down but they were gradually using up the fuel and ammunition in our planes. By the time the torpedo bombers approached only two aircraft were left and it would be another seven minutes before our fresh combat air patrol would be airborne.

That seven minutes was the time that the Luftwaffe needed because at exactly 12:30 a large formation of aircraft was picked up on radar. Capt. Boyd immediately sensed danger and ordered the two remaining Fulmars to fly on and those on the flight deck to take off.

Tragically there was a delay. In order for the aircraft to take off, Illustrious would have to be swung into the wind. Before this could be done, Capt. Boyd was under orders to have permission from the C-in-C to make such a manoeuvre. Permission from Cunningham didn't come for another four minutes and by that time the German dive-bombers were already overhead and preparing to make their attack. By the time the last Fulmar had took off, it was too late. The Stukas were beginning their attack and the obsolete Fulmers were slow to gain altitude and helpless at stopping the incoming waves of aircraft not to mention hopelessly outnumbered.

Back in the keyboard flat at my action station, all our nerves were on edge. We just stood and hoped for the best, praying that we wouldn't go down. At this time there wasn't any more we could do. Unbeknownst to us, the moment of truth was about to descend upon us with the fury of all hell let loose.

Being on top of one of the 4.5 magazines meant we also had an ammunition hoist close by which as I recall held about four shells at a time of whatever was called for; HEs (high explosives), star shells, etc. Adjacent to this in the middle of the flat was the ammunition conveyor belt which had rollers bevelled in the centre to cradle the shells so they wouldn't fall off. When set in motion, the conveyor then carried the shells right through the armoured bulkhead along the wardroom flat to a point aft where there was another hoist. Ammunition supply people would then take them off and send them up to the 4.5 in gun turrets aft. I remember we often lent a hand loading these heavy shells to speed the process up from the hoist

Illustrious alongside Parlatorio Wharf, Valetta, Malta.
Heavy attack by German dive-bombers of Fliegerkorps X,
January 16 1940

to the conveyor up to the turrets but at this time they were
keeping up to them.

Things then began to happen so fast. The whole situation
changed to near chaos as the Germans began to score hits on us.
With each successive explosion and the gunfire up top, a
horrendous cacophony could be heard. Some of the hits were
hard to distinguish as individual explosions although they were
sufficient to vibrate the ship, cause the lights to flicker, and
dust from the pipe lagging would come floating down on us.
God only knows what sort of hell they were inflicting on those
men in other parts of the ship. Even though we were in the after
section as well where many of the hits took place, the armoured
bulkhead had allowed us in the keyboard flat to be spared so far
of any significant damage.

Throughout all this sudden confusion, perhaps by anxiety or
fear, call it what you will, I somehow had shifted to a position
where I could see the keyboard clock plainly above the Marine

sentry's head. It was a few minutes before ten to one.

At an altitude of 12,000 feet the Stukas came down in two groups. One group of 30 headed for Illustrious while ten others went for the Valiant and Warspite to draw away their anti-aircraft fire. The Stukas then dived, twisting and turning to avoid our ack-ack, screaming down at angles up to eighty degrees until they released their bombs at about a thousand feet. Many still came down to flight deck level and strafed the deck after dropping their cargo of bombs. In six and a half minutes they had all gone leaving us a burning mess of twisted metal after six direct hits.

The first bomb to hit us came at 12:38 but didn't cause significant damage. It passed through the loading platform of No. 1 port pom-pom wounding two men but failed to explode until it passed through the ship's side and hit the water where it peppered the hull with shrapnel.

Several seconds later we were hit with our first direct hit for'ard near the bow. A bomb went through the flight deck and burst in the paint store choking the for'ard gun crews with clouds of stinking, acrid fumes. However, it too wasn't serious and was brought under control by the damage control parties fairly quickly.

The second bomb to hit was a 500 pounder with a direct action fuse. That is, it wasn't armour piercing and was meant as an anti-personnel bomb. This bomb missed the superstructure by only eighteen inches and exploded on No. 2 starboard pom-pom which it completely destroyed and killed all of its crew. Fragments from this hit also killed four men in the crew of No. 1 starboard pom-pom.

As bad as those first two hits were by killing a fifth of our for'ard gun crews in under a minute, it was the third direct hit which really caused the first of our serious damage. At exactly 12:40, a second wave of Stukas carrying armour piercing thousand pounders came at us. One of these fell flush on the after lift which at the time was on its way up to the flight deck from the hangar with a Fulmar and its midshipman pilot. In an instant, the plane and its young pilot disintegrated and the lift weighing a massive 300 tons was thrown into the air. It stayed in this position for a second and then came crashing down into the hangar. Meanwhile, fragments from the explosion sprayed the after guns and knocked out three quarters of our 4.5 in turrets aft causing heavy casualties amongst the Royal Marines who traditionally manned the after guns on warships that carried Marines. Inside the hangar, the blast hit parked aircraft of which nine Swordfish armed with a highly explosive cargo of torpedoes and depth charges plus the four recently refueled Fulmar fighters started to catch fire.

Within a few minutes our efficient damage control parties had the fires contained but their valiant efforts were thwarted because at 12:42 another 1000 pounder struck only yards away from where the other one had hit. This bomb didn't burst on impact but ricocheted off the twisted lift platform and slid into the hangar where it then burst. As the hangar was a long armoured box with only the fore and aft lifts as openings, the terrific force of the blast had nowhere else to go except along the hangar causing massive death and destruction in its path. An aircraft carrier is like a floating bomb with all the extra ammunition and Av gas (100 octane) that is carried and so ammo and fuel tanks exploded in the hangar in the wake of this blast. It's a wonder we weren't completely destroyed.

A matter of seconds later the fifth direct hit was scored on us when yet another 1000 pounder exploded beneath our bow near the for'ard lift which was now arched upward fom the blast funneled through the hangar by the previous two hits. The blast from this bomb again swept through the hangar and fanned the fires already raging so that within seconds, fifty foot flames were coming out of this inferno through the after lift well. Up top on the flight deck it was said that the steel deck was white hot in spots from the heat of the fires raging below.

To the rest of the fleet, Illustrious appeared to be covered in clouds of smoke interspersed with licks of flame climbing upward and swarms of dive-bombers bearing down on us. Some sailors I have met who watched us on that day from other ships wondered if we would even come through those attacks or if anyone could survive what appeared to be a living hell. At times they thought we had gone altogether.

After less than ten minutes of battle, the first attack was almost over. Only a group of ten Stukas remained overhead about to press home their attacks. However it wasn't over yet.

Our box barrage of anti-aircraft fire put up little resistance now that most of our guns had been destroyed but our six obselete Fulmars were now coming into action. Due to their lack of speed they were too late to stop the first waves of dive-bombers but still in time to disrupt these last ten Stukas and shoot down five of them by diving at them bravely with all machine guns blazing. They pressed home the attacks at such close range that they were nearly ramming the Germans who were forced to get their attacks over hastily and return to their base in Sicily.

Unfortunately, even their efforts weren't enough for it was from the last enemy plane that we received our sixth and worst direct hit right on the centre line of the flight deck twenty feet for'ard of the after lift.

Down in the keyboard flat we all waited. Suddenly there was a tremendous explosion and the ship shuddered from stem to stern under the impact as if some unknown force had struck us with a gigantic sledgehammer. The lights went out but seemed to come on again shortly afterwards. Everything shook loose, pipes and lagging hung down and the Marine sentry's clock was knocked askew and stopped. The time was exactly 12:50.

I was momentarily stunned with shock and fear as I just stared at the clock. In the next few seconds I felt as though I was suspended in time as if between two worlds. Perhaps that was one of those rare moments where one's life is held in the balance between life and death. In experiences of this type some people say they see their whole life flash before them. Other's have talked about seeing apparitions or the Lord's face for an instant. To me, something quite different seemed to happen in those brief moments which took me a long time after to make sense of but nonetheless it happened this way.

In my mind's eye there appeared as plain as plain could be a vision of my dear old mother. She looked just the way she always did and she wore a slight smile as if to reassure me everything would be alright. Then she was gone. I feel to this day that this strange image had a deeper meaning inasmuch as I came through not only that day physically unscathed but the rest of the war too.

I later interpreted this experience in the only logical way possible by the fact that everybody is born of their mother and as such, is given life if it is God's will. Therefore it seemed to me that this explained the feeling of hanging between two worlds. In those vital moments of that thousand pound armour piercing bomb smashing through the decks above and exploding in the officers' wardroom flat a matter of yards the other side of the bulkhead, I along with the others were mighty close to being completely wiped out or at least seriously wounded. I am now sure the Almighty may have been saying to me that he could also take back that life if he wanted but by His Grace, not now. Who would doubt that miracles happen especially in war.

Shaking myself out of this temporary state of mind, I returned to the grim realities of the situation which now seemed a matter of literally fighting to save the ship, yet I was totally unaware of what was transpiring in other places. The keyboard flat and its surroundings was for now my whole world and I honestly believed then that this was going to be my last day on earth and I would die here if another bomb like the last one hit us again in the flat.

My greatest nagging fear before now had always been how would I react and conduct myself in action should it come to such as this. I inwardly had prayed that I wouldn't be a coward and shame myself by letting my shipmates down. I determined in my mind that at all costs I would try my best to suppress my innermost fears and show a brave face.

Man's first natural instinct of self preservation can be a powerful urge to do some irrational things in a time of crisis but for a sailor trapped in a devastated ship in wartime it's a case of nowhere to run and nowhere to hide. You just have to stand and fight or go down to Davy Jones's Locker.

It appears to me that in times of dire circumstances, the British character shines at its best. Although I don't want to sound biased I feel that people of British stock have an inner quality which enables them to pull together and display enormous courage and fortitude which normally lays dormant until aroused by a crisis situation. This was shown by the fiery speeches of Mr Churchill when he said 'We shall never give in. Never. Never. Never.' So it was on Illustrious that day. We stood and fought.

That sixth armour piercing bomb which destroyed the wardroom flat causing heavy casualties had penetrated the armoured flight deck and the hangar to explode on the deck below flush on the after ammunition conveyor. The whole after part of the ship was on fire and power was cut. As a result our steering gear was damaged and we started to steam around in huge circles at well over 20 knots. Our engines were in good condition but we needed helm control to dodge any more attacks and to make for Malta, 85 miles away. This went on for half an hour as engineers worked frantically to restore control to the rudder but many of the electrical circuits were burnt out.

92

Finally they managed to jam the rudder amidships and Capt. Boyd steered the ship by main engines. We headed for the relative safety of Malta with its harbour defences and some air cover from the Royal Air Force but, we had a long fight ahead of us.

From this point on it seemed that my memory of all the happenings is a little sketchy due to the confusion that was going on around me so I am unable to relate events in exact sequence with precise detail. There are however, a number of incidents that took place which are forever etched in my mind which I will try to relate in context with the overall battle which was taking place to save Illustrious.

After recovering somewhat from our last hit in the officers' flat and our fire and repair party had regrouped and mustered to see if everybody was alright, we waited for orders. Around this time shortly afterwards, I had occasion to go to the stokers' bathroom a few yards for'ard off the starboard passageway. This bathroom as it was called was actually our room for washing and 'dhobeying' with a shower area covered in porcelain tiles. This wasn't the 'Heads' so I didn't have to go in there for that. I have long since forgotten why I had to go in there.

Upon opening the door to the adjacent dressing room I have never forgotten seeing what greeted me. Apparently this room had been taken over as an emergency aid station. Lined up in the middle on stretchers were wounded and some probably dying lads. There must have been at least half a dozen of them just lying quietly. They were not making any noise, no moaning and groaning but seemed to be patiently waiting for someone to attend to them. Perhaps they had already been given morphia injections to deaden the pain. As I walked amongst them and accidently almost on top of them not expecting anyone to be there I couldn't tell who was dead and who was alive neither did I notice what branch they were from, seamen or stokers. All I noticed was that they were lower deck like myself and I just couldn't turn my back and leave without saying or doing something. I knelt down between a couple of stretchers and tried again to put on my bravest face by saying things that might reassure them like 'Don't worry opps. You'll be alright. We're gonna get those bastards'. Deep down though I felt these were just empty words although the deep resentment I expressed towards the Germans was genuine yet I could do little

Illustrious under air attack by Italian high level bombers in the central Mediterranean. The battleship HMS Warspite, Veteran of the Battle of Jutland WW1 and Admiral Andrew Cunningham's flagship CinC Eastern Mediterranean Fleet in background − Autumn 1940

about it. For my wounded shipmates' sake I hoped it sounded good.

As I couldn't stay here much longer having to get back to my action station I asked if there was anything I could do. I was asked if I could light them a cigarette or two. Being a non-smoker still I took a couple of theirs and took some puffs to light them and then I put it in their mouths. Then I had to go with a feeling that I had at least done a little bit. What happened to those lads afterwards I'll never know.

Returning to the keyboard again shortly afterwards, possibly only a few minutes, the armoured bulkhead door on the port side was opened by two people possibly from either the damage control or ammunition supply party. I can't be sure but it's rather irrelevant now. At this point I have to rely on those whose recollections are more specific in detail than mine after so many years have passed and so I refer to some of the accounts in Kenneth Poolman's book *Illustrious* to clarify the chaotic situation prevailing in the area of the wardroom and keyboard flats. I trust the reader will bear with me as to the extreme stress we were all under, not knowing if the ship would even survive the punishing damage already inflicted on her. This chaos may also be partly responsible for my inability to adequately estimate the damage in the keyboard resulting from that last hit.

According to Poolman's *Illustrious*, Commander Tuck himself arrived on the scene after Mr Guttridge, the commissioned shipwright and decided the armoured door should slowly be opened.[5] Tuck was the one who gave the order because only he and other senior officers had such authority as this door sealed off two sections of the ship and to open it prematurely could result in the damage spreading by way of fire or blast.

Besides undogging (heavy steel clips) the door, a large brass wheel mechanism had to be turned by hand which opened the heavy door on a cog-wheel system. Fortunately the door had not buckled during the explosion and was undamaged.

The decision to open the door was made so that Tuck and Guttridge could crawl into the smashed officers' flat to assess the damage. Wearing long-tubed smoke helmets they were able to determine that there was no fire damage to the magazines below thanks to the hangar spray party's quick action but up above through the hole they could see the hangar on fire and water cascading down from the hangar spray system.

What Poolman's account didn't mention was what came through the bulkhead door around this time and which I do vividly remember. There it was, a burnt and blackened apparition of a man staggering through the opening. Two of the party then immediatley dashed to his aid and supported him, one on each arm as he was still walking but making no sound. He was virtually a walking corpse, everything about him seemed to be in shreds. I was horrified to see him but immediately recognized who he was. It was Springbok as we called him, a stoker from South Africa. So they led him away. It was unbelievable that he could still walk but I heard that he later died of his wounds which didn't surprise me considering the state he was in. It was a miracle that he lived as long as he did in that Dante's Inferno.

The condition of the keyboard flat was no less appalling when I read what Kenneth Poolman had to say by the description of Bill Banham the ship's Warrant Gunner when he flashed his torch inside; 'The secondary light lamps had gone, the magazine light boxes, junction, and distributing boxes torn away. Electric leads and cables hung down in festoons, fire-hydrants lay smashed, hoses ripped to shreds, paintwork scorched, blackened, and blistered'.[6]

Everything was happening so fast. My experiences in the keyboard right after that last bomb and the lapse of time between that and the opening of the armoured door could have been in the space of no more than thirty minutes but time to me was now of little significance.

I say it couldn't have been more than half an hour because at 13:20 hours the enemy came back. It was Valiant that spotted them on her radar first and I wonder now if ours was even still working. The aircraft were twenty miles away at 14,000 feet. When they arrived, they turned out to be Italian Savoias and not the dreaded Stukas but we were still vulnerable with no air cover available and half of our firepower was gone. Our box barrage was now open so immediately the fleet closed in around us to give us maximum rate of fire. Fortunately the Ittie attack was not vigorously carried out in keeping with their usual performance. Thank God, they stayed at 14,000 feet and their bombs fell wide, a momentary reprieve.

Strangely enough, the ship's steering gear broke down again at this most untimely moment and we steamed crazily in and out the fleet as though the ship itself had gone mad under the strain. Control was restored again by 14:00 but our speed was now down to fifteen knots though it was at least in the right direction. If it were any less we would become sitting ducks.

This second attack over with, the fight to save Illustrious from being consumed by fire continued. Even though we were now sailing at a reduced speed, our engines were quite intact and it was they that played one of the biggest roles in saving the ship by giving us the power to evade most of the attacks and getting us to Malta later on.

Conditions were bad enough up top and where I was but I must give credit to all those on watch in the ship's machinery rooms. In the boiler rooms for instance, the senior officer had orders that steam pressure had to be maintained at all costs, and that they did. The stokers worked in temperatures that had climbed as high as 140 degrees and the forced draught was sucking in thick, choking fumes from the ventilators up top. Conditions were so bad that men were passing out every few minutes and could hardly read their steam pressure and water level gauges through the smoke. In order for the oil fuel to burn, forced draught air pressure had to be maintained and so they worked on regardless.

Many years later, I met Jim Newton a stoker who was in my training division and he told me that he was below on watch during those first attacks. He said that they hardly knew anything of what was going on topside, even less than me.

To describe what it was like to be in one of these places, especially a boiler room at a time like this was to be like being between two giant kettles of boiling water kept going by two white hot furnaces.* To get a torpedo in the side or a bomb down the funnel would mean dying an excruciating death. Just to stay in these places, one had to exercise immense self control. As some unknown stoker once told a war correspondent who during an action on a warship decided to go down in the stokehold instead of going up top to get his story, 'Now you will find out what fear really is'.

At 16:00, the situation was reasonably under control. We were still on fire and listing to starboard a little but we were steaming

---

*Each boiler had nearly 300 lbs head of steam pressure.

at 18 knots and only forty miles from Malta when the enemy came back. This time it was the Germans again.

The attackers consisted of fifteen Stukas and five Messerschmitts who were probably the escorts coming in from astern in three flights. Up there to meet them in addition to our withering barrage was the Fulmar fighters back from Malta with more fuel and ammo. Our fighters managed to break up some of the attacks and shot down five Stukas. Outnumbered and outgunned it was a case of the old saying about the one that got away. The last Stuka, just like before was the one that nearly did us in with a thousand pounder right on the stern no more than a dozen feet from the after lift which had already taken so much punishment.

I was by this time, having been detailed off to go for'ard and was then commandeered, a part of an ammunition supply party in the galley flat where normally we picked up our 'scran' (food) and daily grog rations.

This was amidships underneath the island (superstructure) on the starboard side. There was a generator room on either side, two out of the ship's six with a killick stoker on watch in each and also nearby was the police office which housed the chief 'crusher' (master at arms) and his staff. This wasn't the most popular place for those who got in the 'rattle'.

Up top was the bridge, the heart and nerve centre of the ship where radar and other devices such as the helm, direction finders, and navigation equipment were located. Flanking the bridge on three sides were five sets of guns called pom-poms. These consisted of two mountings for'ard of the bridge on the starboard side called S1 and S2 and one aft, probably called S3. The other two were on the port side, P1 and P2. These pom-poms were 40mm Bofors guns in mountings of eight, four on top and four on the bottom. Capable of putting up a murderous barrage of 'large, straight banana sized' shells, they were nicknamed 'Chicago Pianos'.

The pom-pom magazines were conveniently located amidships and one of them was a few paces aft of the generator room. Here we made a human chain from the magazine right up to S2 and maybe S3 several ladders up. My position was about the middle of the steel ladder from the galley flat leading to the upper deck. Hand over hand we fed the shells in ammo boxes spacing ourselves a few feet apart.

When the Germans came back at four o'clock, the officer in

charge ordered us to crouch down on the deck so that if we got hit we would make a smaller target for shrapnel and not be knocked over as easily with the concussion and become casualties. I literally flew off the ladder and crouched in a position near the galley amongst a group of men from various branches. It didn't matter who we were. We were all as one right now; Chiefs, POs, officers, and ratings all fighting to save the ship.

Amidst the racket coming from above from the guns and the scream of the diving Stukas, I heard a voice loudly exclaim, 'the bastards are coming at us again'. It might have been me but regardless it reflected what we were all thinking.

Overhead from the loudhailer could be heard the voice of Rev. Lloyd at his action station calmly trying to give those of us between decks an idea of what was happening. To us it was more reassuring than knowing nothing at all, as ignorance is not always bliss especially when somebody is trying to bomb hell out of you.

As we were crouched down, ears straining to decypher the different sounds reaching us and trying to predict in our own minds which one might be the one that gets us, I was still thinking what my chances would be of getting up top if we had to abandon ship. This had been a very real threat all day long with these determined attacks.

Lots of men were lighting up fags to calm their nerves as if it might be their last. Then a chap next to me offered me one as he was getting one for himself. I took it and a light from him as if I was a regular smoker and from that moment on and for the next fifteen years I was.

I started smoking in an extreme crisis situation where nothing else mattered except staying alive and not going around the bend. Much later, in 1956, there was also a crisis situation though not life threatening to me as I was back in 'civvy street'. This was the Suez Crisis where Egypt had prematurely nationalized the Suez Canal and Britain and France with Israel's help had almost succeeded in taking it back by force because of its strategic importance to the Middle East. However, thanks to the world's biggest talking shop, the United Nations with the support of John Foster Dulles, the US Secretary of State, our governments caved in under international pressure and gave up the canal for which thousands of Allied servicemen had fought and died to prevent from falling into enemy hands. This canal and the oil fields around it were almost the whole point of the war in North Africa and the Med. where I had been. Surrendering the canal made it seem that it had all been for nothing and an insult to all those brave men. The bitter irony of all this was that the subsequent blockage of the canal by sunken ships was not the doing of our forces but the Egyptians themselves thus defeating their own purpose. It affected me so much not to mention the price of cigarettes going up when I could barely afford to make ends meet with a wife and family now working at my old job back at the mill. I decided to pack it in with no hesitation and have never smoked since. A crisis made me start and a crisis made me quit — in complete disgust for the latter.

Back in the galley flat a young Stoker First Class from Manchester, crouching low on the deck as the Stukas are making their latest attack is hoping all this will end soon for it has been going on for hours. He then feels the ship shudder from another massive explosion back aft.

This hit which came from the last dive-bomber in its group had penetrated our three inch armour-plated flight deck as said before, near the after lift, and detonated on the quarter deck which was being used as an aid station for the ship's increasing numbers of wounded men. In an instant, twenty or thirty men were wiped out.

In the hangar where the damage control parties had fought so hard to control the fires with water and foamite, the blaze again began to gain on them rekindled by the latest direct hit. By 17:30, the fires aft were out of control and many of the pump motors were burnt out due to the fire and the strain of overwork.

Soon the fire was fast approaching the magazines and Capt. Boyd was informed of the danger. With this knowledge he was asked for his permission to flood them but when he thought of the attacks to come he refused. Every round would be needed and to run out of ammo would leave us virtually defenceless.

Fortunately the magazines weren't overwhelmed but the battle against the fires raged all evening. Sometimes the flames would be winning then, other times we would get ahead. The battle was touch and go and all available hands pitched in. Even the American liasion officer, Lt. Cdr. Opie fought alongside.

Though he was from a non-belligerent country, he was fighting for his own survival the same as the rest and so he proved his worth no less than if it had been one of his own navy's ships.

All through this long and harrowing day, I don't recall ever getting anything to eat or drink nor do I remember anybody getting anything. However, the next day, some of the lads told me there had been mess kettles of rum brought around supposedly for the wounded but apparently there were some that were not that managed to get some, not that I could really blame them for that. I personally would have given my right arm for a couple of good gulpers of Nelson's Blood. It would have done wonders for me. I can't vouch for any of this rum coming around as I never saw any or even smelled it. Regardless, I have always thought why wasn't rum given out generally as there was plenty of it in the spirit room. Why, even at a time like that did things have to be so Pusser where we didn't rate an extra tot. Without it courage was never lacking but it still would have done us a hell of a lot of good just the same. I for one faced that day stone cold sober. As a matter of fact, Capt. 'Johnnie' Walker's famous Second Support Group always ordered 'splice the mainbrace' after each U-boat kill. Weren't we in a situation worthy of such an order? What a bloody shame it would have been for us to go down to Davy Jones's locker and let him have it all to himself not to mention all the officers' wardroom spirits too.

At this point, after that second attack by the Stukas which turned out to be the last by the Germans on us − that day, I would like to quote an excerpt from *Illustrious* by Kenneth Poolman which I think gives a descriptive account of one of the attacks and enables the reader to have some idea what that day was like:

Another thousand pound bomb had plunged into the after lift well. This bomb burst the deck of the lift well and put the steering gear in the compartment below out of action. The ship began to swing crazily round in circles. She remained out of control until Captain Boyd began steering her on main engines alone and headed for Malta.

It was then that her Captain who loved Illustrious so well, went down off the bridge, 'to see', as he said, 'what they had done to my lovely ship.'

He found Illustrious terribly, grievously hurt, her

between-decks torn and blackened, with fires still raging, and a very great number of her men dead or seriously injured. He moved along the wounded and badly burned men trying to cheer them with a personal word here and there.

'But', he said, 'I could not tell one from the other.'

Slowly they fought the ship to Malta, through several more heavy attacks, her stokers maintaining steam in a temperature of a hundred and forty degrees, with the air vents sucking in thick, acrid smoke, her gunners keeping up a fierce barrage with the fury and blind anger of men who were watching their shipmates die and agonize all around them, and their beloved, beautiful ship smashed into punch-drunk helplessness.

About one hour before sundown when we were little more than twenty-five miles from Malta, yet another potentially lethal threat appeared in a day that was full of such unexpected and obviously unwelcome developments.

Illustrious began to list heavily all of a sudden. The cause of this was several thousand tons of water from the overhead sprayers which couldn't escape from the inside of the ship as the scuppers were blocked in the hangar by debris. The sprayers had also been jammed on full output for the last five hours by a piece of shrapnel lodged in the electrical circuit controlling them. This was soon found and the water cut off. In the hangar, another damage control party, crawling amidst debris and smouldering fires, removed the flaps from the ventilators which allowed the water to flow away through the ship's air vent system. By sunset, the list had been partly corrected but only after our damage control system had ironically nearly sunk us.

I don't know how long I spent on the ammunition supply party in the galley flat but shortly before dusk in the early evening after the second German attack, I found myself back in the keyboard with my own fire party. Here, two of us were detailed off to follow my old Chief Stoker Harry Arrowsmith, 'Arrow' for short, through the same armoured door that we had seen poor Springbok stagger through more dead than alive.

I dreaded what I might see beyond that door so I made up my mind that I was only going to see what I wanted to see and not look for all the gruesome sights that surely would be in there.

Those mental defence mechanisms or cognitive screens, call them what you will, did not block out all the desolation which I saw in the dimly lit officers' flat.

There in the wardroom had been a large number of officers who were killed in the first attack while taking a hasty meal. I would presume that many of them would have been the air crew from that combat air patrol which landed back on during the noon hour. This had surely been their last meal.

I had absolutely no intention of looking in there in as much as I had to keep following the Chief though one can imagine what I may have found.

Hurrying along in the gloom through the flat we constantly had to walk over or around debris and through puddles of water which lay everywhere. There wasn't a soul alive in here and there was a deathly silence apart of course from the usual ship's machinery noises. Passing through the bulkhead door at the other end of the flat on the way aft to wherever Arrow was taking us, we turned left into another passage. As we tuned another corner to the right, there on my left was an empty shambles of an office. This had been the Paybob's domain in which our meagre, monthly pay was kept.* Just like the rum ration, I was told the following day that this had been another golden opportunity literally speaking, that I had missed out on because they said money was lying all over the place. Quid notes, ten bob notes, and probably change too, all the money required for a crew of around 1400 for several months. A bit indignantly I said to this oppo, 'What effing money, I never saw any'. This proves that my defence mechanisms were working pretty good, perhaps too good. I could have had a nice pocketful but at the time, that was the last thing I was looking for. Regardless, Chiefy or the other stoker never stopped for anything either, we just kept moving.

Moving further aft on the starboard side we reached a ladder that brought us up near the quarterdeck. This normally hallowed, sacred ground for the Admiral, Captain, and most senior officers was just a smouldering, burning, and blackened area which had once been kept spotlessly clean and its oak decking bleached with salt water. Now in the semi-darkness of the Mediterranean twilight, it was bloodstained from all the

---

*Pay on foreign service was given monthly. At home it was fortnightly.

wounded men who lay there when the last hit from the second Stuka attack wiped them out. The still burning fires cast an eerie glow on vague shapes I could make out lying on the deck and somebody kneeling down. Perhaps it was the Padre trying to comfort the wounded or giving last rites to those less fortunate.

What we had been brought to the quarterdeck for was to play hoses on the smouldering deck which we hooked up to one of the fire-mains.

As we worked our way around the deck spraying seawater liberally, we gradually ended up on the port side when something special happened which has been a cherished memory ever since. I doubt very much if there were many who could actually say something like this.

We were near the port side ladder which led to the next deck when we caught a glimpse of a lone figure coming down. As the person neared the bottom, we recognized him, much to our surprise, as Captain Boyd himself. The look on his face as he looked around told us everything we wanted to know about how he felt. It was an expression of anguish of all that had happened to his ship and his crew.

The Captain didn't walk around when he reached the bottom of the ladder but stood there with one hand on the rail as he looked at us, then past us aft, taking in the scene on the quarterdeck. All this he did in just a few short seconds and then he spoke to us with a few simple words, 'How is everything going?' and were things under control as he could see we were holding a fire hose. I seemed to be standing a little closer to him than the other stoker, a matter of only a couple of feet. We both replied with an 'Everything's under control Sir'. It seems to me that the way he spoke, for a brief moment all three of us were on an equal footing. The difference in rank from Captain of a mighty warship to one of the lowest ranks momentarily seemed to disappear and we were just shipmates trying to save our ship and our lives. All told it was a very brief encounter but it really gave me a new respect for my Captain as he didn't have his usual entourage of Jimmy the One, Commander Tuck, and the Crusher all scurrying around him like he was some untouchable. Normally, to speak with the Captain by request would have to go through most of these people and your divisional officer taking about a week.

A scene such as that may be compared to stories many of us

have heard or read about the Blitz where those in command would share the same fears, dangers, and air raid shelters too with others below them.

After that, Captain Boyd left us with the usual officer's 'carry on' to which would be replied, 'Aye, Aye, Sir'. Then he was gone.

Fifteen miles from Malta, in sight of our safe haven, Illustrious received a message warning of approaching torpedo bombers which found us only five miles from the entrance to the Grand Harbour. As the six Ittie Savoias came at us, our destroyer escort put up a two minute barrage after which the attackers vanished. Then, as we thought we had finally entered the safe haven of Malta, one of our destroyer escorts, HMS Hasty made asdic contact with what appeared to be a U-boat. Hasty responded with a pattern of 'ash cans' (depth charges), after which she lost the contact.* Now it really seemed that we would reach the 'Matelot's Paradise' after all.

As we entered harbour I could just make out the shapes of Valetta and apparently we were cheered in from both sides of the harbour but that detail I'm afraid went unnoticed by me as I felt almost done in. A tug then bumped alongside to help us into Frenchman's Creek and the order was piped 'Secure From Action Stations'. From my position on the quarterdeck I could see a line of vehicles; ambulances and lorries lining the wharf waiting for us to tie up so they could take off the dead and wounded. It was an eerie sight when one thought of the grim task ahead of them.

At 22:15 we secured alongside Palatorio Wharf and after finishing my task, made my way for'ard to my still deserted mess. After all that had gone on, I noticed my dinner plate and cutlery were still exactly where I left them seemingly ages ago.

It was then that it came over the loudhailer asking for volunteers to help remove the killed and wounded. I was in two minds whether or not to go help and even to this day it bothers me that I didn't summon up enough strength and courage although there was no shortage of volunteers. Instead I just flopped down on the narrow mess stool using my gas mask and life belt as a pillow and succumbed to sleep brought on by

---

*HMS Hasty was torpedoed on a Malta convoy by the MTB S55 on June 14, 1942. Sunk by HMS Hotspur the following day.

exhaustion and forgot for a few hours all the horrors of that day. Today at least, I felt I had beaten the odds by surviving.

Although to own one in wartime was forbidden, many men kept diaries, myself included. The entries in it are sparse at best and some written a time after the events happened but nevertheless I would like to include here my own personal entry about the bombing:

> Closed up at action stations while guarding a convoy going through the Sicilian Straits at 7:30. Had forenoon watch; 12:30 went to my action station. 12:40, attacked by German dive-bombers and bombed killing about 80 men in the hangar and destroying all our planes. Attack lasting several hours. Bombed about 7 times, wiped out S2 pom-pom and crew and put out of action all our after 4.5 guns and crews. Making for Malta with a heavy list to starboard. Another formation of bombers attacking but have been drove off. Fires raging back aft and all the planes nearly burnt out in the hangar. Quarterdeck like a slaughter house with dead and dying. Lt. (E) Pitts, our officer in charge of our fire and repair parties killed by a bomb blast. Beyond recognition, had to throw him over the side. Getting near the Grand Harbour of Malta and have come back to quarterdeck playing a hose on the deck to keep the fires from breaking out again. Approximately 10:30, tied up to the wall in harbour. The ship's commander pipes for volunteers to get the dead off the ship, a very nasty job. In Malta for thirteen days, thirteen days of hell. Germans trying to finish us off with their dive-bombers. We got bombed again in harbour but slip out of harbour one night and got back to Alexandria.

Perhaps there are some who may wonder why I have waited so long before writing my story after over 50 years. The answer is simple.

After the war was over, most men just wanted to get back to 'civvy street' and put their service behind them by starting life afresh. The majority did and so did I but yet, one can never really forget. In later years as the pace of life slackens, one begins to reflect and remember the time when we were young and we were all proud to have served.

It has been my experience and has come to my son's attention many times that ex-servicemen do not talk of their military service because their families claim they have no desire to. In most cases this is not so. Those veterans simply have no one who wants to listen except their old comrades at their local Legion hall.

Chapter Eight

Thirteen Days of Hell in Malta

After a restless sleep tossing and turning on the uncomfortable narrow mess stool, I woke up to the pipe of 'Wakey, Wakey'. Nobody was allowed to sleep in, the previous day's ordeal notwithstanding. We were now bottled up in a harbour and the Germans would soon be trying to finish us off so the ship had to be prepared and put back in fighting trim as best we could in our devastated condition.

In situations like this it is essential to maintain routine and discipline for the sake of morale if nothing else so the day started with some semblance of normality. Breakfast of a cup of tea and a fag and a sort of quick mess clean up.

All the time different announcements were being given over the voicepipes to various parts of the ship. Then one came over which applied to everyone, 'Clear lower deck. Everybody muster on the flight deck by divisions'. This meant everybody assembled in their parts of watch for the grim task of roll call. Those who were killed, wounded or missing had to be listed.

Arriving on deck I noticed that the sky which in Malta is usually sunny was now overcast and dull as though the heavens reflected the solemn mood we all felt. As I quickly glanced around, I was able to see the extent of the damage. The deck was pitted and blackened although no longer on fire and the vague twisted shapes that once were the lifts could be seen at either end. Even Jumbo, the little run about crane for towing aircraft and loads was a casualty.

I fell in line with all the other stokers minus those who were down below on watch and was glad to see Eric and Frank at least were alright. One absent face I did notice was Paddy Flynn, the quiet stoker from Southern Ireland. I had heard previously that Paddy had been wounded while working at the steam catapult just below the flight deck when the attack began.

I went to see him the next day with some of the other lads after I got off watch. Walking along the ward where a number of our other wounded were, I spotted Paddy and kidded him about getting wounded just to get out of paying me the ten bob he still owed me for the Bulova wristwatch I had sold him on an installment plan. I never saw Paddy again.

After the usual ship's company coming to attention and standing at ease, everybody dressed casually in working rigs but still wearing the mandatory cap which was considered properly dressed, the roll call began. As the names were called out, some were answered and checked off. Others were followed by silence until the Chief asked if someone knew what happened to them. A voice from somewhere would respond and say that so and so was killed or wounded or still on watch. This was only a preliminary roll call and everything still had to be verified officially later on. This went on until everybody's name had been called out and a rough casualty list had been made. Ship's company was then dismissed and told to stay in our messes.

Very soon after, a Chief or PO came around to each mess and gave everybody a telegram form. We were given a choice of brief statements we could write. Each was just a combination of the same words but in different orders, for instance: don't worry, am alright, or I am alright, don't worry. It all meant the same and it was all we were allowed to send in order to not give away any information. This was then sent to our next of kin who would be extremely worried as news of our bombing was broadcast over the wireless.

During the war, the delivery of a telegram was almost always feared as it so often brought bad news. The poor old telegraph lad was not a welcome caller and news of being killed in action or badly wounded was always sent this way. When Mum and Dad received mine, they were both at home with my sister Florrie. I am told that they wouldn't let Dad open it until they had seen it first as they felt the shock might be too much for him but they were overjoyed and immensely relieved to find out that I was OK and not even wounded. They had heard by the BBC that Illustrious had sustained heavy casualties.

That day I had to pick up my afternoon watch in the control room and start my 24 hours on as we were now at auxiliary steam. Even so I was feeling pretty flakers after a poor night's sleep and yesterday's action. No matter, I still had to go on watch the same as the others who had to be relieved. As soon as

I saw Chief Arrow, he asked me how I was and then he started on a few of his choice comments about the day before, such as: 'What an effing day that was,' and 'I suppose those effing Bastards will be coming back to try and finish us off now'. He used to call me Wings being a Chief who had been in the Andrew about twenty years and close to his naval pension. Being just a young stoker, he regarded me as having been taken under his wing. Arrow was a real crusty sort of chap but easy to get along with and a good sense of humour. Like everybody else, he used to love his tot. When it came time for grog issue while on the forenoon watch he would say. 'I'm slipping up to the mess to get my tot. If any of the officers want me, I've gone to the heads', or some other flannel for an excuse. Needless to say, when he got back he would often tell me to nip up and get mine too while he would fill in for me. This we would do at auxiliary steam but at sea we would have to be relieved to leave our post depending on the circumstances.

Beneath his somewhat tough exterior, Arrow could be quite sentimental. After Illustrious I only saw him once after the war in Plymouth while I was serving aboard the carrier Unicorn in the reserve fleet. About 45 years later though, when visiting Manchester with my family, I heard about another Chief Stoker, Bob Whitworth now about 80 odd years old and living in Ellesmere Port near Liverpool. We decided to visit Bob who we found out had been one of Arrow's closest oppos. Bob was no longer in the best of health and feeling a bit down in the dumps but when he met us he found out I had been one of Arrow's stokers and with him during the bombing in the same fire and repair party. He perked up and related to us some of his story.

When the bombing began, Bob was Chief of the watch in one of the boiler rooms and was separated from his friend who was with me fighting the fires. As I said earlier, Harry took two of us to the quarterdeck and it was there that Bob found Harry once his watch was over. Both had been very worried about each other's whereabouts throughout the action and as soon as Harry turned around and saw Bob, his friend was alright, tears streamed down his face with relief. Just like Eric and myself, we never saw each other until it was over but were worried about each other's safety.

During our brief visit with Bob and his wife we casually talked about our medals and decorations. Bob quite modestly admitted that his medals had lost a lot of meaning to him in as much as he thought others had done far greater deeds than him but as we pointed out, the British Navy doesn't give out decorations for nothing. We must have earned and deserved them and must be proud of them. Somehow this seemed to have an effect and we left him feeling much happier for our visit since we were now Canadians. As Bob stood with his wife at the garden gate as we drove away, I looked back and the last thing I saw was him standing to attention giving the old Navy salute. This made a lasting impression on me because a year later, he passed away after an unfortunate accident in his home. This did not seem a fitting way to go for an old salt who had gven 32 years of his life and had served on most of the famous battlewagons of the Royal Navy.

Lying alongside Parlatorio Wharf in French Creek, having now evacuated our dead and wounded, Illustrious's situation was extremely precarious to say the least and in the following days would become even more perilous. We had become a stationary target, the proverbial sitting duck, without even the opportunity we had at sea of taking evasive action. Only half of our original firepower remained and we had to rely on the dockyard and army ack-ack. The fleet was no longer with us for protection having had to return to Alex with their convoy and get themselves out of harm's way. When the Mediterranean war began, the Royal Navy had virtually been withdrawn from Malta in the belief that the island was indefensible. In company with us, in addition to a few submarines that used Malta as a forward base, was the Aussie light cruiser HMAS Perth who stayed behind to give us some added firepower from her own guns putting herself in the same peril as ourselves. Apart from her and the dockyard, the only other cover available to us was our surviving Fulmars and some RAF Hurricanes operating from Hal Far airfield on the other side of the island. This was all that stood between us and the next onslaught from the Luftwaffe.

Speaking of the good old Perth who stood by us through many terrible days, she reflects the idea that the exploits and courage of the Royal Navy in the Second World War was a team effort that applied equally to the Commonwealth navies as we were all one then. Think also of the famous Battle of the River Plate where two British cruisers and the Kiwi (New Zealand) HMNZS Achilles took on a veritable tiger of the high seas, the Graf Spee which could have easily blown them all out of the water beyond their range with her 11-inch guns compared to the 6-inch 'pea shooters' on Achilles.

Sadly, HMAS Perth would meet her fate a little over a year from then on February 28, 1942, when she was sunk in the Sunda Straits off Java in company with the USS Houston by an overwhelming force of Jap heavy cruisers. The ships had been a part of a multi-national force (British, Aussie, American, and Dutch) hunting for Jap transports steaming between Borneo and Celebes. The day before, the two Dutch cruisers De Ruyter and Java had been sunk by the same Japs and the day after, HMS Exeter, hero of the River Plate which I had cheered into Plymouth exactly a year before our own bombing while I was in the training division. Their gallant action and subsequent loss seemed a futile effort considering the Japs had overrun the entire region. They seemed like a sacrifice in another mission impossible. Those that survived spent three years of hell in Jap prison camps.

Back in Malta I was wondering whether we would manage to get out alive or become a derelict hulk as we waited for the dockyard to patch us up sufficiently to put to sea again and make a run for it back to Alexandria. Being lower deck, I had no idea what plans were in the making but I hoped they would come to fruition as no doubt the Germans were determined to make the Grand Harbour our grave.

Illustrious was descended upon by scores of Maltese dock workers at first light on the morning of January 11. Their task was not to fix our smashed flight deck or lifts or to repair the twisted innards of the ship but simply to make her seaworthy again so we could make our escape to Alex. The main emergency repairs that had to be done on us right now lay mostly below the waterline. Divers went down to inspect the bottom, welders removed the wooden pegs that were used to plug shrapnel and bullet holes then welded metal over the holes. Most importantly, our steering gear which was badly damaged in the first attack had to be repaired at least temporarily.

Within a short time, Illustrious no longer resembled a fighting ship but rather some sort of man-made cocoon covered in ladders, scaffolding, pumps, and machinery punctuated at frequent intervals by the glow of acetylene torches.

All this was a race against time when the Luftwaffe would return to try to finish us off. Fortunately, the dive-bombers did not return right away and Illustrious was granted five precious days in which work was allowed to progress uninterrupted. Had they returned immediately this story could have been vastly different. Vital work could not have been done and we may never have been made seaworthy out of our devastated condition before more direct hits were scored on us.

Why didn't the Luftwaffe return right away? No stories about Illustrious have ever speculated on this yet, in the battle to save our ship, those five days were crucial to our survival in which the enemy lost a golden opportunity. The only reason I can offer which is conjecture at best, is that we put up such a fierce resistance, the enemy may have been hit harder than we realized. Perhaps Fliegerkorps X needed time to regroup too, because obviously, though the percentage of aircraft shot down was comparatively small, in a battle such as that, for every aircraft downed there must be several that return to their base badly damaged or full of holes which must be patched in order to keep the aircraft airworthy.

Regardless, by the 16th, they came back to wreak vengeance on the island and to make up for lost time and punish the Maltese for giving us sanctuary.

The morning after we arrived was dull and threatened rain. After such a long spell without raids, people were beginning to feel confident and I must admit that I was beginning to feel better too. Then to everyone's horror, the awful wail of air raid sirens sounded all around the harbour. Aboard ship, action stations was sounded and those guns that remained intact were uncovered in readiness for the incoming attack. Everywhere, men, women, and children ran for cover. The many dock 'yardies' working on us made a mad scramble for the shelter of caves nearby the ship in Senglea I think.

The initial panic over with, there was a breathtaking silence as everyone waited, servicemen and civilians alike. This was Malta's baptism of fire from the Germans but it wasn't the first raid they had endured after many months of Italian bombings. This however, would be different.

The moment of silence was a fleeting one at best because soon after could be heard the steadily increasing noise of approaching aircraft over the Grand Harbour from the direction of Kalkara. Many people figured they wouldn't be Italian based on the knowledge of what Illustrious went through and the raiders came over in a force unheard of before this time. The attackers in fact consisted of 44 Stukas, 17 Junkers 88's, 10 Messerschmitt 110's, and an Italian fighter escort of 10 Fiat CR 42's and some Macchi 200's.

Then the harbour defences opened up and the scene made it seem as if the gates of hell had been literally flung open.

As on previous days, I had gone ashore on the 16th as I did every other day, being twenty-four hours on and twenty-four off. I just wanted to get away from the ship itself, not that there was anywhere to go or anything to do, it didn't matter so long as I had enough money for a beer, a meal, and a bed for the night. This kind of helped me face the dangers and the fear all over again the next day.

Coming up the after ladder from the stokers' mess after deck intending to catch the one o'clock liberty boat, I was taken aback at the sight of all the 4.5 in ammunition that had been piled up on my mess deck in anticipation of the impending German attacks which we all knew must come sooner or later. Not surprising really, we only had our for'ard 4.5's left and the shells were all concentrated near the ammo hoist ready to go up to the turrets saving the time of getting them out of the magazines. The shells must have been piled up about five feet high and there must have been scores of them.

One look at all that ammo made me all the more determined to catch that liberty boat and get the hell out not that my chances may have been any better ashore. The Germans were out to get Illustrious but weren't fussy what they hit. That's what it turned out to be as this was a total war.

It seemed I hadn't been ashore very long and was in some dive on my own just sitting and having a beer when all of a sudden the sickening sound of the wailing air raid sirens filled the air. This was it. I dashed out of the bar and all I could see was people running in every direction scrambling to take cover. I started running too even though I had no idea where to go. Anywhere that could give me cover would do. Unexpectedly I saw some people running down some stairs into what seemed like a cellar or a basement. I rushed in behind and found myself in amongst many men, women, and children all looking and feeling fearful. As I recall, I was the only serviceman in there but I certainly didn't feel out of place and felt no more confidence than they did. I felt pretty shaky as the effects of our ordeal on the 10th were still vivid in my mind.

We all looked at each other and waited. For an instant

everything was silent then we could hear the drone of the Jerry planes and then the sound of our guns opening up on them.

The Stukas peeled off one by one and began their dive through the curtain of steel and shrapnel being put up by the army who were trying out a new barrage of heavy anti-aircraft guns. Several of the aircraft were hit and exploded in a ball of fire but more followed with their deadly cargoes of 500 and 1000 pound bombs.

Almost immediately, the area around Illustrious in French Creek was a mass of churning water and geysers as near misses exploded. Many of the bombs landed along the Wharf and in the nearby three cities of Senglea, Cospicua and Vittoriosa where there were many civilian casualties and buildings were blasted into rubble. Adding to the bombs were large chunks of concrete falling to the ground which had been blown apart in the dockyard hundreds of yards away.

Two churches were among the blocks of structures destroyed in the raid. One of them was Our Lady of Victories with its lovely basilica which was badly damaged. The other was the Coventual Parish Church of St. Lawrence in Vittoriosa where forty people taking shelter inside were killed, as well as priceless relics and documents dating back to Byzantine times and the Knights of St. John being destroyed

In the harbour itself, Illustrious and Perth put up an intense barrage adding to that put up by the Maltese and British gunners of the Dockyard Defence Battery. Overhead the raiders were met by a number of RAF Hurricanes and our Fulmars operating from Hal Far. Lumbering behind their more modern counterparts were even two old Gloster Gladiators and they all joined in the aerial melee with all machine guns blazing.

Unfortunately Illustrious was hit again. Amazingly it was next to the after lift which had already been hit so many times. Perhaps that was fortunate as that part of the ship couldn't really be damaged much more than it already was. Perth sustained some damage too but the most miraculous part of the whole raid probably involved the merchantman Essex moored near Illustrious. Essex was carrying a lethal cargo of 400 tons of ammunition. She received a direct hit which went off in her engine room killing 15 and wounding 23 but her cargo remained untouched. Had it gone up it surely would have destroyed much of the dockyard and certainly Illustrious too.

The attack was over in a matter of minutes and then fifteen

minutes later it began all over again as a second wave of German bombers returned but this time no more hits were scored on Illustrious though the surrounding dockyard was cratered and on fire. All the tarpaulins and scaffolding surrounding the ship had been blown away and the ship was filled with uncountable splinter holes but at least it had survived.

Ashore the All Clear was sounded and wailing of sirens from ambulances and fire engines could be heard as people emerged from their shelters to see what damage had been done and if they still had homes to go to.

Back in the cellar I was using for a shelter, I took my time leaving having really nowhere to go and there was definitely no 'Harry Grippos' or 'up homers' for matelots like me in this place. I was just another sailor from some ship.

With the feeling of loneliness and far from home I just wandered off down the street indifferent to my surroundings, bomb damage or not. The Maltese I thought were at least in their own country amongst family and friends from whom they could get comfort and consolation for their sufferings, all sharing a common danger.

I was also thinking about how soon we could get out of Malta and not get stuck here. The ship being made seaworthy and somehow avoiding more damage was our only hope. Each day it became more imperative than ever that we get out and any sort of delay added to our nightmare. In the end we would have no choice but to make a run for it and just hope and pray the Jerry bombers wouldn't find us with the distinct possibility of getting sunk this time.

As these chilling and despairing thoughts ran through my mind, I suddenly realized that I had subconsciously retraced my steps back to the same dive I had so hastily vacated when the raid first began. On entering the seemingly empty bar where even Jose, the proprieter was nowhere to be seen yet, I spotted my unfinished beer on the table just as I had left it. Without any further ado, I picked it up and drank it all back in one gulp enjoying every drop. The fact it was flat and had dirt or dust in it was of no consequence then. I was in no mood for niceties.

Idling away the rest of the day, I booked a bed down the 'Gut' having all night leave and Jose woke me up in good time the next morning. I made my way back to the dockyard at around 10:30. Catching up to another shipmate who, like myself had gone ashore to get away from things for a few hours, we talked casually about our situation. As the ship came into view, my heart began to sink. She looked massive and formidable even now but kind of punch drunk like a heavy weight boxer who had gone the full bouts. I couldn't help but say out loud 'The bastards have hit us again. We're never gonna leave this effing place alive. This'll be our graveyard'.

Going aboard and saluting the officer of the watch, I went to my messdeck. Below decks the awful stench of cordite was everywhere even still. That smell stayed for weeks.

Looking at the spot where all those piles of 4.5 shells had been stacked, there was not one left to be seen. All those and probably many more had been used up in yesterday's raid which told me everything I wanted to know about what it had been like and I was glad that I had been ashore.

The one bright spot of the day was of course, 'Up Spirits'. That lovely tot of Nelson's Blood was a lifesaver to us even though it was watered down to 2 and 1. For just a little while as long as the effects lasted, our morale shot up.

However, to repeat a previous comment of criticism about the unbending Pusser's routine, I question the logic in issuing us watered down rum at a crucial time like this when our lives and the ship itself were held in the balance. Giving us neaters would have done us more good morale wise and there was certainly no shortage in the rum locker. Even to this day, I fail to understand yet I suppose ours was not to reason why. It all goes back to the time of Nelson and the theory that 'England Expects'. Jolly Jack expects nothing and rarely got anything.

A short while after I came back aboard, an announcement was made over the tannoy that took everybody off guard. The ship's company was to be evacuated leaving only a skeleton maintenance crew including the auxiliary watchkeepers. That's me.

I would be one of those left behind to face the next attacks while up to 1,000 of my shipmates would go mostly to Hal Far airfield. Furthermore, the ship would not be defended by our own guns.

My first reaction was my wondering of this was another way of giving up the ship not knowing the whole picture. The reason in fact was that the army who was trying out a new box barrage for its harbour defence had complained that our gunfire was getting in the way and they would be better able to defend us without our help.

In the event of further raids, those of us remaining would run to the nearby caves for safety. It seemed we were receiving one blow after another and we wondered how much longer it would go on.

Saddened that all my friends including Eric and Frank would be leaving me the next morning, I picked up the afternoon watch with Chief Arrow.

Promising myself that I would visit them at the first opportunity, I realized that Illustrious now seemed like a ghost ship with her once crowded messdecks almost deserted.

It wasn't too long before the army's theory about our defence was put to the test. Sunday, January 19, the second great raid on the ship took place. This time I was aboard. There was a raid in the morning again with a large number of Stukas, Junkers, Messerschmitts, and Italian fighters. Each time I heard the sirens and the ship's klaxon sounding off the alarm, my stomach turned a somersault. Immediately I dashed up to the main deck and down the gangway at the double, clip-clopping away in my no laces boots. How I didn't lose them I'm not sure. Along with us matelots sprinting for the caves were the Maltese dockyard mateys. These Maltese workers had their own system of lookouts. For every one or two working in the bowels of the ship there were several more all stationed at intervals right up to the upper deck where one had his eye on a red flag or something which would give him the signal that a raid was coming. In seconds, word would be passed right down the line and those working below woud drop everything and race off the ship into the caves with the rest of us. I'd swear that for each worker there must have been at least half a dozen lookouts, not that I blame them. They were still working around the clock trying to get us ready for sea. Without their efforts and their loyalty we would never have got out.

Looking back on Captain Boyd's decision to evacuate most of the ship's company, I am convinced he must also have considered the possibility of much heavier casualties in the event that the enemy made a really concentrated effort and threw in everything they had to completely annihilate us.

118

Having less men running to the caves for protection along with the Maltese would logically involve less confusion and better protection for those still there.

In the caves, I could hear the same things taking place as in the last raid. First there was the deathly silence for a moment after the last strains of the siren died away to be followed by the roar of all the defences opening up. There would be the dull thud of explosions some distance away and then the deafening crack of explosions nearby and overhead. All the while the Maltese who are a deeply religious people would be praying aloud. At one end of the cave they had even erected an altar with a crucifux around which they all gathered. Most of us matelots, myself included prayed silently with them. I make no pretence about being a hero. I was terrified and the feelings I experienced stayed with me quite a long time after the raids were over. There were times when I would go to the heads and suddenly imagine I heard the drone of a plane overhead. Immediately I would jump up and start to run towards the bulkhead door pulling up my overalls on the way only to realize that nothing was happening. Inwardly I would feel a bit foolish at myself.

There was another similar raid in the afternoon and the result was that the ship was damaged again. Two near misses on the port side lifted her out of the water and flung her against the wharf resulting in a hole below the waterline flooding a boiler room and fracturing her port turbine. One can imagine my disappointment and feeling of shock when I came out of the cave and saw her listing. It took a hundred technicians working all night to repair that damage. Even now I wonder how we ever got out at all.

I must mention that there is another side to this story for we took our toll on the Germans too. That Sunday, the Jerries claim to have lost 10 aircraft and four Itties but our reports said 39 were destroyed in addition to 5 probables and 9 damaged. Seventeen of those were accounted for by the RAF Hurricanes and our Fulmars with the loss of only two of ours. Furthermore, the Malta Defences tracked on their radar a Cant Z 506 seaplane with red cross markings which was patrolling the water between Malta and Sicily. Obviously, the enemy had a number of aircraft which were forced to ditch which were not confirmed by our side. Losses like those the Germans could not sustain and so they withdrew to consolidate their forces in order to mass for a final all out assault on the ship.

Keeping the promise I made earlier, I went up to Hal Far about the 20th to see Eric and the others. How I managed to get there as it was a fair distance, I do not know. I do remember that I had very little money left after going ashore every other day. It is doubtful I could afford a paid trip by gharry or other means. Nevertheless, I got there and recollect playing a game of billiards and having a drink in a canteen probably run by either NAAFi or the RAF.

All things considered, it was a pleasant change to see everyone again and it took my mind off things for a bit. If the idea of sending the crew here was to reduce the risk of casualties when we were being bombed then I must point out that apparently they were no safer here as this airfield was a prime target too. On Saturday the 18th, Hal Far was raided by a force of almost a hundred aircraft and received considerable damage along with the surrounding villages where there were quite a few civilian casualties. It looked like everybody somewhere on the island took their turn for a bashing.

As each day passed, work continued at a furious pace to make the most urgent repairs to get us seaworthy. When that would be was anybody's guess because even at this late date I can't recall hearing any buzzes or speculation flying around the messdeck. Not a 'Dickie-Bird' was mentioned. All I can say is that Capt. Boyd and those around him who might know kept it a pretty good secret. Perhaps it was best for all our sakes because the less we on the lower deck knew, the less likely the enemy would find out as they probably had some agents in Malta. We had to leave undetected and we all prayed that the Stukas wouldn't be waiting for us out at sea where we would be little better than a sitting duck with over half of our guns out of action and no harbour defences to give us cover.

January 23rd arrived, a day I'll never forget. At first it seemed like it would be no different to so many previous days. Suddenly, early in the forenoon we found out either by a buzz or the PA, which I'm not sure, that the ships company were recalled immediately. I began to realize that this was it and it would be now or never. We were going to make a run for it but I still didn't know the exact time although it would be very soon.

Everybody was back aboard just before or around noon. The steaming watch bill for sea went up with a few changes for those killed or wounded. I of course, was to remain with my station in the control room. Picking up the afternoon, full watches went below for flashing up all boilers and connecting main steam valves when ready for the engine room turbines. The whole ship was alive again with tension, excitement, and apprehension as to our possible fate once we slipped the cables and headed out to the open sea.

The afternoon wore on with preparations being made to slip out under the cover of darkness. January nights are much longer, especially in lower latitudes which was to our advantage and dusk set in about six o'clock in the evening.

The plan now appeared to be to steam like hell once we cleared the harbour entrance and put as many miles as we could between us and Malta by first light.

As it was about supper time when the ship started to let go from Parlatorio Wharf, I stayed below decks having to relieve the other stoker in the control room for his supper when I finished mine.

Secretly, swiftly, and unceremoniously the ship slipped away with some repair stages still hanging over the side. Scuttles and deadlights were closed tight for darkening ship. Nobody ashore knew that we were leaving but I'm sure those that noticed it passed on the word quickly and there must have been many who were relieved that we had left as we had been the prime reason for the Stukas arriving.

Forty or so years after these events took place, I heard from an ex-sergeant of Marines, Mr Hugh Beaven who had served in one of our after turrets. He enclosed a note which was an extract from a private letter to our captain on the day of our departure from the captain of one of the submarines that had witnessed our ordeal. The extract went as follows:

> . . . we submarines in the peaceful haven of Marsamescetto
> Harbour or the comparatively healthy waters of Dockyard
> Creek have been thinking about you and your brave
> fellows. The Battle of HMS Illustrious has now been
> fought pretty continuously for the past 12 days and I am
> afraid there has been very little we have been able to do to

help but I must express to you our great admiration for a ship so truly named and we all wish and pray that you and your officers and men may have a safe passage to a pleasant refitting base and that we may see the great ship out here again flogging the enemy in all three elements.

Perhaps during your absense, the submarines may have a successful attack on one or more of the three battleships the Illustrious has left us to play with but it seems more possible that they now regard the 'Mare Piccole' as their 'Mare Nostrum'.*

It is evident that no ship in history has withstood such a terrific asault as the Illustrious over such a long period and one may presume that it is equally true to say that no ship has been so feared by her enemies . . .

---

*'Mare Nostrum' refers to Mussolini's reference of the Med. being an Italian lake but after Taranto, this 'lake' shrank to the size of the 'Mare Piccole' − Taranto's inner harbour.

Chapter Nine

Escape from the Med.

Once clear of the harbour the ship quickly increased speed turning east-south-east for Alex. Hearing the deep rumbling vibrations of the engines on the deck had the same familiar sounds as those when turning into the wind for flying aircraft on and off which told me we must have been doing at least 25 knots.

I was glad to be out of Malta at last as it had been a nerve wracking time not knowing one day from the next what would happen. Nevertheless I felt apprehensive and fearful about the coming of daylight tomorrow like everyone else.

My next watch was the First meaning 20:00 hours to midnight. I was then off for four hours to get a bit of 'kip' before picking up the morning watch from 04.00 to 08.00. One could say I spent most of those first crucial night hours of escaping in an engineering nerve centre. Down in that control room we all had our eyes glued to those duplicated steam pressure gauges etc. on the wall panel, not just the engineer officers were watching for any undue changes.

Everything now depended on the engine room branch keeping all the machinery running in order to maintain high speed. Without this, our chances of survival were mighty slim if the Stukas caught up to us. Everybody throughout the ship realized this and it was made evident whenever we were going down below and we would pass seamen or other branches. They would look at us and say 'keep those engines and boilers going Stokes. We're depending on you to get to Alex.' These words of encouragement really made me feel important and that the stokers were being looked upon as those who would save the day. Nevertheless, stokers always had a good rapport with the rest of the ship's company and the Royals too.

Many years later, I wrote to our old Padre who was now the Very Reverend H.M. Lloyd DSO OBE MA who specifically mentioned in his reply about the race for life Illustrious made when we left Malta and said that I must have been proud to have been one of the stokers. Coming from someone who is held in such high esteem and with such decorations for his outstanding service, a greater compliment to our branch could not be wished for.

We kept up our constant high speed all though the night which made it very difficult for our escort* to maintain station and keep up to us. We also missed the rendezvous with the cruiser sent to escort us back to Alex. The first we heard about this was during the next day when word went around that a cruiser squadron had been heavily bombed by the Stukas that were looking for us a mere sixty miles astern. This news worried me as to whether they had spotted us but our luck held as the enemy little knew that their prey had slipped through their fingers and was going hell for leather barely out of sight over the horizon. Hopefully this meant we were just out of their range as well.

By all accounts it seems that the German bombers had flown over the dockyard early that morning intending to give us another bashing but to their astonishment, Illustrious had simply vanished into thin air completely. Almost immediately they had flown out to sea in the hopes of catching perhaps a limping carrier and finally finishing us off at sea where it had all started two long weeks ago. Instead they found the unfortunate cruisers and gave them the pasting we would have received had our rendezvous taken place. Sadly for the cruisers, Illustrious received another blessing in disguise. The bird had flown the proverbial coop to fight again another day.

Eventually we made contact with the covering battle squadron which took us into Alex arriving around noon on the third day of our odyssey, January 25. We had steamed close to 1,000 miles. At one point we had water in the oil fuel possibly attributed to receiving so many near misses which resulted in pitch black smoke spewing from our funnel. This alone could have given away our position as the smoke could be seen for many miles. At another point, we only had three hours of uncontaminated fuel left in our bunkers which proved that even

_____

*HMAS Perth provided the escort back to Alex.

to the last our escape had been miraculous but we were a crippled ship that would require most of the next twelve months in extensive repairs wherever we could get them. Above all, we had defied Hitler himself and his glorious Luftwaffe and survived.

I had hoped that when the ship entered harbour, I could go up top somewhere, perhaps the flight deck, and see what was going on. I could have a look at the old dump Alexandria again although I really hated that rotten, stinking place but at this moment, after all we had been through it seemed like coming back home. I honestly thought a few times recently that I would never see it again.

However I had forgotten about the strict Pusser's protocol which would be in force on this special occasion when we would pass the fleet and the Commander-in-Chief with all the naval dignity and honour that we could possibly muster. Our White Ensign would be proudly fluttering in the wind and the ship's bell displaying its battle scars and shrapnel holes. Even in our battered and blackened condition, we would sail in majestically, and triumphant.

The pipe over the tannoy sounded 'Special sea duty men fall in for entering harbour. Anyone not in the rig of the day (which was full blues, No. 2's) to clear the upper decks'. In other words keep out of sight if you were in overalls like myself.

Getting a 'green rub' I had to be content to look out of a porthole to see as best I could, our momentous reception from the fleet as we passed each ship. Almost to a day, a year ago in January I was among those cheering in HMS Exeter into Devonport giving them a hero's welcome. Now it was us receiving that welcome in similar fashion. As we passed each ship be it a destroyer, cruiser, battler, or even merchant ship, they gave us three hearty cheers. From my limited viewpoint I was still able to appreciate the moment and felt very proud. Those who were cheering us in no doubt realized that in us they had lost the eyes and ears of the fleet except for the old Eagle. This would be a great disadvantage until a suitable relief for us could be sent out from England as we were no longer operational.*

*Two days after we were bombed, on January 12, the Admiralty ordered HMS Formidable, our sister ship then in the South Atlantic to relieve us travelling via the Cape of Good Hope.

Swinging idly round the buoy in some corner of the harbour very forlornly sat the ships of the French Squadron under Vice-Admiral Godfroy and included his flagship, the 11,000 ton 8-inch gun heavy cruiser Duquesne. They were still taking orders from the Vichy French government which had collaborated with the Nazis. I wonder how those sailors who used to be our allies felt when they witnessed such a spectacle of a mighty carrier who was carrying on the fight that they shuld still have been a part of. I wonder if they felt like cowards.

In my opinion, at a time like this I don't understand why we didn't take their ships over completely and man them with British sailors as we were desperately in need of reinforcements and stretched to the limits. Coming to fight with us a couple of years later was no compensation for not helping us now when we really needed them.

In his book *A Sailor's Odyssey*, Admiral Cunningham gave his personal reasons why these ships of the French Squadron were not forcibly seized. On June 29, 1940, he received a signal from the British government advising him that seizure of those ships was under consideration which would coincide with the operation at Oran where French heavy units were attacked by a battle fleet under the command of Admiral Somerville with the result of several French ships being destroyed in order that they wouldn't fall into the hands of the enemy.

Admiral Cunningham strongly resisted the idea of such an action calling it 'utterly repugnant'. He felt that 'The officers and men in the French Squadron were our friends. We had had many most cordial social contacts with them and they had fought alongside us.' Furthermore he felt that 'Suddenly and without warning to attack and board his ships, and in the course of it probably to inflict many casualties on his sailors, appeared to me to be an act of sheer treachery which was as injudicious as it was unnecessary.'

These were a few of Cunningham's reasons and to a point they made sense from a diplomatic and military point of view but the fact remained and the reality of the situation was that these ships were a potential threat to us as Admiral Godfroy had said that they would try to slip out to sea at the first opportunity. This was resolved through negotiations when the ships were de-militarized and de-activated.

All diplomacy aside, the 'cordial social contacts' that Cunningham referred to were all made by the officers. As for the lower deck like myself, I don't ever remember anybody having French sailors as oppos and going ashore with them. In fact, I remember an occasion when a boat full of French sailors on liberty were stepping ashore and some of our matelots were shouting out insults at them like 'Look at those effing Frogs going to the French Quarter in Stanley Bay 'bagging off' in the 'bag shanties' while we're going to effing sea and getting shot up and killed'. The French sailors then turned away towards Stanley Bay, the opposite direction to what all the British matelots would go. We never saw any in our direction, if we did, they probably would have been done for. I also don't ever recall seeing one of their sailors invited to our Fleet Club although many of the lads used to invite soldiers and airmen from the other Allied fighting forces.

Maybe not all the French sailors and their officers agreed with their Admiral even though they were offered the chance to join our side but it was Admiral Godfroy who made the final decision. He was sympathetic to the Allies but determined to be loyal to the French government regardless. History has shown though, how the Free French rallied to our cause along with the Resistance and fought with distinction and saved the honour of France.

After our heroes' welcome, we tied up to the buoy and dropped anchor relatively safe for now under the protection of the fleet. It had been a very harrowing couple of weeks past and in the words I wrote my parents, 'I shall never forget it'. As we now wouldn't be going to sea until our relief arrived from England, I tried to relax a bit.

Nevertheless, we would require further repairs in a dry dock this time to prepare us for our long journey around the Cape to some refitting base. I wish to point out that in the action that had caused us so much destruction, Illustrious wasn't the only casualty. Of the two battlers that were with us that day, both were damaged. The old Warspite, our flagship and veteran of the Battle of Jutland back in 1916, was hit for'ard near the anchor cable. The bomb detonated but it was incomplete and fortunately, no one was hurt. Her sister ship, the Valiant had one man killed and two wounded by shrapnel. It was lucky that these two great ships did not receive more serious damage but it was bad enough.

The following day on January 11, just a matter of hours after we had limped into Malta, the two 9,000 ton, 6-inch cruisers,

Gloucester and Southampton left Malta after seeing the crippled destroyer Gallant safely into port. The two were set upon by a dozen Stukas unexpectedly as they had no radar which was in its infancy at the time. Gloucester which was the flagship of Rear-Admiral Renouf had a bomb strike the roof of the director tower but failed to explode though it killed nine men and wounded fourteen.

The Southampton received two hits and didn't fare as well as her sister. Both hit in the wardroom and PO's mess where most of her damage control heads were killed or wounded. Fires broke out immediately and they were soon out of control. She finally had to be sunk by a torpedo from one of our own ships and her survivors went aboard the Gloucester and the destroyer Diamond. I don't know what her casualties were but they must have been extremely heavy.

That first day in Alex, I didn't do much, having to pick up both dog watches which was 16:00 to 20:00 still being an auxiliary watchkeeper but the next day I went for a run ashore and had a drink in the Fleet Club of that Stella onion beer. It was better than nothing.

The situation in the Med. was now deteriorating with the entry of the Germans with their air support based in Sicily. This was January 1941 and the Italians were still being beaten back by Wavell's 'Thirty Thousand' in the Western Desert but next month, early in February, advance units of Rommel's now famous Afrika Korps would begin arriving to aid their Ittie allies and the situation would soon make a change for the worse. Early in January, the Luftwaffe started attacking the Suez Canal which did not cause any damage or casualties but delayed shipping for about twenty-four hours due to unexploded bombs. Perhaps these bombs were not intended to explode, at least not right away. This development regarding the canal which actually took place on January 18 – 19, was an alarming one. The enemy was trying to block the canal which would, in effect seal up the Med. at both ends if successful with no supplies or reinforcements being able to reach the fleet or the island of Malta which was key to the whole Mediterranean operation.

Soon the Germans began dropping magnetic mines in the canal which was another twist of fate for Illustrious which narrowly escaped destruction by magnetic mine enroute to Liverpool when she was new and again passing through a minefield in the Pantelleria Straits. Now we would have to run the gauntlet against mines again, this time in the Suez.

Before facing this threat, we would first have to wait for the new arrival of our relief, HMS Formidable. Her arrival would be delayed for some time as the canal was made safe for shipping after continually being mined by the Luftwaffe.

The Suez was first mined right at the end of January and not reopened for several days but soon after reopening, a ship struck a mine and sank with the result of the canal being partially blocked. Many of the mines had been removed but a number remained and the canal was closed until February 18 and even then it was restricted to ships under 15,000 tons until the tentative date of March 5. The old Formid was identical to us being our sister and so her large tonnage meant she had to wait at the Red Sea end.

The canal was actually reopened on February 11 but the Formidable would not reach us until March 10 after squeezing through the canal past the sunken wreck with little more than a few feet to spare on either side.

Waiting week after week, wondering when our relief would get here seemed endless. In the meantime, our skipper, Capt. Boyd received a promotion to Rear-Admiral which meant that he would be leaving us and Commander Tuck was promoted to Captain and took over command. One day, I believe it was in February, we were all piped to clear lower deck and muster by divisions on the flight deck. This was to say goodbye to our well liked and courageous Captain Boyd. It was a touching farewell when he addressed the ship's company after we had been brought to attention and then stood at ease. He spoke from the after end of the bridge through a PA system but we could all see and hear him well. In fact, we could detect the emotion in his voice and almost tears in his eyes when he said we were the finest ship's company he had ever served with and he would never forget us. When one considers the number of commands he had taken during his career in the Royal Navy, this was a compliment of the highest order. We would not forget him either.

The ceremony was completed by a final reciprocal gesture by

the ship's company when the 'Chippies' (shipwrights or carpenters) presented him with a beautiful casket made out of the oak planking from the quarterdeck that had survived the fires that ravaged that part of the ship. Coming from that almost hallowed area of the ship which the Captain knew so well seemed the most fitting token of respect we could give him. His voice nearly broke when he was accepting it. I do believe we also gave him three hearty cheers. Then we were brought to attention and dismissed.

It was around this same time we learned the Captain wouldn't be the only one getting a draft chit. So far, nothing had been made official but the buzzes were that several hundred of all branches were to be left behind as replacements for other ships.

For me, the prospect of being left in the Med. was comparable to a huge goldfish bowl with us the fish swimming round and round and no way out. Sooner or later one would get caught and 'catch a packet' meaning getting either sunk or hit and killed or wounded. Regardless, there was no choice in the matter but to just hope for the best.

It wasn't long before the buzzes came true and we would all find out our fate, who would go and who would stay. One day, somebody rushed down into the mess or it was announced, I don't know which but anyway they told us that the lists had been posted up on the notice board somewhere near the seamen's upper messdeck. No matter, I was off watch and with all the other stokers I dashed up the ladder and joined everybody as they crowded around checking the names on the list. Some men were groaning and swearing when they evetually found their name or that of a close oppo, others breathed a sigh of relief and smiled. Finally I managed to get close enough and along with Eric we scanned the long rows of names anxiously looking to see if we were on it. After initially checking, I couldn't believe it and I had to look again just to convince myself. The same applied to Eric, but we were convinced we were not on the list and chuckled at the idea that we would get out of this effing place at last. I could have jumped for joy. We would live a little longer.

We didn't actually know where we were going at this time although Admiral Cunningham and the powers that be did. I knew we would be travelling round the Cape but thought we would probably go back to England. How wrong I was, but I wouldn't be sorry.

Strange things happen in war and peace. One of my shipmates from the training division days, Jim Newton who I have mentioned before was one of those unfortunates who would be left behind.

It wasn't until nearly fifty years later that I found out what happened to him under most unusual circumstances when we happened to meet.

When Jim left Illustrious, he volunteered for naval salvage to become a diver. First however, he was sent to Tobruk which was captured by our forces on January 22. He and a group of other sailors went there by lorry and were strafed by German fighters along the way and was only saved by diving under the truck for cover. At Tobruk Jim went aboard the depot ship Medway which served as a floating barracks. He was put on one of the diesel generators as a watchkeeper but got a sudden draft chit one day to report for diver training. Who should replace him but Albert Melling, the same lad I had had a fight with in Guz barracks over a stamp for marking my kit and later had become friends with. This turned out a tragedy for Albert although it saved Jim's life for within a few hours, the Medway sailed out of Tobruk and was sunk. Albert went down with her. This is an example of what probably happened to many of those who were left behind. In all, about 500 stayed behind from Illustrious.

Anway, Jim became a naval diver and helped clear wrecks that were blocking Tobruk harbour which was under seige by the Afrika Korps and was being held by a gallant band of British, Polish, and Aussie defenders.

He served on a number of other ships and after the war went into the merchant navy for over twenty years. He even got married and emigrated to New Zealand but sadly his wife passed away and he returned to England.

About 1989 – 90, I noticed that Jim had joined the Old Illustrians Association and we renewed our friendship. He was now living in the 'Smoke' (London) and was a Sergeant in the Corps of Commissionaires and doing very well. He even hob-nobs with high dignitaries and royalty during the course of his duties. He also is an international courier escorting documents and packages around the globe several times a year. It was on one of these trips to the United States, Minneapolis in fact which is almost 500 miles from my home on the Canadian prairies that he decided to pay me and my family an unexpected visit though his time was very limited. Jim hopped a Greyhound bus and took the ten or so hour journey to spend only about six hours with us before having to return the same evening, travelling back another 500 miles.

This goes to prove that the friendships forged in wartime lasted a lifetime because I had never seen him since he left the ship in February or March 1941. One can imagine my complete astonishment when I returned home after running some errand to find Jim in our recreation room talking to my son Michael. Instantly I recognized him. Our visit was brief but as promised, he came again about a year afterwards and another visit is planned unless we make it to England first.

The bonds that exist between the Second World War sailors in many associations of the Royal Navy have developed into almost a brotherhood. The Illustrious Association is a good example of this relationship.

Towards the end of our stay in Alex, Eric and I along with one or two others decided to take a day trip to Cairo to see the world famous Pyramids. We agreed that we should go in a small group as some of our oppos had already done because it was more fun to see the sights with your ops and also for a certain amount of security. Now that the Germans were beginning to make gains in the desert war, the wogs (Egyptians or Gyppos as we also called them) seemed to be changing in their attitude towards the Allies in case the Germans made a breakthrough and took Egypt. Before we left, it got even worse where there were incidents of lone sailors getting beaten up, mugged, or even stabbed in black alleys. We were warned to stick together and stay on the main drags.

The train ride from Alex was roughly 100 miles and was an experience in itself. This was nothing like travelling on an English train. The carriages all had open windows and hard wooden seats although this must have been their third class. I seem to recall that we sailors travelled in a different part of the train away from the Gyppos. Riding with those crammed in babbling characters would be too much even for Jolly Jack. We of the lower deck took pride in our standards of hygiene.

Cairo was a bustling, crowded city and the headquarters of the British Army in Egypt. This ancient and historic place had a long association with British rule but for us it was an eye opener. We looked around a bit and then thought we should make our way to the Pyramids. We got on a street car to take us to the city limits.* What a carry on that was. I laughed about it for long afterwards. First of all, we just managed to get on, almost fighting our way for a seat. Each time it stopped, more and more wogs would jump on until it was so overcrowded, they were all hanging onto the sides like flies. We looked ahead and saw a narrow bridge in front of us and just wondered what would happen to all those hanging on outside when we came to it. Almost holding our breath wondering if anybody was going to get killed, just as we were coming up to it, they all started dropping as if being scraped off. When we got to the other end, having not slowed down at all, the tram's sides were completely clear of bodies, clean as a whistle.

Getting off the streetcar outside the city, it seemed as if there were about three different ways to get to the Pyramids. One was a form of taxi, another was by a horse drawn carriage, and the other, most typically was by camel. We certainly didn't bother with the latter being in our spiffy nice white No. 6's.

The Pyramids and the Sphinx were most definitely a sight to behold and many of the lads had their pictures taken at this most celebrated example of Ancient Egypt. I can say it was an education. If I might add, the Pyramids are one of the seven wonders of the ancient world and even with today's technology can't be equalled. When one thinks that the Egyptians built it, but they don't remember how they did it. Our experience of Egyptian engineering was that they couldn't even make a proper lock for a simple suitcase.

Lt. Cdr. Opie, the American liason officer didn't appear to be around the ship anymore now that we were in Alex. At least I didn't notice him with living for'ard perhaps though, because things were moving so fast. His mission aboard a British man-of-war was no doubt a secret and as such, it was desirable to keep it that way.

Regrettably, I never did hear what became of him. I can only hope that he survived the war with the Japs as well and that he rose high up in the ranks of the United States Navy. Even though he wasn't officially a member of Illustrious's ship's

---

*Fare was paid in Ackers. Gyppo money worth about 2½ pence. The Egyptian pound was worth about 15 shillings of a UK pound.

complement, those of us in the Old Illustrians Association would regard him as a shipmate no less equal to any of us.

Fortunately for us and especially in the days to come, the amount of covert cooperation between England and America was steadily increasing thanks to the mutual respect and common heritage between the two countries. Another example of this relationship came in late January 41 when our C-in-C Admiral Cunningham had lunch aboard his flagship HMS Warspite in Alexandria with a Colonel William Donovan. The same Colonel Donovan who in June 1942 was made Director of the OSS (Office of Strategic Services), forerunner of the CIA.* He was on a tour of Europe looking at the overall situation and he offered to send a message back to the US saying they must let us have some fighter aircraft. Cunningham did nothing to discourage him after they discussed the situation in the Med.

Everything on Illustrious was changing. Our complement depleted through casualties was further reduced by hundreds being drafted off for fleet replacements. The air group was no longer with us being left in Malta to bolster the island's air defences. Our ship was no longer capable of operating aircraft anyway due to the wrecked hangar and flight deck. We were left with only enough crew to steam to wherever we would be sent for a refit. Nevertheless, we weren't out of harm's way yet.

One clear, sunny morning on March 10 to be exact, there was great excitement when somebody said that our relief, the carrier Formidable had been sighted on the horizon. This was a sight to behold knowing now that we wouldn't be long in leaving. Double time we all scrambled up the ladder to the main deck to get the first glimpse of that silhouette and make sure for ourselves that she was indeed a carrier. Watching her when she finally came in, the passed us at close quarters so we could see every detail. Formidable was the spitting image of us. Our sister ship, she was identical right down to the camouflage. To me she was a beautiful sight.

Everybody was now speculating how soon we would leave Alex. The idea for security reasons was to keep the enemy guessing until their agents found out that she wasn't the Illustrious reincarnated back into fighting trim.

---

*William Donovan's exploits later earned him the nickname 'Wild Bill'.

The process now was to start preparing the ship for the long voyage and the passage through the Suez.

About a week after the Formidable arrived, Illustrious finally departed from Alex. During that seven day interval everything we didn't actually need or could do without in the way of stores, provisions, spare parts, and valuable ammunition was taken off and left for the fleet. Sadly, as I have mentioned, this included a great many shipmates of all branches and ranks, the majority of which we would never see again.

We slipped out of harbour one day without any fanfare and sailed for Port Said on the Mediterranean end of the canal roughly 200 miles away. When we arrived, we were held up because there had been a raid the previous day which had left mines and/or unexploded bombs which divers were going down to in an effort to either defuse or detonate.

There was at least one remaining afterwards which they couldn't be sure of its mechanism. It wasn't known if it had a timer or was acoustic as several ships had already passed over it without incident. However, these had been smaller vessels and as we were a carrier, if we were to be seriously mined, the canal could be completely blocked. A ship of our size left very little clearance between our sides and those of the canal. There was no sailing around it. The Captain and the canal authorities would have to make a very crucial decision as to whether we should take the chance and glide over it.

The whole affair over this mine I can specifically remember as it happened towards the end of my morning watch in the control room around 07:00 onwards. The Padre kept coming over the loudhailer giving us his commentary of what was going on just before we approached the spot.

Down below, all of us were watching the clock tick away the minutes after it was decided we were going to chance it. Every bit of machinery not essential was shut down to lessen the vibration if it was acoustic. We would literally glide over it as silently as possible.*

I was hoping like the others, we would get off watch in the nick of time and like everybody else, go up to the flight deck where everyone was ordered to minimize the possible number of casualties should this thing detonate under us. Only the watches

---

*For steerage way so close to the banks we were actually towed over the mine.

below were left to take their chances and hope for the best so we thought. The time was ten minutes to eight. My watch ended at eight.

Commander (E) then gave us his bombshell sending word down that all watches that were to be relieved would remain with the relieving watches. In other words, we would be double banked.

As we had an officer in the control room, there was no way we could express our shock and disgust at this reckless and irresponsible order. It showed a complete disregard for all the men below and could result in twice as many casualties.

To have said any word of protest, even just to express an opinion, naval discipline being what it is would have resulted in being put in the 'rattle'. This could also have been construed as being tantamount to disobedience of orders and if more than one was involved, even mutiny. Dumb insolence in the form of a dirty look or grimace was enough to warrant an offense in those days of iron discipline. Being unable to do or say anything about it, we all kept our mouths shut but what I thought to myself was a different matter. In my mind I called him all the names under the sun and to this day, I never forgave Tamplin.

Afterwards, we heard where Tamplin actually was when we went over the mine, sat in a comfortable chair high up on the bridge, higher than the flight deck. No offense to our new skipper Tuck but what purpose did doubling the watches serve except to put the lives of twice as many men at risk. Why did the Captain allow Tamplin to give such an order? After all, the safety of the whole ship's company is the responsibility of her CO.

As we were slowly approaching the mine, the atmosphere below became increasingly tense. Good old Rev. Lloyd relieved some of our anxiety by giving us his usual running commentary about how far away we were and what was going on up top.

First we were five hundred yards away and closing, then it would be four hundred, then three, then two, then one. All engines were shut down and even the circulating water from the fire mains. Us and the ship were silent as we approached the spot. A few yards to go now and I was holding my breath almost, waiting for the explosion any second which would blow a hole in the ship's bottom. God I hope it's nowhere near the control room or a magazine.

Then the silence was broken by the Padre's voice telling us we

136

had passed over it. Nothing had happened. Everything was restarted and the reassuring throb of the ship's engines resumed. Shortly afterwards, we of the morning watch were allowed to go up top having been officially relieved. That fresh air never smelled so good.

This wasn't the end of our worries in the canal by any means.

After a cup of tea and a fag for breakfast and then helping the cooks of the day (two of the lads whose turn it was to clean up the mess after each meal), there was nothing much else to do not being allowed to get my head down at this time of day so I went onto the upper deck to have a look at the 'scenery' as we passed it. What I actually saw was a vast desert wasteland on either side. The only noticeable feature I could see was Bofor guns every few hundred yards staggering along both sides of the canal for air defence. It looked as though some of these guns were manned by Egyptian troops as well as British.

Little did I know at the time but only a few hundred miles from here in desert like this, some of the fiercest and bloodiest battles of the war would be fought between Field Marshal Montgomery's Eighth Army, the Desert Rats, and Field Marshal Rommel's famous Afrika Korps. The following year at El Alamein, west of Alexandria, the battle would be opened up by a terrific, ear splitting barrage as a thousand British guns pounded the Axis lines.

Right now though, the shoe was on the other foot as the enemy was advancing into Egypt and threatening to overrun our defences. They would only be stopped at a place called Mersa Matruh, just outside Alex where I had left.

Much to my relief, I was leaving all this behind but this was only a temporary reprieve as later on I would return to the Med. for two years and eight months continuously aboard a minesweeper and stay long after the war was over doing the deadly task of clearing minefields left over by the enemy and Allies alike.

Steaming slowly along at almost a snail's pace, we couldn't go any faster because of our wash and being so close to the canal banks, passing places with exotic names like Al Qantarah and Ismailia until finally it was decided we would have to pull into the Little Bitter Lake to let a convoy pass. We would also have to spend the night here.

At first I thought this was all very well until we were told by either Tuck or Jimmy the One over the tannoy some very unsettling news. The mesage went almost as follows: 'In the event of an air raid if we are attacked during the night, we have only enough ammunition on board for about half an hour to give them one good burst. After that we will be at the mercy of the enemy if the raid lasts any longer'.

After we de-ammunitioned, why were we left with so little ammo? The powers that be knew the situation in the canal and what might happen. We could hardly believe this. Years after I also found out that in the Indian Ocean where we would soon be, there were German raiders like the Atlantis and Admiral Scheer on the loose. There was no way to defend ourselves if they or even enemy aircraft caught up to us. Perhaps in our present condition we might have been considered expendable. Who knows? Regardless, this made for a very long and worrying night. Fortunately, everything was quiet and we continued our journey next morning down to Port Suez on the Red Sea end. We had been fortunate again.

At the Red Sea, we were entering the trade routes to the Far East. At the moment they were fairly quiet with Japan not yet in the war but in the vastness of the Indian Ocean, more than one German raider or pocket battleship lurked. Here was a good hunting ground for the enemy which pounced on lone merchant ships but always managed to evade the Royal Navy. Hopefully they wouldn't catch up to us in the state we were in, besides these waters were shark infested.

Passing around East Africa and the island of Madagascar we made our way to South Africa and steamed into Durban in the first few days in April. Here was the real matelot's paradise.

Chapter Ten

Out of the World of Darkness

Durban, South Africa, what a wonderful place. Again we heard
stories from older sailors who had done a commission on this
station in peacetime. 'Lovely Grub' they would say meaning
lots of good times.

We sailed into the harbour and tied up at Maiden Wharf.
Perhaps the name Illustrious and reputation we had made over
the last few months had preceded us. It wasn't very long before
they were piping for hands from each mess to muster at the
gangway to pick up boxes and boxes of fresh fruit, apples,
oranges, you name it, to be brought directly down to the
messdecks where everyone could help themselves to as much as
they could eat. There was no Pusser's rationing in this case.

We could hardly believe our eyes. This kind of treatment had
never happened to us before and food of this kind was almost
non-existent back in England due to the rationing and the U-
boat blockade. Immediately we all dug in and relished every
mouthful of this food we had gone without for so long except
on the odd occasion. This seemed to be our first example of
what was to come during our stay here.

The next thing came when the ship to shore telephone was
hooked up. People ashore were ringing up with lots of
invitations for the lads on the lower deck to attend dances,
dinners, or whatever else. These offers were not solely for the
officers as was done in most other ports of call. This was mostly
for us ratings. We didn't expect this kind of a welcome, 'Harry
Grippos' galore.

The first day I couldn't get ashore being twenty-four on but
the messdecks were just about deserted. Everybody who was
not on watch, as we had shut down to auxiliary, were all gone
on the earliest liberty. We that were still on board anxiously
waited for them to get back and fill us in on what it was like and
so we were chomping at the bit for our turn tomorrow.

After I came off watch from the last 'dogs' (22:00 hours) it was dusk but there was no orders to darken ship. Finding this rather odd, a couple of us went onto the flight deck for our constitutional and found out why. What a sight it was. All the lights of the city of Durban were lit up. There was no blackout here. After coming from England where blackouts were in force and the Med. where the war was being fought, this seemed like another world, a world of light after living in a world of darkness and fear. Normally, most people take for granted a simple thing like a lighted street lamp or a neon sign but that sight is something that has always been with me and how I remember Durban on that first night.

The next day couldn't come fast enough for us to get a run ashore. Eric and I along with another lad caught the one o'clock liberty boat. The term 'liberty boat' I must add, is used both when the ship is at anchor and you actually catch a boat and when the ship is alongside and going ashore requires only walking down the gangway after being inspected.

On this occasion, there were that many liberty men we were all lined up in two long lines almost the full length of the ship on the jetty. There must have been close to a couple of hundred men all dressed up in their No. 1 'tiddley' suits. I'll never forget all those smiling faces and bodies fidgetting around waiting for the Officer of the Day (OOD) to inspect them.

As soon as we were dismissed, everybody made for the dockyard gate as quickly as possible and within a few minutes, there was hardly a blue collar to be seen as if they had almost dissappeared into thin air. We ourselves started to walk along the street hoping to make our way to the main drag in the city when a car drove up alongside us. A voice called out and asked where we sailors were going. We replied nowhere in particular. Inside the car were two girls whose names we discovered were Jean and Nettlie Ingles. These two pretty girls in their middle to late teens asked us if we wanted to get in and come home with them to meet their parents and be their guests. Apparently this is how many of the other lads disappeared. They had been picked up by people in cars who took them into their homes. This was the kind of hospitality which was given to us by the people of Durban. I don't know if this was for all ships or Illustrious in particular but since I think that the people opened their hearts to many servicemen passing that way although I can only speak for myself.

Jean and her sister drove us around the city to show us a few of the sites and down West Street, the main thoroughfare. From there they took us home and introduced us to their parents who were extremely nice and made us feel very welcome. After a very pleasant evening in a homey atmosphere with all the comforts and trimmings and getting to know everybody without discussing the war too much, time grew short and they asked when we had to be back aboard. Eric and the other lad were still not twenty years old and consequently not yet allowed all-night leave. They had to be back by eleven o'clock (23:00 hours). If I may digress, this was a bit ludicrous when you think that a man serving in the Royal Navy and has seen action is not allowed to be out all night because he is a few months underage. It just doesn't seem to make sense but those were the rules laid down in the KRs and AIs.

Having said that, young as I looked, I still had all-night leave being twenty-one. I was asked if I would like to sleep there that night instead of going back. I could hardly believe what I was hearing. Tonight I was actually going to sleep in a bed with nice, clean, cool sheets and a room to myself.

Mr and Mrs Ingles then offered to drive Eric and our pal back to the dockyard as it was quite a way away. The room I was given in itself was a significant gesture on the part of this family because it belonged to their only son who was away fighting in the South African army somewhere in the desert. Not only did they give me his room but a pair of his pyjamas and his own bed.

I went to sleep feeling contented and wondering if all these nice things happening to me were truly real. Early in the morning I was awoken by someone knocking on the door and bringing in breakfast on a tray. Jean and her sister came in with a nice cup of tea and an English type breakfast which was better than you would get in England due to the rationing. This was something I never expected. I sat up supported by two fluffy pillows and relished the luxury as warm morning sunshine shone in through the open window. To me this was seventh heaven.

Before they took me back to the ship I couldn't resist asking why they were doing so much for me and I got a simple reply which really touched me and I have never forgotten. Their answer was that if their son was ever to go to England, perhaps someone would take him into their home and treat him the same way. What more needed to be said? With that I went back to the ship in style and arrangements were made for them to pick me up next time I was off duty and go to the beach.

The different stories that everybody was telling each other were fantastic although it didn't happen to everyone. Some just went for a good time and get drunk and there were those who went to places they shouldn't have been in like District Six, the coloured quarter and strictly out of bounds. To be caught there was a serious offense both to the civil authorities and the Navy due to the racial segregation they call Apartheid. This happened to Joe Fitz and resulted in very serious consequences for him including missing the ship I regret to say as he was a close oppo, despite our age difference.

My next twenty-four hours on watch couldn't go fast enough and when it was over, I steamed around as fast as I could into the bathroom for some quick 'dhobiying' and caught the one o'clock liberty.

The Ingles family were there as promised to pick me up in the car. Going around in this kind of luxury was something I had never known before. The best I ever could manage in Depression stricken England was my faithful Hercules model bike which had been a real old faithful to me. I went everywhere on it for pleasure and for work and looked after it as though it was a Rolls-Royce. I parted with it sadly when I sold it for twelve and sixpence to some pawn shop when I enlisted. I have never owned a bicycle since.

That afternoon we all went to Durban beach. The weather was beautifully sunny and warm and the beach was clean with its bleached white sand and cool sea breeze from the Indian Ocean. I had never felt happier.

Strange to say, the same style of deck chairs were used here as you would find at the English seaside but the similarity ended there as most beaches back home except for a few days are mostly cold and breezy and the water very chilly. However, Durban beach was also for whites only.

With us on the beach were two brothers named Fred and Noel Whittaker who also became very good friends of mine and treated me with a great deal of kindness allowing me to sleep at their flat a time or two. I don't recall for sure but I think that one of them was the boyfriend of Nettlie but it doesn't really matter now anyway.

Out of our twelve days spent in Durban which seemed to pass

as fast as a whirlwind I made about five runs ashore. I didn't manage my sixth although I had everything planned because the ship was under sailing orders suddenly on April 17 and all shore leave was cancelled. Jean, Nettlie, and her mother were going to pick me up for another great time ashore but I couldn't even tell them I wouldn't be able to make it. Ties with shore were cut off. When the ship cast off all lines and pulled away from the jetty I just looked longingly out of a porthole and felt the same sadness as if I was leaving my own home. Tears were almost in my eyes and this is how I always want to remember Durban, a home away from home.

After leaving I wrote an entry into my diary about our stay in Durban and this is an extract.

> Went to Jean's house and met her father and mother who were exceedingly nice and asked me to stay the night having seven bell leave. Jean and I went to the 20th Century Bioscope (pictures) in style. My friend Fred Whittaker took us in his car. Went home with her after the show and stayed the night. Made arrangements for seeing her on the 17th, her mother and sister calling for me at the ship at one o'clock with the car. Hope I can make it, ship under sailing orders.
>
> News has reached the ship lying alongside the wall called Maiden Wharf, Durban of the death of Jock Cree (stoker) who died of the wounds received in the action which turned gangrene. We trust and pray to God he will not have died in vain for the cause which we fight for.

Our rather hasty departure from what to me seemed a little bit of heaven in a world on the verge of sinking into the abyss, meant getting the ship safely to its ultimate destination for a refit. Secrecy of movement was of paramount importance although in all common sense, one could hardly expect to hide an aircraft carrier. Where we were heading few outside of Capt. Tuck and those close to him actually knew. I know I and those on the messdecks didn't but conjecture was ripe.

The enemy had agents everywhere and South Africa with its Dutch Boer (Afrikaner) community no doubt had its German sympathizers. It's worth a mention that the hospitality we received came mostly from those people of British descent if last names like my benefactors are anything to go by.

The bottom line was that if our whereabouts were transmitted to one of the commerce raiders or U-boats being a crippled ship, we wouldn't stand much of a chance without an escort. I don't even remember if we had one up to that point.

I make these points to remind the reader that we were still not on a pleasure cruise even though we were no longer in a war zone. Our stopover in Durban had been for very good reasons such as minor repairs or whatever necessary. We were still a valuable asset to the RN in that once repaired and put back into fighting trim we would rejoin the fleet and give another good account of ourselves, and we did. By staying afloat until now, we had scored a moral and psychological victory against the enemy and for anything to happen to us now after all we had been through would have been a terrible shame.

Our next port of call was Port Elizabeth, a little over halfway between Durban and Cape Town, perhaps four hundred miles or so and right on the bottom of the African continent.

Nobody got ashore so it may have been just to take in water and the stopover was hardly a day long. We then sailed on to the Cape where we stayed a couple or three days. I was able to make a run ashore and enjoyed the sights including the famous Table Mountain but we didn't receive the same amount of hospitality as we had in Durban.

I must pay one last tribute to Durban. Although I never knew or saw her, there was a famous lady named Perla Siedle Gibson, better known as Durban's Lady in White. I first heard about her in the 50's when listening to Wilfred Pickles's show Courage and Adventure series over the wireless. She was featured on one of his shows as a special guest.

Her contribution to the war effort was by singing with the aid of a megaphone from a vantage point on the coast outside Durban whenever she heard of a troopship or convoy passing to and from the Far East. This was intended to cheer up the troops who were far from home and homesick on their way overseas. Of the many songs she sang, I believe one of them and other ex-servicemen may remember was Land of Hope and Glory, a song that was unmistakable in what it stood for. It was symbolic of England and its fight for freedom.*

This lady with her powerful voice and long white dress became a familiar figure in Durban and represents the type of

---

*Perla Gibson never missed a convoy including the one that sailed out the day she learned her son was killed in Italy. Sadly she died in 1971.

144

hospitality given the Allied forces by that city. Regretfully, she didn't seem to be there when Illustrious was passing. Perhaps she sang more to convoys rather than individual vessels.

I would feel somewhat amiss in not speaking of another story from South Africa which has now taken on folklore proportions. Many and varied are the tales of Able Seamen Just Nuisance, a Great Dane officially on the books as a naval rating at HMS Afrikander, the naval base at Simon's Town, just outside Cape Town. In 1939 at the age of two, he volunteered for service in the Royal Navy. After he commenced his duties he was registered as a 'Bone Crusher' and his religious denomination was the 'Canine Divinity League, Anti-Vivisectionist'.

As the story goes, Just Nuisance was the friend of all ratings and wasn't very disposed to the ladies – human ones, very uncharacteristic really for a sailor. One of his functions was to escort drunken matelots back to their ship after a run ashore and he was a common sight strutting up and down the corridors on the Simon's Town to Cape Town train.

Just Nuisance was no saint and he did have a number of run ins with authority after such misdeeds as travelling without a ticket, going AWOL, sleeping on a POs bed, and getting into fights with mascots of other vessels resulting in their death. So I was told the story goes that his punishment came in the form of stoppage of bones.

The yarns that have been spun about the exploits of this unusual canine one can only imagine that Jolly Jack who tells his version will make the most of it.

Sadly, Nuisance came to an untimely demise as a result of a motor accident which paralyzed him and he had to be put to sleep on April 1, 1944, his birthday.

Finally, to add credibility to this legendary hound, a thirteen part television series is being made in South Africa of his adventures. An exhibition is on display at the Simon's Town museum and to this day, a rating is detailed off to tend his grave.

Leaving all this behind, Illustrious embarked on the last leg of her journey. For security reasons, I believe we were not told our destination until we left Cape Town and were well into the South Atlantic. When I found out the location of our refitting base I was thrilled. We would go to the Norfolk Navy Yards in Virginia, the US of A.

Chapter Eleven

Stateside

Illustrious's stay in America would be the end of an era in her career but the beginning of a new chapter. For myself and Eric, this would be an experience which would have a profound effect on both our lives later on.

After an uneventful trip across, despite the risk of running into the 11-inch gun pocket battleship Admiral Scheer now operating in the South Atlantic which could have blown us out of the water with ease, Illustrious stood off Cape Henry Virginia on May 14 just out of sight of land and in international waters to avoid prying eyes.

I once met a few years back in the Isle of Wight an ex-Chief Tiffy who told me he had been on one of our two escorting destroyers and all aboard had been looking forward to an anticipated run ashore after following us in. Much to their chagrin, they got a 'green rub' after handing us over to a pair of US Navy minesweepers then turning right around and headed straight back out to sea.

When the American sea pilot who would guide us through the swept channel came aboard, he was almost speechless at finding out that we were not some old, beat up merchantman but an aircraft carrier bearing the damage sustained in battle showing how good the secret was kept.

Rounding Cape Henry Lighthouse we were spotlighted by the brilliant glare of four searchlights revealing who we were and putting an end to our security. Past Virginia Beach we sailed into the entrance to the Elizabeth River shortly before midnight and at one o'clock we approached a darkened jetty. As we tied up the lights were switched on and a reception committee came aboard including Capt. McCandlish USN, Captain of the dockyard bearing a bottle of whisky and a basket of flowers from his wife. We had reached the safety of a neutral port at last.

Fortunately for us, back on March 11 when we were just leaving the Med. President Franklin D. Roosevelt whose sympathy to Britain was not disguised, signed the historic Lend-Lease agreement between the US and the UK. This act came at a time when Britain was running out of money and our resources were stretched to the limit. Lend-Lease which was Roosevelt's idea would allow Britain to buy arms and services on credit. In exchange for allowing the US to use bases in Newfoundland, Bermuda, the Bahamas, Jamaica, St. Lucia, Antigua, Trinidad, and British Guiana on 99 year leases, fifty old four stacker destroyers had been transferred to the Royal Navy as a prelude to reaching an official agreement. The first eight were transferred over in Halifax on September 9, 1940 fully provisioned and ammunitioned.* Appropriately, the first one renamed was called HMS Churchill.

Now that Lend-Lease was official, Britain was able to buy arms in large quantities and the use of American dockyards for repairing ships became available as in the case of Illustrious. At the risk of breaking their neutrality the Americans were going out of their way to openly assist Britain in every way possible.

To give an example of their generosity, I read a story about a matelot who was among a party who went to Halifax to pick up one of those first eight destroyers. They found the ships scrupulously cleaned from stem to stern and full outfits of shells, torpedoes, and depth charges. There were full sets of navigational equipment, high powered binoculars, paint, silverware and good china in the messes. Best of all, the ship's stores were provisioned with the finest and tastiest tinned foods including spiced ham, sausages, corn lobster, and fruit juices. There was even a big fridge full of juicy big steaks. These provisions given in the best generosity were meant for all the ship's company and the changeover took about three days with the American sailors familiarizing our ratings with the workings of the ship. After this was all over and the White Ensign replaced the Stars and Stripes the menu for the Lower Deck reverted back to Pusser's 'scran'. Apparently the new mouth watering food was taken off and some given to the officers' wardroom to be replaced with regular Naval rations, 'Pusser's Peas' diet etc.[9]

---

*Halifax, Nova Scotia, Canada.

Being one who remained with the ship as C&M* party it would be like missing a page of history, an incomplete story as it were about the ship itself if I didn't recount some of the highlights of our stay in Norfolk. It would also provide continuity to the story until recommissioning with a new crew and returning to England to get back in the war.

Some of the things that took place are personal experiences and fond memories because they had a bearing on both mine and Eric's future. Other events have either been not very well recorded or hardly been mentioned. Therefore, hopefully all this put together will be of interest and informative to the reader.

After our late night arrival, the day began by all hands mustering on the flight deck for a pep talk from Tuck or the Commander but seemed to be more like a warning of Pusser's retribution to any 'stroppy' Jack who was put on 'defaulters' for misconduct ashore. Stress was laid on in no uncertain manner that we were in a friendly port and the United States though strictly neutral by international law was giving very valuable aid to Britain so behaviour ashore befitting the Royal Navy was the order of the day. In other words we were all supposed to act like ambassadors.

The point was well taken by us lower deckers in so far that on our meagre scale of pay we preferred to look for 'Harry Grippos' rather than trouble as the little money we had would go nowhere fast here.

America to us ratings who had come from the working class was the land where glamorous film stars and amiable gangsters like Cagney and Bogart lived. These we had seen often in pre-war days at our local 'Flicks' (picture houses) paying threepence for a cheap seat at the front or a 'tanner' (sixpence) for a posher one at the back where the courting couples usually went. These favourite stars had, if nothing else helped to brighten up many people's dreary lives by taking their minds away for a couple of hours from the misery of the dole and the Means Test, escaping in the fantasy of Hollywood.

With these thoughts I was looking forward to a run ashore. We had now shut down our machinery and were hooked up to shore lighting and a 'donkey boiler' which provided steam and

---

*C&M – care and maintenance.

hot water for our cooking and cleaning etc., a killick's job usually. As for myself it meant no more auxiliary watchkeeping in the control room and all night in the 'flea bag' (hammock) from now on. Believe me, this was a luxury indeed.

The Navy Yards at Norfolk and Newport News across the way were and are massive facilities which means this was a naval town housing thousands of US sailors and marines even though they weren't at war yet. This was a problem which would catch up to us matelots later on.

'Here comes the Limeys' is the best way I can describe our first night ashore. Except for those who were duty watch aboard it seemed that nearly everyone else put their 'tiddleys' on and headed for the 'beach' (ashore) myself and Eric included. I suppose each had their own expectation of the New World.

To my recollection, as for money no special provision was made to give us any at that time. We got paid once a month on foreign service and that was it so we had to make do. Admittedly, a small concession to our pay was forthcoming but not yet.

Once outside the dockyard, three or four of us stuck together and soon spotted a diner which we decided to go in for a drink. Our first experience of America and its lifestyle came in the form of sitting in a booth and the waitresses eyeing us with curiosity not having seen a British sailor before. We could see they were anxious to serve us and they giggled to each other as they decided who would talk to us. Eventually one of them did come over and laughing at our funny English accents she figured that we would probably want some tea. Before the tea came we glanced around and the very colourful gadget with neon coloured water running all around it caught our attention. This was a Wurlitzer jukebox or nickelodeon or automatic record-player what have you, they all meant the same. We had never seen anything like this before, an automatic gramophone that changes records on its own and would play the selection of your choice when you put a nickle in. I had often heard that modern conveniences that came out in America wouldn't come to England for another ten years. This instance seems to prove that point.

When the tea came, we noticed to our horror that it had lumps of ice floating about in it. 'What is this?' we said, 'Is this tea?'. We didn't want to embarrass the waitress but this looked ridiculous. Who ever heard of iced tea before? Tea is a drink meant to be consumed hot, by our standards. We got a lot of laughs out of this and we did get our hot tea after all.

After a while, we left the diner and made our way to the main street which was typical of most Naval ports with US sailors and marines all over the place. Right now the girls were more interested in us Limeys as we were a novelty which got us a few dirty looks from our American counterparts.

The big surprise came when we decided to go to a movie. The person in the box office wouldn't take our money and said we could go in for free. This was a most generous gesture on the part of the management. Perhaps those in authority may have already known or heard about our inadequate pay and felt sorry for us, I don't know which. Nevertheless, we never did pay to get in for a show the whole time we were in Norfolk.

It was about the end of May and we had been here a couple of weeks. Buzzes had begun to circulate that most of the ship's company were going to be drafted off leaving only a skeleton crew as care & maintenance party.

By now we had pretty well settled down to dockyard routine which was as usual a bit chaotic. There was the cacophonous sounds of banging hammers, riveters going like machine guns accompanied by the flashing lights of acetylene torches all over the ship not to mention all the paraphernalia lying across the decks and passageways, hoses, pipes, electric cables, and what not. Strangely these noises gave me an odd sense of assurance in that we were in a safe place for the time being, no bombs, planes, guns, or action stations that might all end in a flash or an explosion. Malta and the Med. were still fresh in my mind yet.

The day soon came as it did in Alex when the big list went up telling us who would be going and who would be staying. As before everybody crowded around and strained to find their name. Inwardly I longed to go back to England to see my parents and family of course assuming those leaving actually would go home and get some leave before being drafted to other ships. We didn't know where they would be going. Being single and having no ties, another part of me hoped I would stay. With America not being in the war I might stay alive longer. Besides, I had got used to this ship and knew my way around. To be drafted off would be an unknown quantity kind of like moving into a new home that you haven't seen yet and you don't know where it is. As always, we had no choice whatever happened.

The matter was settled when I found my name on C&M party list along with Eric, Frank, Sid, Kenny, and several others from the training division. I was glad but it was odd how we always seemed to be kept together.

Our complement by now was approximately six or seven hundred at most but it wasn't long before the big draft of around five hundred was taken off leaving about a hundred and fifty or two hundred men. We would be the nucleus of the new crew when we eventually recommissioned.

Those that left I believe went to New York to steam home a battleship which had been refitting there. The name of her escapes me. There were also a few who went to other odds and sods of ships like the chap I met in later years, Arthur Barlow an ex-seaman. He told me that he went aboard a US Coast Guard cutter which was only thirty odd feet long and sailed it across the Atlantic back to England. Apparently they had a terrible crossing hitting dirty weather and the vessel leaked all over the place. It's amazing they even made it at all.

May 1941 had been a terrible month for the Royal Navy losing many fine ships sunk and damaged with heavy casualties. Back in the Med. the Germans had invaded Crete and in a lightning attack with paratroopers on the 20th took the island in under two weeks from the British, New Zealand, and Greek defenders. Two days after the invasion began, Stuka dive-bombers sank the cruiser Gloucester with a loss of almost seven hundred men and crippled the cruiser Fiji which had to be abandoned. Sunk also was the destroyer Greyhound and the flagship HMS Warspite was damaged. The following day the Stukas took their toll again by sinking the destroyers Kelly and Kashmir and then machine gunning the survivors in the water as they were being rescued. HMS Kelly had been the flagship of Lord Louis Mountbatten our future Commanding Officer from the Fighting Fifth Flotilla.

On the next day, the 24th, the battlecruiser HMS Hood pride of Britain and the Navy was sunk in the Denmark Strait near Iceland by the Bismark with the loss of 1,419 men and only 3 survivors before going to the bottom in 90 seconds after her magazines blew up. In company with her was the brand new battleship Prince of Wales which broke off the action after receiving damage from a number of hits. A massive sea hunt was mounted to avenge the loss of the Hood and regain England's honour. Every available unit in the Atlantic was deployed in the search and she was finally sunk by the battlers Rodney and King George V on the 27th with the loss of 2,200 men.*

Our relief, the old Formid didn't fare much better than us in the Med. On the 26th she launched strikes on the Stuka base at Scarpunto Island east of Crete but payed for it by being dive-bombed and badly damaged along with her destroyer escorts. After we left, the Med. had virtually become a killing ground.

Finally, on May 29, the destroyers Imperial and Hereward were sunk in an air attack while taking part in the evacuation of Allied troops from Crete. Hereward had been in company with us on January 10 when we were dive-bombed during Operation Excess. No wonder I was not very anxious to get back in the war. I needed time to recover if I could before going back into the fray again.

The ship now reduced to a skeleton crew meant a change of jobs for many of us. I got detailed off as the Chief Tiffy's messman along with another lad. This wasn't too bad a number really as I had no duty watches aboard, we could go ashore anytime we had finished clean up after supper. If there was any 'gash' (extras) left over, we could have it. Of course everything had to be done according to a strict routine and we had to get up early but we also enjoyed the little bit of privacy which the pantry provided and which we regarded as our little domain One door to the pantry opened up to the upper deck which was open but covered in up top by the deck above. On some warm southern nights we used to sleep there in the fresh air.

The cushiest number as the Captain's driver went to 'tiddley' Sid Nuttall, the car probably being lent by the US Navy. How he got it I don't know but Sid seemed a pretty competent all round guy and must have had his driver's license from civvy street. In pre-war years, the average working class chap didn't have a license as they never had the opportunity to drive a vehicle unless they had that sort of job. However, Sid had to be in his No. 1's all the time being on call and the lads used to

*Bismark was finished off by three torpedoes from the cruiser Dorsetshire who then picked up survivors.

often kid him about what a soft number he had and how he managed to pull it off being a stoker. Sid took it all in good humour and had his witty replies ready when one of us asked him if he was the Captain's 'winger'. Still, he seemed to be well suited for the job as he was always very smartly dressed and had a lot of street sense along with an outgoing personality.

The question of a pay adjustment was announced just after the big draft left, probably so that they would have less men to pay more money out to. I assume it was done in an effort to make us appear to the Americans that we were better paid than we actually were. The increase was given in proportion to rank with a First Class rating (stoker, seaman etc.) getting 50 cents a day extra, a Leading Rate 75 cents, a PO one dollar, and a Chief a little more than that. These numbers are approximate but it still only meant that I was getting paid a dollar a day altogether and my monthly pay after an allowance home worked out to $28. This money had to pay all my expenses including personal items, kit upkeep, and runs ashore. No wonder they let us in the movies for free. I nearly flaked out when they charged me 50 cents for a haircut ashore, half a day's pay. Remember, old Joe Fritz our messdeck barber had missed the ship in Durban.

Our standard of living in America had improved somewhat with the increase in pay but as for our diet, very little change had taken place. I mentioned earlier about how the Americans had put the finest victuals on board these destroyers they gave to Britain but this didn't mean to say we were living high off the hog now we were in the US. US Navy cutlery, crockery, and mess gear was provided but not their mouth watering food other than a couple of Coca-Cola machines aboard the ship and Lucky Strike and Camel cigarettes in the NAAFi. As a messman I was in a position to testify to this and that for the most part it was Pusser's 'gorge' (eating) of 'squeaks, rushes, and duffs'. This food was wholesome at least if not too appetizing.

Buzzes, always buzzes, the adrenalin that kept the blood in the messdecks flowing with anticipation of what might be happening, where we were going, or who had heard this, that, and the other. Every ship big or small had its grapevine. For openers, somebody would ask 'What's the latest?' This time was no different. Word had gotten around that our new skipper was going to be none other than Lord Louis Mountbatten, cousin of the King and Captain of the destroyer Kelly that had just gone down off Crete. As far as I was concerned, this was not very good news. Other seemed to be of the same opinion and things were said like 'Oh no. We don't want that effing dare-devil. He's already had one ship shot up from under him. What'll he do with an aircraft carrier? He'll be sure to get us sunk too.' This was not meant as something personal on our part and he was a fine commander but his reputation for going where the action was had preceded him, but as always, no choice for us.

It was sometime in August that we heard officially that Mountbatten was going to take command. I personally witnessed him coming aboard from my usual vantage point, a porthole and saw something that I never thought I would see or am likely to ever again. A guard of honour was formed on the jetty at the bottom of the gangway to receive him. On one side was a line of Royal Marines and opposite was a line of United States Marines, the 'bootnecks' and the 'leathernecks' facing each other. This scene has always stayed with me as something very significant and its meaning was not lost on me back then. I believe this said it all with regards to the close relationship between Britain and the United States. By the way, I often wonder if it was Sid who drove him up to the ship being the Captain's chauffeur.

However, Lord Mountbatten almost literally went up one gangway and down another. He did stay a few days and long enough to look around the ship and have a photo session when journalists and photographers from Life magazine came aboard to do a story on the ship. Mountbatten had his picture taken with Captain Tuck on the flight deck petting two black cats which were ship's mascots and surrounded by a bunch of hairy a – – –d stokers including none other than big Bungy Williams and Taff Davies. I knew every one of those stokers in that picture and several were close oppos of mine although I never got the opportunity to have my picture taken.

The magazine actually printed an extensive account covering the bombing and our refit in the States adding a little colour of their own. Many photographs were taken or used including a special one of our ship's bell full of shrapnel holes.

The full story of Mountbatten's departure from Illustrious was revealed many years later in his personal memoirs.

Knowing the ship would not complete the repairs for at least another three months he decided to tour the US. Only a person in his position could do this for whatever reason but shortly afterwards he was recalled to England by Winston Churchill who told Mountbatten he had another important job lined up as Commander of Combined Operations to prepare for the eventual Second Front. At first he was not too keen on his new command telling his boss that he preferred to be Captain of the 'crack aircraft carrier Illustrious'. The great man's instant reply was 'Do you mean to tell me that you would rather go to sea on a bigger and more expensive ship and get sunk again?' Mr Churchill seemed to share the same opinion as the stokers when we first heard about Mountbatten taking command. Also it seemed that the life expectancy of Illustrious was not considered to be very long either.

Lord Mountbatten went on to greater things. After combined operations which carried out famous raids like the ones on St. Nazaire and Dieppe he became Supreme Allied Commander Southeast Asia Command. After the war as Viceroy of India he oversaw the creation of the new countries of Pakistan and India given their independence from Britain in 1947. From 1952 – 54, Mountbatten served as Supreme Commander of all NATO forces in the Med. except for the US Sixth Fleet and in 1955 became First Sea Lord of the Admiralty. From 1959 – 65 he was Chief of Defence Staff and finished his career by becoming governor of the Isle of Wight. Lord Mountbatten met a very tragic end in the early 1970s at the hands of the IRA who murdered him by blowing up his yacht off the coast of Britain. To meet a fate such as this for a man with such a distinguished career was not befitting his stature in life. It seems strange how men of this calibre sometimes seem to meet inglorious deaths. General Patton died of injuries sustained in a simple automobile accident. Lawrence of Arabia was killed outside Bovington Camp in the south of England while serving in the RAF in a motorcycle accident and finally to give one other example, Audie Murphy, America's most decorated World War Two veteran who later became a famous film star died in a plane crash. Such incidents defy comprehension.

We had been in Norfolk about three months by now and somehow I had made my small money spin out going ashore as most others did. Not surprising 'Jack' found the haunts and dives for entertainment like dime-a-dance joints, places called

Albert Jones (right) with shipmate Eric Taylor (left) and photographer
Bud Miller, their host in Steubenville, Ohio, USA – September 1941

road houses, and many other types of bars. Where else could a
sailor go in this huge naval metropolis.

So far us Limeys had not quite worn out the welcome mat
with the USN but it was getting a little thin with a fracas here
and there. With the arrival of the Formidable in late summer
1941 after her bombing at Crete we considered her to be our
reinforcements against the Yanks as we were badly
outnumbered.

I must now talk about what happened to myself and Eric
when we managed to get some leave and went on one of the
wildest and wackiest trips to a place called Steubenville in Ohio
hundreds of miles inland. Towards the end of August Eric went
ashore one night with another lad, I think his last name was
Richards. They came back with a story of meeting a real 'Harry
Grippo' and his wife who were in Virginia on holiday. They
invited Eric and the other lad to go and spend a few days with

them at their home in Steubenville if they could wangle some leave. Other than paying the train fare it wouldn't cost them a dime. Listening to this it sounded unbelievable, almost too good to be true, an unexpected opportunity and rare at that to get away from Norfolk and explore a bit of America before the ship finished its refit.

Richards didn't appear to be too inclined to go saying that it sounded very chancy and putting obstacles in the way. Eric was just the opposite. He was very enthusiastic and disappointed that his friend wouldn't go so he asked me if I would take Richards' place. Without hardly any hesitation I agreed.

It seems now that fate and providence began to play a hand in both our futures that only time alone could tell.

The two of us decided to take the risk and put our request chits for leave through the usual channels of Divisional Officer, Jimmy the One (First Lt.), and the Commander yet thinking we hadn't a hope in hell of getting any on such a flimsy story.

To our astonishment we were granted six full days in which to get there and back. This was to commence on September 4, 1941. I always wonder what considerations were taken into account for the Commander to grant us this leave when going so far away we might have decided not to even come back. Perhaps the fact that we were twelve year volunteers, we weren't 'skates' (troublemakers), and had good conduct sheets. We had also been through the bombing and had been selected to stay behind as C&M and as such were probably deemed good risks. One final note to this was that it had been impressed on everybody that we had to do everything we could to make a good impression on the Americans for all the help they were giving us. It may have occurred to the Commander that to have two young looking and rather handsome sailors if I may say so going around the American heartland would do some good in invoking the sympathy and support for England's struggle since we were still fighting alone. Who could be better ambassadors at a time like this? This turned out to be the exact result which was achieved.

We sent a telegram to our benefactors, Mr and Mrs Charles 'Bud' Miller who owned a photography studio and let them know our date of departure.

We caught the train about midday for the six hundred odd mile trip but we would have to change in Washington DC. The fare was $13.50 one way and on what money we had this was a

157

large chunk of a month's pay and didn't leave us very much to spend.

Unlike British trains we didn't board from a platform but climbed up steps from the tracks. These kind of trains were large and roomy and not divided up into little compartments like those at home. The whistle blew signalling the beginning of our latest adventure and Eric and I watched with keen interest the passing American countryside which was a vast expanse of never ending scenery. It was also a change from the vastness of the sea.

We pulled into Washington's Union station just after dark and had a two hour wait. We didn't hang around there as this was the nation's capitol and home of President Roosevelt himslf. Although we didn't have time to go see the White House we wanted to make the most of our short stay here so we looked around the vicinity of the station.

I felt this was history in the making being here at a time like this. I had never even seen my own country's capitol, London, yet, never mind America's. Talk was in the air of impending war with the Japs as at this stage her intentions were not clear and she was a member of the Tripartite Axis with Germany and Italy.

Wandering down the well lit streets, many people turning to stare at us wondering whose navy we belonged to, we finally went into a small restaurant. Though our funds were limited we had to eat and so decided to order a nice juicy steak. We hoped this mouth watering morsel would be the main thing above all to remind us of this great city. So it was but not in the way we had hoped for. The speed with which it was cooked and served to us we really appreciated on our tight schedule but as it was done so rare which we hadn't bargained for, it was that tough it was like chewing the soles of our shoes. At first we felt a bit 'browned off' (annoyed) but we ate it anyway having a long way to travel yet. We paid the check/cheque (take your pick of spelling depending on your nationality) which was a couple of bucks, a lot of dough to us without complaining. We didn't want to hold it against our host country who was really sticking their necks out to help us. Being two sort of mini ambassadors from His Majesty's Royal Navy though without a portfolio as it were this was our first lesson in the art of diplomacy.

We caught the connection for Steubenville and as it was late at night everybody in our car was settling down for a sleep. Eric and I rented a pillow for ten cents each from the black porter who came around periodically. We couldn't afford a sleeper berth. For us it was back to hard layers, nothing new.

On through the night our train chugged its way along across the relatively flat corn fields of Maryland where some of the fiercest battles of the Civil War had been fought, and on into the rugged Appalachian mountains before crossing a small stretch of West Virginia and the Ohio River on one side of Steubenville.

Early in the morning we finally pulled into our destination and found Bud and his wife waiting for us as promised. They took us home right away and we freshened up ready for the whirlwind of activities which were to come.

To try to describe all the events in detail of this leave would be impossible but the least to say it was one big merry-go-round which would last twice as long as we had originally expected.

To most Americans the war seemed far away though it was two years old by now. All of Europe was overrun and under German occupation. The latest conquest at least in part was the invasion of Russia codenamed Operation Barbarossa in June.

Only England was left holding out barely hanging on by the skin of its teeth. This much even small town America like Steubenville were aware of through the media though understandably they didn't want to get mixed up in it themselves. With the appearance of two British sailors the likes of which few had ever seen before looking no older than their own high school and college kids yet being veterans already from a battle scarred aircraft carrier. it's not surprising we were soon to become somewhat of an attraction. Perhaps our very presence brought this far off distant war a little closer to home.

With having only three days after our travelling in which to paint the town red, there was no time to waste. Our first invite which had come even before we had arrived was to the policeman's ball that weekend. Bud joked with us about how we could get out of it if we couldn't make it and saying they might start giving us tickets. I don't believe we ever did go.

Our visit really got off to a start when Bud and his wife began to introduce us to their circle of friends as they seemed to be well known in the community. Among the people we met were two girls, one of which who was named Wanda Martin really took a shine to us and made no bones about both of us being cute and all that jazz in the typical American manner. However

Portrait of Albert Jones taken by Bud Miller, Steubenville, Ohio,
September 1941. This is one of the photos sold to raise money for the
British War Relief Society

we couldn't afford to get caught up in anything other than a
mild flirtation as we were too much in demand elsewhere.

Evenings we indulged in entertainment at the local night
clubs and taverns namely the Yacht Club and the Red Horse
Tavern and others. We didn't realize it at the time as we had
seen it all and didn't care but in later years I was told that
Steubenville was a wide open town back then. One can imagine
the sort of goings on there must have been but we did enjoy
ourselves.

Everywhere we seemed to get treated almost like celebrities
and one place asked us to do the honours of a ribbon cutting
ceremony in their night club but for what I can't remember. All
I know is that somebody handed us a pair of scissors. Drinks

were of course plentiful and those that we managed to pay for ourselves cost a dime a shot for the famous rum and Coca-Cola. It might only be coincidental but it hadn't been all that long since Prohibition had been repealed and people might have been trying to make up for lost time.

The days of this hectic activity began to fly by as it took on the appearance of a Hollywood type comedy. Even the traffic cops would hold up the traffic when they saw us coming in order for us to cross the road.

All too soon it was time to start thinking of returning to the ship yet it seemed like we only just got here. However sometimes events taken an unexpected turn as it did with us.

We were contacted by a Mr Frank Smith, president of the British War Relief Society Inc. asking if we could appear as guests at one of their meetings. This local organization which was probably part of a national fund raiser was officially registered with the US State Department, No. 208. These people were for the most part of direct British descent who felt this was one of the ways they as individuals could help Britain in her time of need by raising money to buy supplies such as medicine, food, ambulances, and other humanitarian aid to send overseas. They also worked to promote awareness of our situation and our cause in the fight against the Nazis.

Time was now too short to accept the invitation though we really didn't want to turn it down. Again however, we had no choice. Desperate situations call for desperate measures. The Millers put their heads together and came up with the idea of calling the mayor's office and explaining the problem. The mayor who was an acquaintance of Bud's was sympathetic and told us all to come down to his office right away. His worship, after hearing what we had to say suggested that he send a telegram to our Captain asking for an extension of our leave but the working had to be such that it would be convincing and difficult to refuse.

Eric and I soon hit on the idea of making use of the Anglo-American goodwill and cooperation that had been drilled into us when we arrived. This seemed to be the key to the diplomatic arm twisting strategy we would use in the telegram which went roughly as follows:

To Commanding Officer
HMS Illustrious

Request extension of leave for stokers Albert Jones and
Eric Taylor who are doing good work in raising money for
British War Relief Society and fostering good relations
with America etc.

After the mayor sent the telegram we went back to Bud's
home and kept our fingers crossed that a reply would soon
come as we would have to leave in a few hours if we were not
successful.

Unbelievably, as requests like this are almost unheard of in
wartime, the mayor's office phoned Bud with the reply that we
had another six days granted to us. We were all nearly on the
verge of jumping up and down with joy and relief. Now we
would have the time to make our appearance and do whatever
else we wanted.

Extra leave without pay to go with it normally wouldn't be
exactly an enjoyable combination in our position where we were
more or less dependant on chance generosity. However, the
whole idea of coming here had right from the start been an
adventure into the unknown and we were willing to rely on lady
luck who had not let us down so far.

We showed up at a local community hall for the meeting of
the British War Relief Society. This was a rather informal affair
with a fair sized crowd of ordinary people who wanted to meet
and talk with us and find out if all the stuff about the war they
were hearing on the news was really true. It would be a sort of
confirmation of their own worst fears if they became involved.
Just the sight of us two boyish looking sailors brought
comments about how hard put England must be to be calling up
such young lads. We obviously looked younger than we actually
were which was in itself a compliment.

People were soon gathering around and making a fuss of us
and needless to say the attention never made me feel so
important in all my life. After a while doing our best to answer
people's questions and satisfy their curiosity, somebody asked
me for my cap. Not quite sure of the reason I gave it anyway
and what I saw happening simply astonished Eric and I. The
cap was being passed around to all present who were putting
money in it. In a short time the cap was given back to us with
many nickels, dimes, quarters, fifty cent pieces, and even
greenbacks. Eric and I were speechless as we looked at each
other and tried to comprehend this unexpected show of

162

generosity. A mere thank you didn't seem enough but they explained that the collection was because they knew our pay was not very much.

Of all the attributes I might have had, speech making was not one of them though obviously at this particular time it seemed almost expected. Turning to my oppo I whispered 'One of us has got to say something'. By nature Eric was a shy person and he replied 'I can't do it. You get up'. With my knees nearly knocking together with nervousness I plucked up enough courage and rose to the occasion. Standing on a chair so as to be seen and likewise glancing around at the crowd wondering how I should start I began in my broad Lancashire accent and naive way, having never done this before. I spoke simply from the heart and thanked not only the people of Steubenville but all of America for everything they were doing to help England fight the war and how much it was appreciated. I went even further adding that Britain couldn't hold out indefinitely unless the States came into the war with them soon. I doubt that being so blunt would have won me any prizes for diplomacy but I was being realistic and felt this was a sympathetic listening audience notwithstanding the American characteristics of no nonsense and saying it like it is. By the applause it didn't appear to be taken out of context.

I have wondered since if, in our own little sphere of this community of about 25,000, Lord Mountbatten on his tour was doing better than us two ordinary stokers at promoting more active involvement to our cause if indeed this was his intention. We'll never know because Japan decided the issue when she launched a sneak attack on Pearl Harbour three months later on December 7, 1941.

Our extended furlough passed just as quickly with basically meeting people and having a good time. As it had inadvertently taken on a patriotic aspect, we of course tried to conduct ourselves accordingly being aware of whom we represented.

Toward the end of our stay a sort of finale to everything we had done put the finishing touches on to our hilarious visit. Bud's photography business was put to good use when he decided to take portraits of us as permanent reminders of our stay since we may never meet again. The idea further developed into a brainstorm about using the portraits as a fundraiser picking the best pictures of each of us and putting them on display in the studio window for sale. The proceeds would be donated to the British War Relief Society if any were made. We all howled with laughter at the absurdity of us matelots being treated like mini film stars. Who would buy them anyway? We underestimated good old Yankee know-how, even at the local level because after we returned to Norfolk, Bud wrote to tell us they had raised over $300 from the sale of our pictures. This may not sound a great deal of money now but in those days of ten cents for a coffee, it was worth a lot more.

The quality of the photographs was such that the ones I still have today are as clear and unblemished as they were fifty years ago. They haven't even begun to go yellow. This brings me to wonder whether in some attic or bottom drawer, somewhere in America someone still has the pictures of two British sailors who once visited a small town in Ohio but are now unknown and long forgotten.

The time came to return to the ship, September 14. We opted for a change and save a bit of money by going by bus. All thoughts of asking for still more leave was abandoned. We didn't want to kill the goose that lays the golden egg and overstay our welcome here. We had already done things that exceeded our expectations and it is doubtful we would have got any more. This is the only leave I have ever gone back from with more money than I went with. That one night when the money was collected for us had given us a good fifty dollars or the equivalent of two months of our pay.

Our hosts and some friends took us to the National Bus Station to see us off. We couldn't thank them enough for giving us a leave we never would forget. Unlike the way I left my 'up homers' in Durban, at least I had the opportunity to express my appreciation for everything they had done. Bud took a last minute photograph of us together and we said a sad farewell considering these wonderful people were complete strangers a short time ago. Bud said he would try to pull some strings to get us another leave.

As the bus rolled off down the highway and we settled down for the long ride, Eric and I began to talk and reflect on what had happened. We wondered if we would ever come back here again or see those people. The chances were one in a million against with the way the war was going. We never reckoned with the role fate would play. As for myself, I realized that I had had a good time but felt no special desire to come back. Unknown to me, it seemed my oppo had other ideas which would alter the rest of his life and Steubenville would become his final resting place eventually. Forty-seven years later I would return as well to see my friend Eric for one last time after piecing his life story together.

Back aboard Illustrious we were not called to give an explanation of why we asked for extra leave and we settled back down to the chaotic dockyard routine.

Work was steadily progressing on the ship and improvements over the original design were being made. I went back to my messman's duty and it was here that I received the only wounds I would ever get while serving aboard ship but it had nothing to do with the war, only my own clumsiness. While carrying two large tea urns full of water almost boiling from the galley tanks, I tripped over one of the many cables strewn across the decks resulting in scalding both my arms. This put me out of action in the sick bay for over a week. Fortunately it left no permanent scars but I was a little annoyed at myself for not being more careful.

One other incident took place while on these duties which I am not too proud of but I might as well mention. Messdeck life was always rough and ready but no matter it was for the most part fairly harmonious. Even though it isn't human nature for people to get along all the time especially in close living quarters, disputes most often were settled amicably. When a matelot would come back from a run ashore in an inebriated condition, for example, he would do his best not to disturb those trying to sleep in their hammocks if it was late at night. If he was too far gone, one or two of the lads would even help him undress and put his uniform away. Then they might tuck him away in his own hammock or at least under a table to sleep it off.

To those who have never served in the Navy, the following incident may seem insignificant but for us, there was an unwritten code of conduct. Besides, we lived under a strict naval discipline far harsher than the civilian criminal code. Brawling on His Majesty's ships was considered prejudicial to good order and naval discipline as things like that might get out of hand and were therefore not tolerated. Ashore was a different matter.

What basically happened was that I got into a bit of an

argument with the other messman over something rather trivial like who would go ashore first after cleanup. The result was that I lost my cool and I threw a punch. He was in some pain and went off to the sick bay. When he returned a little while later he had a bandage around his head and he told me I had dislocated his jaw. Well I felt pretty bad and apologized though it did nothing for his pain. I have always regretted this as it was inexcusable of me.

We were alone near the pantry when this occurred. Had we been on the messdeck with the other lads, it is doubtful it would have gotten that far. My point is that those on the lower deck whatever their background for the most part showed a lot of consideration for their messmates. We all had to learn to live with each other's shortcomings.

As a contrast, what happened ashore was a breakdown in relations with the Yankee 'Gobs' (sailors) and Marines which had been steadily deteriorating. A number of us matelots including Eric, Frank, and I were drinking in some dive in Newport News one night. Everything was going alright when all of a sudden we started to see people jumping over tables and fighting each other. Before long we were all embroiled in a genuine knock down, drag-out bar room brawl with the American sailors. It got to the point where they were even breaking off bottles to use as weapons. The sight of that jagged glass scared hell out of me and I made for the door into some side alley. Several of them pursued me into the dark alley and cornered me. I thought I was done for. After surviving the bombing I didn't think I would get killed or maimed this way. I yelled out at the top of my voice, 'Eric, Frank. Give me some help'. I don't remember how I got out of it but somebody must have come to my assistance because I lived to tell about it.

Towards the end of the refit, the situation with the US Marines especially reached very serious proportions with a lot of our lads getting beat up. Our Commanding Officer had to take the matter up with the Commandant of the Marines who laid the law down to put a stop to it. Things settled down a little and our lads started to stick to certain places not frequented by the marines and avoid trouble. Right from the start there was one place that the lads had always been in the habit of visiting just outside the dockyard gates. I forget whether it was the proprietor's name or not but it was called Jack's Bar and later nicknamed 'the Limey's Bar' because many of its patrons were from the two carriers. In addition to Illustrious and the Formid, our brand new sister even showed up, HMS Indomitable around the middle of November required some repairs after running aground in Kingston, Jamaica while still on her sea trials. Providence may have dealt her a lucky hand because she had been slated to go out to Singapore with the battleships Prince of Wales and Repulse which were sunk by Jap aircraft only a month later.

Back to the topic of Jack's Bar very briefly which catered to the British, I wish to mention another Jack's Bar which we discovered many years later. This bar located on the border between Canada and the US in the state of North Dakota just an hour and a half's drive from our present home in Portage la Prairie, Manitoba caters mostly to Canadian customers who go there for cheaper beer prices and steaks that are known for miles around. It's rather unusual how two businesses of the same name both cater to a clientele other than Americans.

As the old saying goes, Eric and I tried for one last kick of the cat when Bud wrote and told us the mayor was sending another one of his arm twisting telegrams to the ship in an effort to get us one more leave. We both knew this was really stretching it but no matter, after it arrived we got sent for and through channels saw the Commander. He firmly told us he had replied to Steubenville denying the request because the ship's refit was near completion. We half expected a 'bollocking' for trying to pull what seemed a fast one but instead it almost appeared like a bit of a recommend the way he was putting it. We never did know what exactly had been said in the telegram but this marked the conclusion of our war relief work.

A few weeks before we were due to sail back to England the bulk of our new crew came aboard from the old carrier HMS Furious which was refitting in Philadelphia. As expected a mixed crew generated a degree of inter-ship rivalry until we all settled down. Naturally they were proud of the old 'Fu' as they called it and I made some very good friends amongst them. There was one in particular. He was a 'townie' of mine from Manchester by the name of Johnny Salt. He was an HO and a real comedian. A real 'flannel face' too who would go to any lengths of 'BS' to get something but good natured. We all called him 'Salty'!

Along with the crew of the Furious came our new Captain, their former CO, Captain Arthur George Talbot who proved to be something which left much to be desired.

By late 1941, America was slowly but surely being drawn into the war. Lend-Lease had paved the way for the US to give material aid to Britain but now she was beginning to give military aid too by escorting British convoys up to Iceland and conveniently going on manoeuvres near British merchant ships in areas known to be places of U-boat activity. On October 31, Halloweeen night, the destroyer USS Reuben James was torpedoed and sunk by a U-boat with the loss of 95 men while escorting a convoy. This incident further strained relations with Germany which like its partner Japan where the situation was also deteriorating was putting an end to American isolationist opinions.

The general opinion that the Yanks had of the Japs as we were told more than once a little over confidently by the US sailors was that they could 'lick the Goddamn arses off the Japs in six weeks if they attacked'. We were also told the odd time during our stay, 'Don't bring your effing war over here. Keep it over there in Europe'. Little did they know the time was fast approaching when we would all be in the same boat together.

It all started on the quiet Sunday morning for us on that day of the December 7 which F.D.R. called 'A date which will live in infamy'. Everything went as usual. The refit was coming to a close and the buzzes told us we would be leaving any day now. Lunchtime rolled around and I was doing my messman's duty as usual listening to a local station on the radio in the background. All of a sudden the music stopped at a few minutes to one and the announcer said that Pearl Harbour was at that very moment being attacked by Jap aircraft. Our immediate reaction was one of almost satisfaction in as much as we finally had the Yanks in the war with us. In a strange way it was a crowning glory to the end of our refit. We felt like something else besides the ship being repaired had been accomplished. Sad as it was, England would no longer be fighting alone.

Later we too were shocked at the extent of the damage. The US Pacific battlefleet had been crippled with eighteen ships sunk or damaged, 188 planes destroyed and three and a half thousand sailors killed and wounded. Fortunately the two aircraft carriers which the Japs had hoped to sink in harbour were both our ferrying aircraft. That same day, the Japs also bombed American facilities on Guam, Midway, and Wake Islands plus the Philippines. Landings were made in Thailand and Malaya.

Apparently when all the senior officers of the Jap fleet were celebrating aboard the flagship of Admiral Yamomoto upon learning of the damage inflicted on the US fleet, the Admiral grimly responded to the effect that all they had done was awaken a sleeping giant. He was referring to what would happen when the American military and industrial might which was awesome was geared to war production. In other words, Japan was going to pay a high price. Ashore, the Americans we met were stunned. There also seemed a quick change in attitude by those who had claimed they had wanted no part in the war.

All this mattered little to us except that they were at last in it with us. Even in the darkest days before, no one ever doubted we would win. With the Yanks alongside us it would be only a question of time before we would gain the upper hand on the enemy.

Meanwhile, this latest bombshell had made things take a serious turn for the worse. Here I had been thinking perhaps the war might be over before the ship was ready to leave. What a bloody hope. The war had switched into high gear overnight It was now a truly global conflict which would leave no corner of the world completely untouched.

Chapter Twelve

Homeward Bound

About a week after Pearl Harbour, Illustrious and Formidable left Norfolk to head home to England. We were now longer and sleeker looking than we had been before being completely rebuilt aft and lengthened. In addition our radar had been improved and our armament increased. The Americans had even given us little buggy cars for towing planes and equipment around the flight deck.

Having a new crew aboard meant a new steaming watch bill which found me back in the centre engine room and living on the lower stoker's messdeck below the waterline.

The days before we sailed everybody was frantically shopping ashore buying anything that was rationed or unobtainable in England to take home on leave providing one could afford it of course. Obviously there were limits to this buying spree. Not surprisingly, to get the biggest bang for their bucks, Jack made a rush to snap up items like silk stockings, lingerie, perfume, cosmetics, and the like for wives, sisters, and sweethearts. Little imagination is needed when mentioning the raucous laughter this brought to the messdecks plus the fact we were going back home to 'Blighty' which put everybody in high spirits.

Plenty of other things were purchased in the food line too numerous to list other than tea, coffee, and sugar but which were scarce at home where rationing was in full swing. Anything and everything got snapped up. I decided my dear old Dad would enjoy a box of good cigars though he usually smoked a pipe which were quite reasonably priced in the States but ended up costing me three times as much to get them through customs.

While provisioning ship a stoker came staggering down the for'ard messdeck ladder under the load of a hundredweight sack.* In it was pure white sugar. Where he got it from nobody asked or cared. It was simply dumped on top of the stowed hammock rack and swiftly slit open for distribution amongst all who scrambled to find a container or tin of any kind to get a share, me too. Its fine white granules quickly trickled away and disappeared like gold dust into lockers and countless hiding places.

The Atlantic to any old salt has produced tales akin to the cowboys of the American Wild West especially about the weather one can encounter. For those who fought the war in it, shipboard living could be downright miserable at best. This was particularly true for the small ship navy, destroyers, corvettes, frigates etc. hence the saying 'Hard layers Jack', and it certainly was.

Now two carriers were braving the elements and making the crossing in the dead of winter. Inevitably, a couple of days out, Mother Nature caught up to us as well. Big ship or small ship meant no difference to her and we were tossed about like corks.

One night in the midst of this foul weather, due to the risk of submarine attack Illustrious and Formidable were zig-zagging without an escort. How it actually happened I don't know although we must have lost each other due to poor visibility and got too close. The result was that Formidable struck us on the port side a glancing blow which fortunately caused only superficial damage. The potential for a major disaster was narrowly averted, not to mention we were two badly needed carriers fresh from extensive refits. If we had both gone down or heavy casualties caused the price would have been colossal. This was hardly a good omen for Capt. Talbot's new command. I'll bet he and the Formidable's skipper put somebody in the 'rattle' for it. On the lighter side, Illustrious immediately sent the signal, 'If you touch me there again, I shall scream'. Somebody probably did.

When the mishap occurred I was fast asleep. Having come off the first (8 – 12) watch and as the weather was rough and the ship was pitching and rolling, I decided not to sleep on the messdeck which was for'ard. Instead I brought my hammock midships and slept on the steel deck just above the engine room. It was kind of stinky with the smell of lube oil

---

*A hundredweight (CWT) equalled 112 lbs.

171

but it was warm and fairly stable. I soon drifted off to sleep and didn't hear of the collision until next morning when I went to the mess. Everybody was talking about it. The rest of the trip was uneventful but we had been lucky again. Not just because of the crash but on December 21, HMS Audacity, an escort carrier was sunk by U-751.

Oh to be in England now that Christmas was nearly here and 'Roll Out The Barrel' of fun. We were all excited like kids at the prospect of going 'up the line' (home). Leave at any time was always cause to celebrate as one never knew when your next one might be. For too many it was often their last.

There was only a handful left aboard of the original commissioning party sent up to Barrow from Guz. The rest had been either killed, wounded, or scattered throughout the fleet. This was my first time seeing Devonport since Illustrious left for the Med. what seemed like an eternity ago. It had actually been only a year and a half but so many things had happened to us. I knew my family would be overjoyed to see me especially after the shock of nearly losing me in the bombing. I couldn't wait to see my Mum and Dad again.

With these thoughts running through my head Illustrious sailed into Plymouth Sound. Soon we were passing Drake Island and entering the River Tamar. If I remember right we took up a berth alongside one of the jetties and within a short time most of us were given leave.

The night before going home everybody was busy 'dhobiy-ing' and packing away all the goodies and souvenirs they had accumulated. Soon there were cases, wooden and cardboard boxes, and parcels sitting all over the place ready for the morrow.

Just before going ashore the next day we got paid in the first British currency we had seen for some time minus the so called cost of living allowance we had been given in America. We also received our ration cards which were necessary if our families were to get extra food to feed us. Everybody then converged on the NAAFi to buy up bars of chocolate, soap for washing and scented soap plus our duty free exemption of 200 cigarettes.

I was given about 14 days leave which meant I would spend Christmas and New Year at home but when it was piped for all those proceeding on leave we were told to muster ashore in a big warehouse shed where we would be inspected and searched by the Customs. Even in wartime one had to put up with the BS protocol of going through Customs and being picked out at random to be searched for contraband. Anyone caught would be hauled back aboard and probably have his leave cancelled. Only the foolhardy took such chances. As for myself I had to wait with hundreds of others in several long lines for over an hour until finally we were dismissed and allowed to proceed.

The eleven hour train ride back to Manchester in a carriage crowded with matelots and all their gear couldn't pass quickly enough but eventually I saw the signs for London Road station. Everything was all blacked out but I found a taxi which took me back to Trafford Bar. When I knocked on the door everybody was up waiting for me. I was back home at last safe and sound. Mum and Dad were nearly crying when they saw me and were delighted when I told them I had until the New Year.

After a wonderful time with the family on a leave which was most difficult to obtain in wartime with both Christmas and New Year, I began to feel a little depressed as it drew to a close. I was lying in bed one morning when my Mother came running upstairs looking very worried after just being handed a telegram for me. I dreaded opening it wondering whether it was a recall or something worse like a draft or 'pierhead jump'. Anything was possible in those days. When I opened it I couldn't believe what I saw as this hardly ever happened. I was given another seven days leave and told to report to the ship in Liverpool only 36 miles away. It seemed that Illustrious had to go into the Gladstone Dock which was the only one big enough to take her probably because of the damage received in our collision with the Formidable and perhaps to inspect the repairs made in Norfolk. It made no difference to me what the reason was. I was home for another week.

It goes without saying, Eric also got the same telegram as we had come on leave together. We spent a lot of time doing the rounds in our local pubs and making the most of it. As close friends we were more like brothers as well as shipmates having gone through so much.

All too quickly it was over and we had to say our goodbyes. Nobody knows unless they have experienced it personally how hard it is to leave those you love in wartime as that goodbye could be forever. For the moment we had the consolation that the ship was nearby in Liverpool and hopefully there would still be the opportunity for a few quick trips before we finally sailed.

The Second World War as a global conflict with its sheer magnitude of human suffering and untold millions of displaced people has changed the world for all time. England the island fortress and last bastion of defence in Europe was now literally an armed camp accommodating all the armies of the Allied and Commonwealth countries and the Free Forces from Occupied Europe.

In such a setting like other wars before it love and romance inevitably blossomed as though the Almighty in his infinite wisdom wanted to ease the pain and agony of it all somehow. So it happened there were the war brides and perhaps vice versa the soldiers, sailors, and airmen concerned might even be called war grooms. No matter, mixed marriages with all our allies took place on such a scale never imagined.

I was not immune either for I met somebody one dark and foggy January night at London Road station. By coincidence we had both missed the train back to our respective bases. She was a Free Pole serving in the ATS (Auxiliary Territorial Service – British Army). What had happened was that I had been home for the evening and had stayed too long missing the last train back to Liverpool.

This chance meeting took place in the Station Master's office where he and a 'Bobby' were having a hard time decyphering the broken English of an ATS girl upset at getting back to her training depot at Warrington late. Her train was delayed due to the fog and this required getting her leave pass signed.

Going inside to make enquiries it turned out that my next possible train would be the one she was taking but only going as far as Warrington, which still left me in a bit of a fix.

Seeing me, another serviceman going the same way seemed to be their way out of an awkward situation as they asked me to look after her as it was late at night and she was very young. Jolly Jack is always one willing to help a damsel in distress so I agreed.

On the short ride we had the opportunity to get to know a little about each other. Her name was Inge Hirsch and had only been a few months in the army. Her English foster parents lived in Romily, Cheshire but she was a Jewish refugee from Danzig on the Baltic Sea.

At Warrington we had to part company but not before I suggested we meet again at the YMCA at a certain time a few days later as I knew I might be on defaulters for being 'adrift' (AWOL) the next day. YMCAs catered mostly to the armed forces providing tea and cheap meals, mostly beans on toast or bangers and mash! Above all they were a place to go and they usually had a piano for a sing song for anybody who could 'tickle the ivories'.

After leaving the station I headed onto the East Lancashire Road hoping I might get a lift from any army lorries going to Liverpool but without any success I just plodded on through the dark, chilly winter's night and vowed to myself I would never try to hitch-hike again as long as I lived.

Eventually I left the road when I came to villages along the way and caught odd very early morning buses taking people to work. Finally after numerous buses I reached the outskirts of 'Scouse land' and from there made my way to the dockyard getting back aboard sometime after 08.00.

At the gangway I reported to the OOD (Officer of the Day) and being sent to the Crusher's office was immediately put in Jimmy the One's report.

After that I went down to the mess feeling flaked out with being up all night but no matter, I changed into the rig of the day and turned to for work.

Later on in the morning I lined up for defaulters and saw Jimmy who after I had given him my excuse for being late gave me one and one. This meant loss of one day's pay and one day's leave. All things considered I felt I had gotten off light.

Once again our time in port was running out before we sailed to an as yet unknown destination. I talked to some of the lads about who I had met and they kidded me that she wouldn't bother showing up and I was wasting my money. Nevertheless I decided to take a chance and hope the Polish ATS would be waiting for me at the YMCA in Warrington as I felt an attraction.

When I got there, a little late, I think both of us were just

175

as surprised at seeing each other. We sat down for a little snack and I offered to buy her a meal from what was available although there was little to choose from. She tactfully declined although she was hungry because she knew how small the service pay was with only getting eleven 'bob' (shillings) a week. I did convince her to have a tea and I had the proverbial bangers and mash.

The remainder of the evening we strolled about in the blackout getting to know each other's background. Mine of course was fairly straightforward but her's was a different story altogether.

Her home, the Free City of Danzig which had been jointly administered by Poland and Germany after the Versailles Treaty of 1918 had been taken over by the Nazis when Hitler came to power in 1933. Being half Jewish on her father's side meant her family was persecuted long before the war started as part of the Nazi's ensuing 'Final Solution'. In one of their purges her father who actually was a First World War German veteran and winner of the Iron Cross First Class was attacked and beaten to death by the SS to make an example of him.* His murderers then paraded his body around the city in the sidecar of a motorcycle before finally leaving him with his family to bury him. He had been one of the first of many Jews that would suffer in Danzig.

On November 10 1938, a date known as Kristall Nacht or Night of Glass in English, her family's clothing business was completely destroyed. At the time, Inge was a nanny to two children in a high ranking SS officer's home in Sopot a few miles away. Although his wife treated her fairly well, he was another matter and after seven months she ran away and hitch-hiked all the way home. She was only 14 at the time.

The deteriorating situation in Danzig for the Jews resulted in the creation of an underground movement to smuggle out children to the West. Inge and her sister Margot were among the last group of children to escape through this network destined for America originally. They ended up in a refugee camp in Rotterdam and the plan changed so that they went to England instead. Soon she was adopted by a Fred and Doris Holmes of Romily who wanted a sister for their only child

*The Iron Cross First Class is roughly equivalent to the VC and Inge's father was wearing his ribbons when he was beaten.

Maureen but also wanted to do something for one of the many orphaned children coming from Europe. Her foster dad enlisted in the army when war broke out and served with the 8th Army in Africa and Italy and later on in France. When Inge was old enough she took nurse's training in a Manchester hospital. At the age of 17½ she joined up because she felt that it was a way of repaying England for giving her safety. Her first choice of service had been the WRENS (Women's Royal Navy) but as she was not British born could not go in and could only join the ATS or the WAAFs (RAF).

On a lighter note, an odd thing happened that evening I met her. Using an old Lancashire expression when we were walking together in the blackout so as to appear more friendly I asked her, 'Do you want to put your leg in bed'. This simply meant linking arms as couples do. Naturally I forgot that she came from the Continent and had a poor working knowledge of English colloquialisms. She took it literally and felt my intentions were not honourable and quickly moved away from me until I was able to catch up to her and tried to explain. Things were patched up quickly and saved our relationship from getting off to a bad start.

I only managed a couple more meetings with Inge as the ship would very soon be sailing. I took her home for a quick visit to my Mum and Dad and family and once more in Warrington where I gave her a sealed letter. This I had written in case I couldn't come back again and she was to give it to my parents. In it I asked them to make her feel at home if she ever came over no matter what might happen to me should the ship be sunk or hit. The buzzes were that we might be going out to the Eastern Fleet now that the Japs were in the war. We agreed to write to each other. On that note our last brief encounter ended and the ship was put under sailing orders and all shore leave cancelled.

Illustrious sailed from Liverpool at the end of February 1942 to begin working up trials under the command of our new skipper, Arthur George Talbot. Apart from our mishap in mid-Atlantic it seems that Arthur George was getting off to a bad start in his relationship with the lower deck. During our stay in 'The Pool' he decided to have his daughter's upcoming wedding take place aboard the ship in the chapel. This sanctuary probably by design was strategically and perhaps diplomatically located on the dividing line between the officers' quarters and the rest of the ship which was the bulkhead next to the keyboard flat. This floating House of God as it were, was open and available to anyone 24 hours a day who might be in need of prayer and meditation particularly in these turbulent times. As the chapel was being readied for the wedding, our Illustrious Captain deemed that it should be closed until the ceremony was to take place. Only a person of his position of power and privilege could attempt to deny access to this Holy place to the rank and file resulting in much resentment.

To compound the issue, significant quantities of food were brought aboard and taken aft, presumably for the reception afterwards. This did not go entirely unnoticed by us and more so by the civilian dockyard mateys. Considering that Britain was under a strict system of rationing and items could only be obtained by using ration cards, it led us to wonder where and how this extra 'scran' was acquired.

This would not be the last example of Talbot exerting his authority in ways that did not endear him to the hearts and minds of the ship's lower echelon in the weeks and months to come.

As to be expected for security reasons our usual abrupt departure left me once again feeling homesick especially now I had met somebody. I wondered how long it would be this time before we got back and I saw my family again. My Dad was getting old and the war was beginning to tell on him with me always going away. With the Far East now completely overrun by the Japs there was no forseeable outcome in sight. At this point in time, the Allies were in fact losing the war and things were still going from bad to worse.

With all this in mind the Illustrious headed for the Firth of Forth in Scotland where we would pick up a convoy and prepare for another major operation.

Chapter Thirteen

Madagascar and the Eastern Fleet

Illustrious arrived in the Firth of Forth near Edinburgh and here we were able to get one or two runs ashore. This was my first time visiting that great Scottish city, home of the famous poet Sir Robert Scott and old kings like William Wallace and Robert Bruce who had led their armies against Edward I many centuries before. Their spirits are said to be still a part of Edinburgh Castle and provide the stirring 'voice of the Castle' at the annual Edinburgh Military Tattoo.

In the city we met soldiers and wrens who were part of the convoy we were to escort to Durban. They were much relieved to find out from us that an aircraft carrier would accompany them and give air cover.

The ship was now up to full complement again though there were many different faces. The messdecks were as crowded and lively as before although nobody was rejoicing about going away, least of all me. Quite a number of the old crowd were still there, like Sid, Eric, and Frank but there were new ones like Salty from the Furious and Alf Spiny. Alf was not too young, in his mid-thirties I believe and a real Cockney from the 'Smoke'. These two were characters who helped make life more bearable with their wit and funny stories, particularly the latter. The inter-ship rivalry with the old Fu was gradually fading away and these were as good a shipmate as anyone could ask for in the trying days ahead.

Although we didn't know it at the time, as it turned out we would be taking part in the first of the Allied invasions, the capturing of the island of Madagascar in the Indian Ocean codenamed Operation Ironclad.

This island is about twice the size of England at nearly 1000 miles long and 3 or 4 hundred miles wide. Held by th Vichy French, our former allies, intelligence reports indicated that it might be turned over to the Japs or at least used as a base by them for submarines operating in the Indian Ocean and Mozambique Channel. All the supplies and men going to the Eastern Med. and Far East had to pass the Cape of Good Hope and the island used by Jap and/or German submarines threatened to cut off this essential route and put our whole strategy in the Middle and Far East in peril.

At this point in time most of the western Pacific and South-East Asia had fallen under the Jap onslaught. On February 15 our fortress Singapore had surrendered to Nippon in addition to Sumatra and Hong Kong two months before. In the Philippines, American forces were still holding out on the Bataan Peninsula and Corregidor Island but these too were only weeks away from capitulation. The Japs were moving rapidly south towards New Guinea and even Australia was faced with the threat of invasion. Back in February, the Japs made numerous strikes against Darwin on the Aussie's north coast and their planes roamed at will with devastating results. By May most of Burma had also been captured and Jap advance would soon threaten India.

This was the crucial situation that Illustrious was now entering for on March 23 in company with the convoy OS23 we sailed bound for Durban. This slow convoy held the supplies and motor transport for the three infantry brigade groups and No. 5 Commando which had sailed as convoy WS17 a couple of weeks before. Along with convoy OS22, we would eventually link up with warships from Force H in Gib. and the battleship Ramilles sailing out of Kilindini, Mombasa, Kenya.

Illustrious and her convoy reached Durban in mid-April, just about a year since we left on our way to the States. I noticed that things had started to change since my last visit with this being on the main route for troopships heading to and from the East. I managed a few runs ashore with my new oppo, Salty. One of the more likeable aspects was going into the bars and lounges for a few drinks and being seated next to officers, even some of our own much to their visible dislike. In this country we were treated as equals being white in a place where the population was predominantly Black or Coloured. This was Apartheid and segregation was strictly enforced. As bad as it is, from Jack's point of view we enjoyed no class distinction which was discrimination in itself. Wherever else we went, not just in England, lower ranks in all the services were looked down upon

HMS Illustrious serving with the Eastern Fleet, en route to
Madagascar and Operation Ironclad — 1942

almost yet expected to be the defenders and put their lives on
the line when it came to the church. In social circles of the
British elite we were outcasts forced to find pleasure and
entertainment for the most part in places of ill repute.

Being back I felt a certain obligation to look up the Ingles
family again who had treated me so well. They wouldn't know
that I was still on the ship but they were pleased to see me. I
only went to see them once and I don't remember exactly what
was happening with Jean. She may have struck up an
acquaintance with someone else by this time and I didn't want
to spoil anything. Besides I had somebody now to think about.
The visit was brief but it satisfied my desire to look them up one
last time. Nevertheless, to this day I have never forgotten that
family or their hospitality.

The fleet massed for the invasion of Madagascar left Durban in
two convoys. A slow convoy consisting of special landing ships,

supply transports, a tanker and a hospital ship escorted by the heavy cruiser Devonshire, three destroyers, and the 14th minesweeping flotilla sailed on April 25. A fast convoy with the assault troops under the overall command of an Admiral Syfret left on the 28th. This was escorted by us, the cruiser Hermione, six destroyers, and the battleship Ramilles. On May 3 we were joined by Indomitable and two more destroyers from the Eastern Fleet.

By the evening of the fourth, the two convoys rendezvoused 95 miles west of Cape Amber on the northern tip of the island.

Down in the engine room we knew little of what was going on except what we were told. The next morning in the early hours the attack would take place and it seemed that the Vichy French defenders were mostly colonial troops with white officers and therefore would offer little resistance. That they did. When our forces stormed ashore at 04:30 hours, the enemy were literally caught napping.

At first light our Swordfish dropped leaflets on the Antsirane Peninsula across from Diego Saurez urging them to surrender without bloodshed. We then sank the armed merchant cruiser Bougainville and the submarine Beveziers and damaged the sloop d'Entrecasteaux.

Meanwhile our fighters which were now Grumman Martlets replacing the old Fulmars flew cover over the beaches.* Sea Hurricanes from the Indom attacked the airfield and caught the French aircraft in their hangars and burnt them out.

After a couple of days our troops had advanced a long way but ran up against a strong defensive line at the southern end of the Antsirane Peninsula but couldn't get naval support because the entrance to the bay was guarded by batteries of large guns at Oranjia Pass. The destroyer Anthony was given the job of sneaking into the harbour with 50 Royal Marines from the Ramilles. Anthony slipped past the French batteries and was noticed by the enemy gunners too late. When they opened fire their shells missed the destroyer who replied with her own 4.7 in guns and successfully landed the marines ashore. Speaking from a personal point of view I can only say it must have taken great skill and daring for that destroyer to have raced past those monstrous guns as later I was put on motor boats and went ashore with a survey party where I was able to see them myself.

---

*British Version of the US F4F Wildcat.

The batteries consisted of 18-inch guns in fixed mountings, that is unable to turn or elevate. These two guns were positioned such that they covered the mouth of the bay and anything else that came into their line of sight would be blown to hell.

Not knowing exactly what was going on with the Anthony, the Ramilles and Devonshire opened up on the French guns wth their 15 and 8-inch guns. Meanwhile, negotiations were being made for the enemy's surrender and the bombardment was soon called off but not before the French had been given a good shaking up. Soon after the enemy forces there and at Diego Suarez capitulated, a mere three days since the first landings had taken place. The breeches from the huge guns guarding Oranjia Pass were later noticed to have been removed and hidden somewhere on the island. Apparently the Vichy French had no intention of us making use of them. I don't think they were ever found either.

Our minesweepers arrived shortly afterwards and swept a safe channel into the bay where our victorious fleet then sailed led by Ramilles.

Diego Suarez was a big open harbour with no boom defence to prevent enemy submarines from entering. When the operation ended most of our destroyers and anti-submarine vessels left leaving the fleet virtually unprotected against an underwater attack.

While Illustrious lay at anchor I was put on the motor boats as part of the cutter's crew. The cutter which was the smallest of the ship's boats was about twenty or so feet in length and powered by an in-board six cylinder engine. Used for a variety of jobs including liberty men ashore and running errands for provisions and odd jobs the lads referred to it as the 'gash boat'. The other boats were pinnaces, bigger and wider for liberty men and the officers' motor boats. There was also the Captain's barge with its two Rolls-Royce V8's. These other boats were not required at this point as no liberty took place. The cutter however was required for the job of surveying for a boom defence.

Our crew including myself, the coxswain, bow and stern sheetman, and the survey party of an officer and two others loaded up one morning with all the instruments and a day's provisions and we set out for the harbour entrance. The weather was beautiful and the bleached white sand of the beach looked really enticing like a tropical resort by the sea. As we ran the boat ashore and pulled it up on the beach one of the seamen, Harry Metcalfe and myself were ordered to stay behind to guard the boat until they returned. As there was nothing really much we could do during the long hours we had to wait we decided to take turns having a swim in the turquoise water. All the time we kept an eye out for any stray shark that might venture close in hoping for a free snack on one of our legs.

It was on one of these trips that we came across the blockhouse that held the two 18-inch guns. Although they looked pretty old they still seemed formidable and would have made mincemeat out of HMS Anthony had they caught her directly in their line of fire as she sped past.

Again with being an open harbour, Diego Suarez Bay was prone to tropical storms and offered little protection. One dark night as we were heading back to the ship with the survey party something got caught around our propeller and we were unable to get over the side to deal with it as the water was getting rough. Consequently we had to stop the engine and were drifting away into the night, helpless. Fortunately we had an Aldis lamp and one of the seamen gave a distress signal which was seen by the ship. After a while of bobbing up and down drifting farther away we saw a pinnace coming to rescue us. With a few ribald remarks about the cutter being the 'gash boat', they took us in tow and slowly hauled us back to the ship. They managed to manoeuvre us to the after gangway so the officer could go back inboard. Before we could tie up to the boat boom a few yards further along, we broke away and again had to be retrieved by the pinnace.

Getting back onboard on stormy nights like these was no easy task and took a bit of doing until you got used to it. You first had to grab hold of the swinging jumping ladder tied to the bow of the boat which was heaving up and down. Then you had to climb up sideways and grab the top of the boom swung out about twenty odd feet from the ship. This boom less than a foot wide was like walking a tightrope in a high wind with only a single thin guide wire to hold onto while doing a balancing act running along back to the ship's guardrail. Later on when the ship was at Kilindini I saw one of the seamen lose his balance while on the boom and fell smashing against the side of a couple of the boats about fifteen feet below. He was taken out of the water unconscious and rushed to the sick bay with extensive injuries. It was lucky he wasn't killed or drowned but it made me be extra careful after seeing that.

When I got back to the mess after our mishaps with the cutter and being out all day I was pretty tuckered out but still got a few remarks 'taking the Mickey' out of me and the old gash boat. Best of all my tot of bubbly had still been saved for me and was sitting in the mess cupboard covered over with a saucer. The lads really were very considerate and tried to look after each other.

Our vulnerability without a boom defence or anti-submarine vessels was made evident on May 30 when two Jap midget subs entered the bay and destroyed the tanker British Loyalty (6,993 tons). Ramilles was also badly damaged by a torpedo which blew a thirty foot hole in her port side for'ard of 'A' turret. These midget subs had been launched from two submarines of the Jap 8th Submarine Squadron ten miles from Oranjia Pass. These large vessels also carried a seaplane which had flown reconnaissance flights over the harbour before hand. After the attack, the crews of the midget subs landed ashore but were all wiped out in a brief fight with the army.

It seems that we had underestimated the Japs' innovations and tenacity despite the fact we had dealt with similar attacks by the Itties at Gib. and Alex. Unlike the Italians however, the Japs were operating a vast distance from their own bases. Regardless, it's a wonder they didn't go after us, a carrier. The poor old Ramilles was crippled and it took until the beginnning of June for her to be patched up enough to limp to Durban for more extensive repairs. Illustrious would now take more serious precautions in which even the cutter would play an important role.

In response to the torpedoing of Ramilles and the risk that the Japs might have other plans with frogmen and limpet mines from their midget submarines, it was decided to do boat patrols around the ship during the night hours while at anchor. Starting somewhere around 20:00 hours we loaded up the old 'gash boat' with rifles, grenades, and Lanchester submachine guns plus an officer and PO with the regular boat's crew to patrol around the ship, constantly shining an Aldis lamp on the waterline looking for tell-tale bubbles or any undue movement which might suggest a frogman. Never more than a few yards from the ship's side we kept up a slow, methodical search chugging along being challenged by a sentry stationed fore and aft on the ship for two hours non-stop before being relieved for two hours rest. Then we were on again armed to the teeth ready to lob a pineapple at anything that looked suspicious and give them a burst. As boring as the task was it was still a tense time for everyone knowing that the Japs had submarines in the area. I remember that the water in the bay was very calm making it easier for us to detect any little waves, indicating trouble.

All's well that ends well for nothing happened, but who knows if our presence deterred any would-be attackers on the several nights we patrolled?

Judging by the fact that we had to mount an attack on Madagascar seems that our former staunch ally, the French had now become a liability to us where a lot of the time we were fighting them instead of the Germans or in this case, the Japs. First we had to sink the French fleet at Oran. Then their squadron at Alex wouldn't come out and fight with us and then an operation was mounted against Dakar where the battleship Resolution, sister of the Ramilles was hit. Finally when the Japs came into the war Indo-China under Vichy was virtually handed over to the enemy in South-East Asia and now they were narrowly stopped by us from letting enemy subs use Diego Suarez as a base of operations. There seemed no end to this brand of treachery being committed under orders from the Vichy government who was collaborating with a barbaric enemy which in my opinion was completely reprehensible. It was about time that we took off the kid gloves and stopped trying to fight this total all-out war by the Marquess of Queensbury rules.

After things were secured in Diego Suarez, Illustrious sailed east to operate from Colombo on the island of Ceylon (now called Sri Lanka) and from that tropical dump, Trincomalee on the northern end of the island. Trinco could roughly be described as the Far East equivalent of Scapa Flow. I never bothered to go ashore there as there wasn't anything to see or do other than a canteen.

The weather in this part of the world was bloody hot and the ship was stifling between decks made worse by the extremely high humidity and being battened down for darkening ship. On the messdecks the unofficial rig of the day was uually a towel around the waist or under your shorts but on watch overalls were still compulsory. Cockroaches and heat rashes were common. I was fortunate not to be plagued with this itch which could keep you awake all night because I always tried to wear something under my overalls to soak up the sweat when I was down below. The cockroaches were a nuisance too. Every ship had this problem whatever part of the globe they are in with always being closed up but in the tropics they are even worse and got into everything. One Old Illustrian commented that we were on a high protein diet. When the cook would make a big tub of soup in the galley the roaches would be attracted by the odour and congregated on the deckhead above. The cook would then come along to stir the soup and when the lid was removed a big waft of steam would rise up and a few of the roaches would lose their balance and fall into the bubbling contents. 'Cookie' just kept right on stirring. He figured we on the messdeck wouldn't know the difference anyway.

Then there were the flies and other insects which prompted somebody to bring a chameleon aboard under the pretence of being a pet but which benefitted everybody. This little member of the lizard family with its big popping eyes and lightning-speed tongue used to crawl around the deckhead ducts and hammock bars and do its stuff catching its prey which would otherwise be buzzing around our heads while we tried to sleep and eat.

On the whole however, Illustrious was a very clean ship. Unlike many other vessels which got overrun by those four legged vermin we know as rats, we never had a single one that I know of. We had that at least to be thankful for.

Nevertheless we had another irritant in the form of our Captain. We noticed the 'chippies' one day were working just inside the capstan flat a little for'ard of the lower stoker's messdeck. It turned out they were building extra cells made of canvas and wood and we already had six permanent cells further up.

There was a period which lasted maybe six months when Illustrious was not the happy ship it had been under Boyd and Tuck. It seemed that men were always getting put 'in the rattle' for something. These cells were being constantly used and even extra ones had to be built for the increasing number of lads being put on defaulters. There seemed no valid reason yet there were always a lot on 10-A. This form of punishment involved doubling up and down the flight deck with a rifle and full pack for about an hour when there was no flying. In this scorching climate the heat itself provided additional punishment. It got to the point where a lot of discontent was brewing and I even heard the word that I feared the most, mutiny. The thought of such a thing made me cringe. The lower deck called him Captain Bligh.

To give an example of what was going on, one of the stokers did something, I don't know what, and was given three month's stoppage of pay and leave. After going through this ordeal and trying to make ends meet by scrubbing hammocks for some of the lads to make a few shillings the time came when he had to go before Talbot to review his punishment.* Instead of getting off it, he was given the same thing all over again for another three months. He was so 'browned off' he was almost fit to be tied. We all sympathized with him and calmed him down. He eventually got off the punishment by sticking it out but this kind of discipline wasn't good for ship's morale. By late summer 1942, all the discontent seemed to stop as suddenly as it started. We had been given a new skipper, Capt. Robert Lionel Brooke Cunliffe. Things then went back to normal after what had been a very trying and unnecessary time.

I wonder if Captain Boyd who was now Rear-Admiral Aircraft Carriers, Eastern Fleet knew about Talbot's goings on and if he had anything to do with Cunliffe taking over. It was mighty coincidental considering Boyd had flown his flag on the Indomitable during the Madagascar landings.

After he left Illustrious, Arthur George Talbot went to command, of all ships, the Formidable. After this as some form of recognition for his efforts he was promoted to Rear-Admiral and made the Flag Officer in command of Force S covering the assault on Sword Beach on D-Day. He didn't lack enthusiasm and sought out the action by going ashore often and loading a jeep up with food to give to army forward units. At least once he put his personal safety at risk by his zealousness. However he really showed his true colours when he was given the command of a motley task force designated Force X which went out to the

---

*It wasn't uncommon practise for enterprising stokers to start up their own 'dhobying firms' to earn extra money even under ordinary circumstances.

Pacific. The mission was almost doomed to failure right from the start as the Americans neither wanted or needed them. Conditions on the ships, and the treatment of the lower deck was poor and resulted in bad morale, so bad in fact that a mutiny ensued. Talbot made his 'Jimmy the One' the scapegoat by court martialling him. He retired from the RN a Vice-Admiral with the CB (Commander of the Bath) in 1947. For a while he tried pig farming in Yorkshire but was not very successful with those four-legged critters. I guess they proved too much for him. He then moved into a small flat in Bournemouth where in 1960 he died of a brain tumour at the age of sixty-eight.

Mail from home was always exciting and a definite morale booster. One could say it was the fuel that kept the home fires burning for everybody but there were times when letters brought sad news too as in my case.

There had been a spell of two or three months at one point since we left England where the mail hadn't caught up to us. In war one can only speculate as to the reason. Sometimes the ship carrying it would get sunk and then it would be completely lost.

However, in a letter I was told by my Mum that Dad had passed away peacefully many weeks back. I was quite upset but not really surprised as the strain of the war took its toll on older folks having their loved ones away in the forces. This left a great emptiness in their lives. As for my dear old Dad, I've always felt it broke his heart and he lost the will to live mostly. He had been the best father anyone could wish for and would have literally given me his last penny, poor as he was. Nevertheless there was nothing I could do about it out here and had to get over my grief best I could as others had to do.

On the more cheery side, Inge and I continued to correspond as much as possible. Her command of the English language was slowly getting better so there was no problem in understanding each other. As the situation in the Far East was still deteriorating I didn't want to give her any false hopes. The way things were going anything could happen to me or the ship so I gave her the option of seeing someone else if she wished.

As Illustrious patrolled around the Indian Ocean and we called in at Colombo, I went ashore and on the spur of the moment decided to go into a jewellery shop. The East of course is famous for its jewels and precious stones which were unobtainable in England at the time. The name above the shop was 'Abdul Kaffour' but English was widely understood as this was an important British base next to India.

Sitting at a table, Abdul who was the proprietor and wearing the fez typical of the East, asked me what my pleasure was. I told him I wanted a ring with some stones in for my girl friend. Very obligingly he gave a couple of claps with his hands and seconds later one of his servants came through the beaded curtain near us carrying a tray full of glittering gems. I wasn't sure if they were all real or not. I was just taking a chance as out in these places one had to be careful. These people could be very tricky as one knows who has travelled to the East. To cut a long story short Abdul seemed pretty genuine and went to the trouble of explaining to me about the language of stones and their meaning. Each one symbolizes a different month of the year and as such I decided to pick something which would relate to Inge's birthday month of March. This was an Alexandrite, a kind of red stone which would go in the middle of the ring. Surrounding this went six white sapphires which resemble diamonds symbolizing my birth month of September. I hated to ask Abdul the price of this ring which was set in 18K gold considering my matelot's pay. When he said £3 10s I inwardly breathed a sigh of relief thinking it would have been much more and left him a small deposit. Abdul promised to have it ready in three days which left me in another bit of a quandary as I didn't know how long it would be before we sailed. So it began a race against time as each day passed. After the third day I went back to the shop and to my relief the ring was ready. It looked a real 'bobbydazzler'. I paid him the rest of the money, went back to the ship and the next day we sailed. I never returned to Colombo again.

This ring that I intended for an engagement had an odd effect on me in as much I vowed that no matter where I went I would always have it on me. I carried it around in my pocket on and off watch, kept it in my hammock while I slept and said to myself if we got sunk, the ring would go down with me.

Being a little suspicious about it being genuine I later on had it appraised at a jeweller's in Durban who said it was worth twice what I paid. The stones were definitely real, and so was the bargain!

While in Ceylon we had heard that two or three months

previous a Jap carrier force had bombed Colombo and sank the cruisers Cornwall and Dorsetshire not far away. Four days later on April 9, this force raided Trincomalee and sank the carrier Hermes, the Aussie destroyer Vampire, a corvette, and two tankers. Sadly they were only 65 miles away from an Allied airfield but no help was received. HMS Hermes became the only British carrier to be sunk by air attack. That same day, 35,000 American soldiers defending the Bataan Peninsula in the Philippines surrendered to the Japs. Less than one month later on May 6, the day after our troops landed in Madagascar, the American island fortress of Corregidor, last bastion of defence in the northern Philippines surrendered giving the Japs twelve and a half thousand more POWs. Things were in very bad shape for the Allies in the Far East in 1942.

A 'Buzz' went around the ship. A couple of us were on the messdeck 'shooting the breeze' when a stoker came down the ladder looking a bit glum. After hearing what he had to say I felt 'chokka block' too and wondered when it would all end. He asked if we had heard the 'latest' and we said 'No, give us the gen'. Of all the buzzes I ever heard, I always remembered this one. It was standard practice if you were lucky enough to be a survivor from a ship that had been sunk and if you were sent home you would be given fourteen days survivor's leave. This 'buzz' said that apparently you would have to be a survivor twice before you would get leave now. How lucky can you be to escape death twice in a row? Even if you were fortunate enough to live through a sinking you would probably end up as shark meat or be taken prisoner by the Japs and live a life of torture and degradation as so many others did. Thankfully I never had the misfortune to test the authenticity of that 'Buzz'.

It was in this atmosphere of uncertainty that Illustrious literally put her head in the dragon's mouth by making a patrol up into the Bay of Bengal near Burma well within striking range of Jap land based aircraft. Luckily we didn't meet up with anything.

In August we made diversionary raids to distract the Jap attention from the American landings at Guadalcanal in the Solomons on the 7th. This was the first of a long series of island hopping invasions by the Allies and US in particular to retake the Pacific.

I never really knew how close we were to Guadalcanal until I saw that old American movie recently, *Guadalcanal Diary* with

Lloyd Nolan and William Bendix. There is a scene in which the landing force is forming up with its escorts and a group of marines were watching from one of the assault ships. Not knowing the names of the ships one of them says, 'Get Jordan up here'. This was a Black marine who was familiar with all the names. He rattles off a couple of names, Pensacola and then of all ships, Illustrious. I guess we were there after all and we even made it into a Hollywood movie.

After the Madascar operation I was given a change of jobs for sea on the steaming watch bill being taken out of the centre engine room to take hourly temperatures on the plumber blocks.

A ship the size of Illustrious with its 113,300 shaft horsepower required three huge propellers attached to its own shaft three or so feet in diameter in places running half the length of the ship. To keep these huge shafts steady and in place were things known as plumber blocks which acted as a form of bearing. A part of these plumber blocks was made of one of the hardest known woods in the world called Lignum Vitae. This wood comes from Central and South America and is so dense it won't even float.

To get to these plumber block mountings one had to go down several decks to the ship's bottom involving three separate compartments for both outer shafts and four in the centre being longer. Each deck had a heavy steel hatch or a manhole in the centre which required opening and closing and then dogging. With the pitching and rolling of the ship sometimes there was a certain amount of personal risk in the event one slipped and the hatch fell back on you it would be sufficient to cut your hand or fingers off let alone falling down onto the next deck. I was extra careful believe me.

When I eventually reached the plumber block spaces I walked along a catwalk alongside the shaft spinning around at hundreds of rpms until I reached the mountings where I took a temperature reading with a 14 inch long thermometer in a steel casing. I recorded every reading on a slip of paper and reported to the control room every hour. This job was essential for monitoring whether the bearings were overheating and was done 24 hours a day by three of us. Being in the tropics this task was especially fatiguing as we were on the go all the time, not that we had it worse than anyone else. I must admit there were times when we would intentionally miss one of these readings and took a chance by guessing because it was difficult to get around to all of them in only an hour. It's scary to think now how little chance one would have had down there if we had been hit by a 'tin fish' without a hope in hell of getting out, but the job had to be done just the same.

In early September we returned to Madagascar for the occupation of the southern end of the island. Our 45 aircraft provided air cover but the operation met with little resistance and our aircraft fired no shots in anger.

The last two or three months in the Indian Ocean we spent hanging around for some reason in Mombasa, Kilindini. This was another dump if ever there was one but I was back on the cutter again and this helped take the edge off what would have otherwise been a very humdrum stay. It seems that there were plans for us and Illustrious was being saved for some other important mission.

Being on the cutter did have its perks. Sometimes we would be detailed off to go and collect some officers' provisions or extra goodies like tomatoes or fresh fruit like pineapples etc. These were items we didn't get on the lower deck. Having quite a ways to return to the ship gave us enough time to select a few of these tasty morsels for ourselves to take back to the mess. These we would stash in a locker near the engine where they wouldn't be seen by the officer of the watch and then after we tied up to the boom we would sneak them inboard in our pockets or caps. Pineapples we would eat on the way as they were a bit awkward to conceal in one's cap or under your shirt. Carrying a pocketful of juicy tomatoes, one also had to be careful how you went up the jumping ladder and got onto the boom. These I shared with Eric and Frank and others sometimes.

One weekend afternoon we were called away to pick up a 'shower' (group) of WRENs who were waiting at the jetty. They weren't our guests but had been invited to the officers' wardroom. These WRENs were not officers but rather ratings like us. Obviously we tried to put on a smart appearance to make a good impression and joked a bit with them as they came inboard but didn't get any great responses. It seemed right away that these gals were immune out here from Jack's wit and charm. We loaded up and pushed off. Again we tried to make a little conversation on the way. Apart from the odd smile it seems that now away from old Blighty's shores that they were a little different and acted above us. Jacko had a plan up his jumper. When we reached the gangway and they all filed off and climbed the steep steps we suddenly had a bit of 'difficulty' pulling away. In those few timely moments when Coxswain was vigorously opening and closing the buckets around the 'screw' and I was having some 'trouble' with the engine not to mention the bow and stern sheetmen were trying to push us off Jacko had the chance of casting some very fast glances straight upwards. This was enough to produce the desired results of seeing what we wanted to see. When we tied up to the boom we were laughing and making lewd comments about their drawers. For instance 'Did yer see that redhead/blond and what colour her bloomers were?'. All the way back inboard we joked about that and then told the other lads about it. In a way we had the last laugh and even got to take them ashore later on that evening.

This brings to mind what happened a while back when I tried to look up one of the WRENs in Mombasa that had seemed so friendly in Edinburgh before leaving with our convoy. Eventually locating her billet somewhere just otside the town of Kilindini seemingly on the edge of the jungle I enquired if WREN so and so happened to be there. One of her oppos called her name and to my surprise she appeared.

I'm afraid the reception though polite was rather cool in contrast to the hot climate we were in. I asked her if she would be free for a date sometime but was told that almost every evening she was booked up with some social engagement or other invitation. I soon took the hint but not before purposely going through the whole seven days of the week and more to let her know I had really got the point. I left in disgust. Jack has his pride too.

Another down side to our time in the Eastern Fleet concerned our 'scran'. For a period of about three months we ran out of spuds, that staple element of the Western diet. These were substituted by yams (a Middle East form of sweet potato) and rice. We soon got fed up with these but could do nothing about it. We still had to eat. To make matters worse we even ran out of the good rum from Jamaica and Trinidad. That was replaced by rum from South Africa. They had to give us something but it didn't go down as well and we nicknamed it banana juice. For all I know that was what it was made of. Later on they finally gave us the proper stuff again and everybody stopped 'dripping'.

In this God forsaken place of Mombasa, to help relieve the boredom we got the occasional movie, usually American. This we watched in the hangar. Some of us sat in the 'balcony', sitting on the flight deck with our legs dangling over the edge of the lift well. At least nobody's head got in the way.

With all due respect to ENSA (Entertainments National Service Association) we never saw any entertainers coming out here even by 1942. If they did they didn't come to us or any other ships nearby. I only saw one throughout the entire war later on in Bari, Italy I believe, and it was so packed out I left long before it was over.

'Swinging round the buoy' in Mombasa for whatever reason was okay by me and better than going out and perhaps 'catching a packet'. Nevertheless it was a stinking hot hole and the messdecks were like a sweat box. Shipboard air conditioning was unheard of in those days and we only had the small overhead duct louvres for ventilation so most nights I took my folding camp bed up to the cable deck to get a decent sleep amongst the giant anchor chains. Others did the same but the snag was that we had to be up pronto in the morning when the seamen came to swab the decks.

For the sake of morale and to keep our minds off things an entertainment officer was detailed off by Jimmy, or he may have even volunteered but it doesn't matter, to organize a skit show put on by members of the ship's company from all branches. There were stokers taking part including Sid who was an outgoing character with a good sense of humour.

The night of the show, the hangar was packed with a large, enthusiastic audience. As one can imagine, a good thousand swearing and sweating matelots throwing in their own brand of humour, shouting and whistling made for a bit of a boisterous atmosphere as to be expected.

The show was a big hit with a lot of laughs, jokes, skits about Navy life, and a sing-song. The biggest laugh came at the finale when the cast all joined together on-stage to sing their own made up version of that old Irish melody 'The Emerald Isle'.

The exact words I only vaguely remember so I must be forgiven if I have to put in a sub here and there but it went something like this:

Sure a little bit of heaven fell
From out the sky one day.
It nestled in the Indian Ocean,
A spot not far away.
But when the angels found it,
They said 'Oh what a bloody shame'.
'We'll give it to the Navy,
And let them take the blame'.
So the Andrew sprinkled it with matelots,
A carrier and battleship or two.
There was no other place quite like it,
No matter where you go.
Though when they had it finished,
It still looked so bleak and bare.
They had to name it something,
And sure they called it Mom-ba-sa.

There were a couple of other verses attached to this skit which I have long since forgotten but this was the one that got everybody roaring.

There were other common songs we used to sing on the messes with our own lyrics as a kind of relief for pent up feelings when we were chokka block. For instance:

Roll on the Rodney,
The Nelson, Renown.
This one funnel bastard
Is getting me down.

Then there was also the lower deck version of Bless 'em All.

There's a troopship just leaving Bombay
Bound for old Blighty's shore.
Heavily laden with time expired men
Bound for the land they adore.

There's many a matelot
Just finished his time.
There's many a fool signing on.
You'll get no promotion

196

This side of the ocean.
So cheer up my lads eff 'em all.

Roll on my effing twelve.

One last thing while on the topic of entertainment, I was passing through the seamen's mess with another stoker when we noticed a group of sailors on a conducted tour with an officer. The difference with this bunch was that they all had white bands around their caps which denoted they were officer candidates. Straight away my oppo pointed one of them out to me and said 'Do you know who that is?' I replied 'No. What about him?' He then said 'That's Michael Redgrave the actor'. I didn't realize the significance at the time as the British film industry was in its infancy and we saw mostly American pictures. However, he later rose to stardom and became Sir Michael Redgrave acting in many fine movies which I have seen. It seems rather unusual that he was aboard Illustrious while I was there. I think he stayed for about three months. Famous people did cross our paths from time to time.

The ship spent Christmas 1942 and the New Year in Kilindini. No white Christmas here in this climate. We had no idea what 1943 would bring except another year of war. I now had my first good conduct stripe for three years service and some of the lads had even got their hooks. For me I would get threepence a day extra. As for promotions, I didn't really care at this stage. All I was concerned about was surviving this lot and the last thing I expected was we'd be sent back to England. Nevertheless, in January the ship flashed up the boilers and got under way. Lo and behold the buzz went around that we were heading back home. I really couldn't believe it was true.

Illustrious steamed like hell, faster than what we had done to escape Malta after the bombing. Our escorts could hardly keep up to us as we maintained an average speed of close to 28 knots.

What we were leaving behind may have been a fate worse than death had anything happened to us like many other ships, but the carrier still had its share of misfortune. A few months back we had a series of accidents for about a week which caused everybody to get the jitters and believe we were jinxed. Sailors are traditionally very superstitious. It all began when one of the after 4.5 turrets manned by the Royals somehow fired into

Crash on deck. Swordfish torpedo bomber about to be removed from the flight deck of HMS Illustrious while in the Indian Ocean – 1942

another turret killing and injuring several. Committals to the deep followed and I personally saw the eerie sight of the bodies sewn up in their hammocks being slid over the side to their watery grave. Then a member of the Fleet Air Arm got caught up in the props of one of the aircraft and seriously injured. We also had an unusual amount of planes crashing or going over the side. It got to the point where nobody wanted to go up to the flight deck for their constitutional including me. I figured that if I had to go it wouldn't be in an accident caused by some jinx. I stayed below where I thought it would be safer or just up as far as the gash chute even though it did stink. I suppose it was just one of those things and the mishaps settled down after a while and we got back to normal.

I think the ship only made one stop which was for fuelling in Freetown, Sierra Leone, West Africa. This place was known as 'the white man's grave' because of its climate and tropical diseases but we still had ships on station there. It was here that the natives would come out in small boats or canoes like outriggers and would dive for coins tossed over the side but only if you threw them in a certain direction. The locals knew the currents so well that they would retrieve the penny before it sank. If you threw it the wrong way they wouldn't even bother diving for it.

So we steamed on to England after a brief stop and crossed the line along the way. This was about my sixth time going over the equator. My first time had been back in March 29, 1941 when we were escaping the Med. and at longitude 45°36′E Illustrious crossed that imaginary point which divides the earth into North and South. In peacetime and to a lesser extent in war this is accompanied with a special ceremony and a certificate in the form of a proclamation from the court of King Neptune, the mythological ruler of the sea. This transcends international differences and is recognized as a turning point in a sailor's life by most Western seafaring nations. Even the German Navy does it.

The ceremony is meant to be a fun affair involving members of the ship's company being dressed up in all kinds of costumes representing Neptune's court and kingdom. A public dunking of all the new members after being duly initiated then follows. Illustrious did have the ceremony but I only watched, having just come off duty. The whole thing is quite hilarious and various games follow afterwards. I too was presented with a scroll highlighted at the top with a drawing of the carrier flanked by two of our battle honours, Taranto and Pantelleria. Later on of course, the ship was to earn more honours.

I still have the certificate which is in remarkably good condition after being stored many years in a long, skinny box which held a thermometer for taking the temperature of the plumber blocks, both probably priceless relics now.

What a relief as we sailed north and the temperature gradually got colder. It was a great feeling to be going back even though it was winter and the rig of the day was blues and jerseys after constantly sweating for a whole year.

Illustrious steamed at a breakneck pace to cover nearly ten thousand miles in twelve days. Soon we were entering the Western Approaches and we would be going on leave shortly.

What had the 'nuthouse' got planned for us to get this great ship here so fast? Little did I know I wouldn't be aboard for her next operation. They had something planned for me too.

Chapter Fourteen

A Whole New War

Illustrious arrived back in the UK in early February and some time was spent that month up in the River Clyde doing aircraft trials. I have an excellent photo of the ship taken by the Fleet Air Arm at Ailsa Craig in the Clyde. On deck is a single aircraft which an old shipmate, John Atkinson who now lives in Ryde, Isle of Wright, told me is a Blackburn YA5 Firebrand. This particular plane was a prototype on trial and only one was ever made.

Around this time, our air group were starting to take delivery of the modern American made Vought F4U Corsair fighter. This type with its 18 cylinder radial engine was the first plane to reach 400 mph. They later won fame as the aircraft used by the US Marine Corps Black Sheep Squadron commanded by the ace Gregory (Pappy) Boyington formerly of the American Volunteer Group – Flying Tigers.

On March 1st my diary tells me I went home on 22 days leave and found an extra pleasant surprise waiting for me. My Mother and sisters were there and gave me a big welcome but sadly no Dad this time. Then everybody laughed when Inge appeared from another room.

To see England again so unexpectedly gave me much to be thankful for and especially now there was somebody I could give this ring that I had carried around on me day and night for months on end. One had to make the most of each opportunity then and live for today only as there was no tomorrow with any degree of certainty, so it was on this leave that we got engaged and out of the blue I suggested we get married if I could arrange a few days. We planned for April 24. As Inge was Polish there were a few formalities to get permission from their government in exile in London.

Returning off leave it wasn't long before I received a blow

when told I was to be drafted back to Guz barracks. I immediately wondered to what ship and how soon, but I tried not to think about it for fear it was for foreign service again. As the hymn tells us, 'One day at a time Lord', that's all I ask.

Time, things always seemed to race against time. With the plans to get 'spliced' (married) on Easter Saturday and now getting a draft chit it would be nip and tuck whether we could pull it off.

I visited Inge at her camp in Swindon, Wiltshire for a short weekend. Then another unexpected thing happened. After coming out of the YMCA canteen into the blackout I fell over the edge of the lawn which was raised up about three feet above the pavement and badly sprained my ankle so I couldn't walk. Inge ran back inside to get some help and a bunch of Kiwi soldiers came to my rescue picked me up and carried me back in. I believe an ambulance took me to the hospital and they kept me overnight. At least I didn't have to pay for my bed and breakfast.

The next morning the nurse told me they wanted to keep me there for the next two weeks and they would notify the ship. This was a great idea at first because I would get two weeks leave for nothing except that I would miss my draft and possibly screw up my plans to get married. Reluctantly I had to turn it down. This was the first and only time I ever refused leave. The funniest part of it all was when I was hobbling around on crutches. People were stopping me and making remarks about 'that poor, wounded soldier'. They thought I was too modest when I tried to explain it was just a sprain.

I returned to the ship on crutches and on time.

I finally left that great ship Illustrious on April 21 after spending three years of my life almost to the day aboard her, which I will never forget. Saying cheerio to the lads on the messdeck was not easy. As for Frank Lord and Eric, I never saw either of them again. I didn't find out what happened to Frank but did find out Eric's story which had a sad ending which I will relate in the Epilogue.

As I walked onto the gangway I put down my bag and hammock, turned aft and saluted for the last time.

Back in Jago's Mansions which was teeming with matelots, mostly HOs, I was able to get some marriage leave and set off for Manchester on Good Friday, April 23. The next morning it was still a close shave because it was only a few hours beforehand that permission was received from the Polish government. In the afternoon we were married in St. Alphonsus Catholic church in Old Trafford, Ayres Road. This church still stands there to this day. When we were just coming out of the door a notion came over me to run away with the bride to the astonishment of all the family and onlookers. I grabbed her hand and ran like hell all the way home. This of course was just up the street. We couldn't afford a taxi anyway. What a carry on.

In war time you had to catch those few fleeting moments of happiness while you could. All too quickly they were gone and became just a memory when you went away again to face whatever lay ahead. So many never returned.

Those heart warming songs of Vera Lynn like 'We'll Meet Again' and 'I Never Said Thanks For That Lovely Weekend' reflected everybody's feelings. Even the Germans had their sentimental side too it seems in the famous 'Lili Marlene' which is about a girl waiting underneath a lamp light by the barrack gate for her soldier friend who couldn't come, being under orders for sailing. It happened to us all.

My leave as always just flew by. Though I suppose it was only natural, it was getting harder all the time to say goodbye. With gut wrenching emotions, the only way was to get out of the house and walk away without looking back.

Getting back to Devonport and seeing those cold, grey, granite slabs sent a chill of deep depression over me as I entered the barrack gates and reported to the guard room to hand in my leave pass.

After just getting married I now found myself in the melancholic surroundings of having to stay at this 'stone frigate', HMS Drake. I didn't know anybody and felt almost friendless. At least aboard ship there was a lot of company you got to know like family, but here you couldn't even get a sleeping billet unless you slung your hammock by four o'clock in the afternoon after coming off a working party. You couldn't leave anything lying around. If you were lucky enough to get a kit locker it had to be left locked and the same with your kit bag. I once had my money stolen, so I know!

After several weeks of this plus physicals and swimming tests I was fed up. Then I received a letter from Inge who was now in a holding unit in Aldershot telling me they were forming a Free Polish Brigade to be sent to the Middle East. As she was now married and a British subject, she had the option of staying behind but she was considering it.

I was really 'browned off' and wrote back telling her not to go, knowing what the situation out there was like. On the strength of this I devised a little plan to fiddle some leave which was taking a big chance. I forget whether I produced a telegram or letter but went to the Officer of the Day and told a good story about my wife being sent (I neglected to mention the option) to the Middle East. Thankfully they never checked up on me otherwise I would have been thrown in the jankers. I was given seven days compassionate leave and Inge was given a leave to be with her husband which was a consideration often allowed for the women's forces.

Somehow this sort of second honeymoon made me feel better when I returned and it was just as well because I had narrowly missed one of the big raids on Plymouth on June 12 later known as the Plymouth Blitz.

By coincidence not long after I walked into the mess one dinner time to get my tot and as happened every day there was always a bunch of draft chits waiting for somebody. This time it was my turn. There it was for me to report to the drafting office at 08:00 where they gave me Job No. J219.

This was the Illustrious all over again. There was the uncertainty of guessing what was J219. Was it a destroyer, a battlewagon, a cruiser, or maybe even another carrier? Nobody with me seemed to know and those in the drafting office wouldn't tell us even if they did.

The morning of June 25, 1943 saw me as part of an advance party of about 20 others of different branches mustering at Mill Bay Station for our train bound for Stranraer to take the ferry across to Belfast, Northern Ireland.

In charge of us was a seaman PO known as the 'Buffer'. When talking to him we called him 'Buffs' which he didn't mind because it respected his rank though he wasn't really Pusser anyway as such, even with his nearly 20 years service.

There was also a young HO seaman called Wally who had only recently come in. Rather quiet and likeable we kind of took to each other. We were all strangers and had to make new oppos. It all seemed to bode well for a friendly crew and a good ship.

Landing at Larne later in the day we were shepherded to the Harland & Wolff dockyard. There we walked alongside the wall past many ships in different stages of construction all looking alike. At last we spotted the number on the bows of one which seemed nearly complete, J219.

This turned out to be an Algerine class deep-sea minesweeper. I would now be part of the small ship navy, which would be a bit of a shock after spending the last three years aboard a massive aircraft carrier.

HMS Rosario was to become half-leader of the newly formed 19th Minesweeping Flotilla. Aboard her I would return to the Med. to fight the rest of the war and for a year afterwards clearing the sea of that deadly underwater menace, mines. Rosario would take me back to many of the places I had been aboard Illustrious including Malta, Alex, and even Taranto which we had bombed back in 1940. I would take part in the landings on Elba Island where Napoleon was exiled, Operation Anvil, the South of France landings coinciding with the Second Front, and I would fight the Italian campaign from Naples to Trieste where we were given a sample of the Cold War in its very early days when Marshal Tito's partisans tried to grab Trieste for the Communists.

The crowning glory if one can put it that way, would come while being sent to a rest camp in the mountains of Sicily, Taormina. Here we were billeted in a building near the village called the Hotel Schultz which had been a Luftwaffe headquarters, possibly the one that issued the orders to bomb Illustrious back in January 1941. What an irony.

God willing this may be another story for another time but right now I was being faced with a whole new war that was as dirty, deadly, and dangerous as anything could be, with little or no glory.

Epilogue

After I left her, the ship HMS Illustrious went on to earn four more battle honours making a total of eight during the Second World War. The reason for being recalled so suddenly was in order to take part in Operation Husky, the invasion of Salerno. In 1944 she operated in company with the carrier USS Saratoga in the Indian Ocean making strikes against Sabang, Sumatra and Surabaja, Java.

In 1945 she undertook devastating attacks against the oil refineries at Palembang as part of the British Pacific Fleet. In March and April she helped support the American landings at Okinawa launching 443 combat sorties. During this battle she fought off attacks by Jap Kamikaze aircraft. One in particular was shot down after clipping the island and exploded under water causing more damage than was realized at the time. Being relieved by Formidable on April 14 she put into the US forward base at Leyte Gulf where an investigation of her hull revealed cracks in the outer plating and internal frames. This required her to return to England via Sydney where she received temporary repairs in dry dock.

Illustrious which had been a brand new ship when the war started was completely worn out by continuous service and had never really recovered from the crippling wounds received from the Stuka dive-bombing at Pantelleria. Ironically she missed the Jap surrender in Tokyo Bay in September 1945.

After the war until 1954 she was deployed as a trials and training carrier doing initial deck landing trials with the RN's first generation of jet aircraft.

In 1954 she was laid up in the reserve fleet and on November 3, 1956 that magnificant ship bearing one of the Royal Navy's proudest names and having been one of the most distinguished ships of the Second World War went to her final resting place at the breakers yard at Faslane.

On 20 June 1982, the Invinceable class ASW (Anti-Submarine Warfare) carrier HMS Illustrious was commissioned at sea into the RN. This was a Royal Navy first. Completed three months ahead of schedule she sailed directly to the Falkland Islands to take up patrol duty.

Armed with Sea Dart missiles and the Vulcan Phalanx radar controlled super accelerated Gatling gun and operating Sea King helicopters and Sea Harrier V/TOL fighters, she is a state of the art warship capable of being a command centre for an entire fleet with her radar and communications equipment. This fifth Illustrious would no doubt give an equally good account of herself as her predecessor given the opportunity.*

In July 1983, Inge and Michael were on holiday in England when they saw a placard at a Portsmouth news stand that read 'Illustrious to host old boys'. This concerned the very first Old Illustrians reunion which was held aboard the new ship September 9, 1983. Out of this reunion an association was formed.

Upon their return from the UK, Inge and Michael excitedly informed me and I was in two minds whether or not to go. Because it involved too much expense at short notice I decided against it, regrettably. However I did telephone the ship the day of the reunion and spoke to the OOD who then handed me over to the Second in Command, Cdr. G. Sullivan. He and the skipper, Capt. J. B. Kerr put me in touch with several people who were forming the association. Through them I made contact with other old shipmates by mail and eventually with a Wallace Needham, who with his wife Ethel and a number of others worked diligently to make the association a reality and what it is today.

In June 1985 there was another reunion aboard the new carrier which we managed to attend. Here we met many of the old shipmates I have referred to in the book including Sid Nuttall, Kenny Baker, Harry Thomas, and of course Joe Fitz.

The one face that was missing which I had hoped to see was Eric's. Nobody knew what had happened to him.

Early in the new year, 1987, Wallace and Ethel and my sister Flo both sent me letters saying they had seen a classified ad in

---

*Vertical Take Off and Landing.

Wallace and Ethel Needham of Bury, Manchester, who helped found the present Old Illustrian's Association. Without their enthusiasm and persistence, the Association would never have been formed

the Manchester Evening News written by a Mrs Alma Bennett of Bangor, Wales asking the whereabouts of Albert Jones who had served as a stoker with her brother, Eric Taylor aboard HMS Illustrious. We immediately wrote to her and the following summer went to visit and spent nearly two weeks with her and her husband John, an ex-Dunkirk survivor.

Alma told us the story about her brother. Eric had died in 1982 in Steubenville, Ohio, the very place we had spent a leave back in 1941. Sadly, his American wife who he must have met unknown to me, although we were together most of the time, had passed away twenty years before in 1962 leaving him with two young sons to bring up alone as he never remarried.

Those years apparently were very trying to Eric, his sister told us. One might even say there was a culture clash. His boys it seems felt a certain embarrassment at their Dad's broad English accent in contrast to their own pronounced American one.

207

Without going into too much detail it can only be imagined there were many difficult times during their teenage years.

Without a doubt he was a good father and worked very hard in the steel mills of Wheeling, West Virginia, eventually becoming a foreman. His gentlemanly attitude and characteristics earned him the respect of his fellow workers who gave him the nickname 'the Duke'.

Unfortunately he was not to enjoy the good life that he worked so hard to build for himself and his family in another land for he succumbed to cancer and passed away in 1982. It had always been his dream to own a brand new car and so in his dying days he bought one, thought he didn't live long enough to even sit in the driver's seat.

After listening to Alma's sad account of Eric's life, we resolved that the next year we would tour part of America and visit Steubenville to re-live that which I had talked about for forty-seven years.

Setting out in August 1988 in our big old navy blue Mercury we drove through the American heartland stopping in places like Minneapolis, Chicago, and Cleveland all the time heading south-east on our 'sentimental journey'. In the state of Indiana we found Eric's eldest son Ronny and his family who, when showing up like a ghost from the past, said he instantly recognized me from his Dad's photos. For me, when I looked at him likewise, I could see my old shipmate in his features.

We only spent a few hours with them but a lot of ground was covered and had a lovely visit. That day we carried on to Ohio. Strangely enough, their address was on Ohio Street.

In a couple of days we reached Steubenville entering the city with a feeling of nostalgia. Looking around for different landmarks, I vaguely remembered some, but much had changed. The night clubs we had frequented and even Bud's old studio were no longer there. Very little remained to remind me of those twelve hilarious days we both spent so many years ago. Nevertheless we found Eric's house and spoke to a lady who had been his next door neighbour. She spoke most kindly of him.

Finally after staying overnight in a local motel, we determined to find his place of burial, though we weren't sure of its location. We made extensive enquiries at all the local cemeteries and eventually found it at the last one, Ft. Steuben cemetery. With the help of the caretaker the site was pinpointed on the

charts at the office. His grave lay alongside that of his wife Marjorie. It was well tended but obviously it had not been visited for some time as there were no flowers on it. As we all looked down at Eric's final resting place I felt we had met after all, but not in circumstances either of us would have wanted. On leaving, Inge remembered we had a small Stars and Stripes flag in the car. She thought it would be fitting if it were placed on his grave as he was an American citizen when he died.

After leaving the Navy, my life and Eric's ran almost a parallel course by emigrating to North America. Having lost contact with each other we had no idea how close we really were and could have enjoyed many reunions together but God and providence would have it that we lived so near and yet so far.

As we close this book we wish to mention that we are about to embark on another trip back to England. Jim Newton will be meeting us at Heathrow Airport and after a short time in London we will be driving up to Manchester for an Old Illustrian's barbeque which is held every July.

Albert Jones receiving the Malta George Cross 50th Anniversary Medal from Mr Victor Sant, Deputy High Commissioner to London from Malta. Kensington Place – London – July 28 1993

The author's wife Inge, co-author and son Michael, and Mr Jim Newton, Old Illustrious shipmate, another ex-stoker. Taken outside the Maltese High Commission, Kensington Place, London – July 28 1993

By a remarkable coincidence we received a phone call this morning informing us that my Malta George Cross Fiftieth Anniversary Medal will be presented to me at the Maltese High Commission in Kensington Place, London. Those surviving veterans of the Siege of Malta from all the Allied countries are eligible. Sadly the many others like Eric and Joe never lived long enough to share in this honour of which they are equally worthy. We will remember them.

Appendix 1

The following description of Illustrious' commissioning and of her Captain, Denis Boyd was taken in part from *Taranto* by Don Newton and A. Cecil Hampshire.

Slimly built and of slightly less than medium height, Captain Denis William Boyd, DSC, was fair-haired and keen-eyed.

A torpedo specialist, he had served with distinction in the First World War in submarines and surface craft earning his decoration for gallantry in the destoyer Fearless.

Between the wars, he had held both staff and technical appointments and had earned an official commendation for making certain improvements to British torpedoes.

In 1931, he was promoted to Captain and served as Commander of destroyer flotillas in the Home and Mediterranean Fleets interrupted by a spell at the Admiralty as Director of the Tactical Division. In 1938 he was appointed Captain of HMS Vernon, the Navy's torpedo school.

Despite this position, he desired an active service job afloat. The Admiralty promised him this in the form of the new aircraft carrier Illustrious.

After the outbreak of war, Hitler's new 'secret weapon', the magnetic mine was posing a grave menace to shipping. This was the same menace which could have sunk Illustrious on the way to Liverpool in January 1940 but was only averted by the minesweeper trawler Thomas Leeds.

One day, the then First Sea Lord, Winston Churchill sent for Boyd and asked him what he knew about magnetic mines. Being in command of the undersea warfare school HMS Vernon, Boyd replied 'Nothing sir. But I have plenty of officers who do'. Churchill then told him he was to come up to the Admiralty and help in the magnetic mine investigation.

Boyd protested that he had been appointed to Illustrious.

Realizing what he had done and that his plans were about to fold up before him, Boyd explained to Churchill that Illustrious would not be ready for sea for three months and if the problem of the magnetic mine was not solved then, it never would be. Churchill thoughtfully conceded and promised Boyd command of Illustrious.

In November 1939, a magnetic mine was recovered at Shoeburyness and stripped down by a team from Vernon to discover its secrets. Counter measures were taken and Boyd was able to depart for his new command.

In January 1940, Capt. Boyd arrived at Barrow to review his new command and get to know his key officers. They were:

Cdr. Gerald Tuck
Lt. Cdr. Herbert Ackworth, Gunnery Officer
Lt. Cdr. Ralph Duckworth, Torpedo Officer
John Tamplin, Commander (E)
Lt. Cdr. Richard Tosswill, Navigating Officer
'Rosie' Baker, the First Lieutenant
'Doc' Keevil, Surgeon Commander
Ian 'Streamline' Robertson, Commander (Flying)
Chaplain Henry Lloyd

Boyd's new command was the fourth Illustrious to bear the name. The first Illustrious was built at Buckler's Hard in 1780. With 74 guns and 1,600 tons she had fought the French in the Mediterranean and was lost by stranding in 1794.

The second Illustrious, also with 74 guns was launched in 1803. Six years later she was present at the attack on the French Fleet in the Basque Roads. This attack was conceived and executed by Lord Cochrane and involved a daring attack on an enemy fleet in a defended harbour at night.

The third Illustrious was built in 1896 and was one of a class of nine battleships. She took part in the First World War but was outdated by the end of the war and was sold for scrap soon after.

This fourth Illustrious being completed at Barrow in 1940 was destined to perform a similar feat to that of the second Illustrious although with much different weapons.

Illustrious was commissioned into the Royal Navy on 16 April, 1940. As part of the ceremony, Capt. Boyd addressed the ship's company on the flight deck;

We commission today one of the finest ships in the Navy.
I hope it will be my privilege to bring her into contact with
the enemy. What happens then depends upon everyone
doing his duty with efficiency and courage. Let us prepare
for this test by enthusiasm, zeal, and keen understanding
and with a sure faith in the justice of our cause let us place
our work and our future in God's hands.

It was small wonder that under the command of such a man
the Illustrious was to live up to her name in no uncertain
manner.

Appendix 2

Aircraft and Crews in the Attack on Taranto

First Wave

Aircraft	Pilot/Observer	Warload	Decoration
L4A	Lt-Cdr K. Williamson	Torpedo	DSO
	Lt N. Scarlett-Streatfield		DSC
L4C	Sub-Lt P. Sparke DSC	Torpedo	Bar to DSC
	Sub-Lt J. Neale		DSC
L4K	Lt N. Kemp	Torpedo	DSC
	Sub-Lt R. A. Bailey		DSC
L4M	Lt I. H. Swayne	Torpedo	MID
	Sub-Lt J. Buscall RNVR		MID
L4R	Sub-Lt A. S. D. Macauley	Torpedo	DSC
	Sub-Lt A. L. O. Wray		DSC
E4F	Lt M. R. Maund	Torpedo	MID
	Sub-Lt W. Bull		MID
L4P	Lt L. J. Kiggell	Flares &	DSC
	Lt H. R. B. Janvrin	Bombs	DSC
L5B	Lt C. Lamb	Flares &	MID
	Lt K. Grieve	Bombs	MID
L4L	Sub-Lt W. C. Sarra	Bombs	MID
	Sub-Lt J. Bowker		MID
E5A	Capt O. Patch RM	Bombs	DSC
	Lt D. Goodwin		DSC
L4H	Sub-Lt A. Forde	Bombs	MID
	Sub-Lt A. Mardel-Ferreira		MID
E5Q	Lt J. Murray	Bombs	MID
	Sub-Lt S. Paine		MID

Second Wave

L5A	Lt-Cdr J. W. Hale	Torpedo	DSO
	Lt G. A. Carline		DSC
L5H	Lt C. S. C. Lea	Torpedo	DSC
	Sub-Lt P. D. Jones		DSC
L5K	Lt F. M. A. Torrens-Spence	Torpedo	DSC
	Lt A. W. F. Sutton		DSC
E4H	Lt G. W. Bayly	Torpedo	MID
	Lt J. H. Slaughter		MID
E5H	Lt T. W. G. Wellham	Torpedo	MID
	Lt P. Humphreys		MID
L5B	Lt R. W. V. Hamilton	Flares &	DSC
	Sub-Lt J. R. Weekes	Bombs	DSC
L4F	Lt R. Skelton	Flares &	MID
	Sub-Lt E. Perkins RNVR	Bombs	MID
L5F	Lt E. W. Clifford	Flares &	DSC
	Lt G. R. M. Going	Bombs	DSC
L5Q	Lt S. Morford	Bombs	MID
	Sub-Lt R. Green		MID

MID – Mentioned in despatches

Appendix 3

Specifications of HMS Illustrious and HMS Rosario

HMS Illustrious (as built)

Displacement:	23,000 tons (standard)
	29,110 tons (full load)
Length:	740 ft
Beam:	95 ft 9 in
Draught:	29 ft
Machinery:	3 sets geared steam turbines, 3 shafts
	110,000 shp – 32 knots
Armour:	3 in flight deck, 4½ in main belt and hangar walls
Armament:	16 4.5 in DP, 48 2-pdr (40-mm), 8 40 mm,
	8 20 mm Oerlikons
Aircraft:	36
Bunkerage:	4,850 tons Petrol Stowage: 50,540 gallons
Range:	11,000 nm at 14 knots
Complement:	1,500 (varies)

HMS Rosario

Displacement:	950/1,000 tons (standard)
	1,250/1,300 tons (full load)
Length:	225 ft
Beam:	35½ ft
Draught:	10¾ ft
Machinery	2-shaft geared turbines, 2,000/2,400 ihp
Speed:	16½ knots
Range:	6,000 miles at 12 knots
Armament:	1 4 in QF Mark V, 4 20 mm Oerlikons,
	4 depth charge throwers, 92 depth charges
Complement:	104 (often more)

Appendix 4

*List of Personnel Killed in Bombing Attack on HMS Illustrious, January 10, 1941**

Alan, J	AB	Hoskins, L. G.	OD
Anstis, W. R.	Gnr	Hughes, E.	Ldg Ck (S)
Barnes, E. C.	Ldg Wtr	Imrie, R.	Ck (O)
Bascombe, S. D.	ERA 3	James, F.	PO Stwd
Bleasdale, C. W.	Ldg Sea	Jones, T. L.	Ldg Sto
Blundy, S. F.	Mne	Kerby, A. J.	PO Stwd
Bray, T.	AB	Luddington W. G. E.	MAA
Briggs, W.	AB	McNeill, R.	AB
Burness, C.	OD	Maltby, A.	AB
Butler, S. E.	PO	Manistry, A. G. E.	Lt RM
Carter, R. E.	LSA	O'Neill, F. J.	Sto 1
Charlton, J. G.	Asst Stwd	Packer, T. J.	AB
Clarke, C	LSA	Parkin, E. H. R.	Ldg Sea
Cockburn, J. R.	OA	Parson, S. J.	OA 4
Cole, H. A. R.	Asst Ck (O)	Pascoe, H.	Ldg Stwd
Cook, H.	Sto PO	Pitts, N. H.	Lt (E)
Crocker, T. W.	RPO	Rice, M.	Ldg Sea
Drew, W. H.	PO Stwd	Rollinson, L.	AB
Duggan, J.	Sto PO	Salter, S. C.	Sto 1
Elford, W.	SBA	Seldon, T. H. G.	Mne
Eubank, M.	AB	Smyth, J.	CPO
Evans, D. W.	Ch Ck (O)	Stephenson, R. L. C.	Sto 1
Featherstone, C. S.	Stwd	Tall, A. E.	AB
Fletcher, E. R.	Sto PO	Taylor, M.	AB
Floyd, A.	Mne	Thomas, J.	SA
Fowell, K. G.	Ldg Wtr	Thomassin, A. L.	OD

French, R. J.	Mne	Todd, E. M.	Sto 1
Goodman, W. B.	OA	Tomlinson, L.	PO
Hadley, J.	Mne	Trenchard, C. W. S.	Sy PO
Hallam, S.	OD	Westmacott, V. T.	PO Ck (O)
Harrison, T.	PO	Whitehead, F.	AB
Hedgecock, K. C.	SA	Whyler, G.	Mne
Henshaw, L.	OD	Williams, G. E.	Sto 1
Horrell, A. H.	Mne	Wilson, P. G.	Mne
Horton, L. H.	Sto 1		

Fleet Air Arm Personnel

Allwright, K. G.	L Airn	Burney, F. W.	AM
Barnes, W L LeC, DSC	Lieut (A)	Bushell, J. D.	PO Airn
Beales, F. D.	Licut (A)	Clifford, E. W., DSO	Lieut
Bennett, T. V.	AF	Cook, R. L.	AM
Broad, A. C.	AM 1	Cray F. T.	L Airn
Donaldson, R.	AM 2	Loudon, H. N.	Sub-Lieut (A)
Dowdles, F.	AM 2	McLeod, D. J.	AF
Finnigan, J.	AF	Mardell-Ferreira, A.	F X Sub-Lieut (A)
Fitzpatrick, H.	L Airn	Marsh, T. R. I.	AM 1
Garton-Stone, D. C.	Lieut (A)	Marshall, J.	Sub-Lieut (A)
Gilson, J. F. X.	AM 1		
Grantham, J. E.	AA 4	Mowbray, H. R.	AM 1
Gregory, P. M.	Lieut	Oaten, T. R.	AM 2
Griffith, A. S., MID	A/Sub-Lt	Perkins, E. A.	Sub-Lieut (A)
Hall J. W.	LAM	Skelton, R. G.	Lieut (A)
Hancock, S. J.	AF	Tallack, N. E.	PO Airn
Hanscombe, A. J.	AM 2	Tapp-Smith, G.	L Airn
Hastie, J. MCC W.	AM 1	Taylor, R. J.	AM 1
Heede, J.	AF	Ward, B. D.	LAF (E)

Kemp, N. MCl, DSC	Lieut	Waterman, I. J. G.	AM 1
Kensett, R. D.	Airn 1	Woan, A. R.	AM 1
Kingswood, R. H.	AM	Wray, A. L. O., DSC	Sub-Lieut (A) RNVR
Kinslow, P. H.	AM 2		
Lane, W. A.	AM 2	Young, J. B.	AM

RAF Personnel Killed Aboard HMS Illustrious January 10, 1941

Behan, W. J. T.	Cpl	Longmore, J. H.	LAC
Ellerington, C.	Cpl	Morris, N. L.	LAC
Goddard, C. J. Z.	LAC	Robinson, F.	Cpl
Harley, F. A.	Cpl	Tyson, H.	F/Sgt
Hough, E.	Cpl	Vignaux, V. R.	F/Sgt
Hyslop, C. D. S.	Sgt	Wilby, J. F.	Cpl
Jarvis, R. E.	Cpl	Willan, J. B.	Cpl
Leach, A. C.	Sgt		

*Complete list of casualties killed in the dive-bombing attack obtained from: Malta, Defiant and Triumphant, Rolls of Honour 1940 – 1943. Edited by Capt. E. A. S. Bailey, CBE, DSC, Royal Navy
Copyright 1992 by E. A. S. Bailey, Somerset.

Glossary

Adrift − AWOL, absent without leave
Aft − Back end of the ship, where the officers usually live
Andrew − Nickname for the Royal Navy. Derived from Lt Andrew
    Miller, a successful press-gang officer of the 18th century.
Ash Can − (American) A depth charge
ATS − Auxiliary Territorial Service, the women's army

Bag Shanty − A brothel
Bangers − Also snorkers, sausages
Barrack Stanchion − One who tries to stay in the barracks to avoid
    sea time
Beach − Shore, land
Bob − Shilling
Bobby − A policeman
Bollicking − A good telling off
Bows − Front end of the ship, the sharp end
Browned off − Fed up
Bubbly − Rum
Bunting Tosser − Signalman
Buzz − Rumour

Catch a Packet − Ship being hit or sunk
Chippies − Shipwrights, carpenters
Chit − A piece of paper with some form of official instruction or
    permission on it, eg. A Draft Chit
Chokka Block − Full up or really fed up
Civvy Street − Civilian life
Clubs − PTI − Physical Training Instructor
Crusher − A member of the Regulating Branch, Navy Police

Defaulters − To be in trouble
Dghaisa − Maltese row boat, water taxi, like the Venetian Gondola

Dhobeying – Doing your laundry
Donkey Boiler – Small auxiliary steam boiler on the jetty when the
    ship is in dock

ERA – Engine Room Articifer

Flakers – Tired out
Flannel – BS, buttering up or story telling
For'ard – Front end of the ship, forward

Gash – Anything disposable, rubbish
Gen – News
Geordie – Someone from Newcastle
Gorge – Term for food, eating
Green Rub – An unfair deal
Grog – Daily rum ration
Guz – Devonport, Plymouth

Harry Flakers – Very tired
Harry Grippo – Someone giving something for free
Heads – Ship's toilets
Hooker – A leading hand

Island – The bridge on a carrier
Ittie – Italian, pronounced eye-tye

Jack mi Hearty – Someone who likes to show off
Jack Stropp – Someone who gets rambunctious, rowdy
Jago's Mansions – Devonport barracks, HMS Drake
Jankers – Being put on punishment, provo
Janner – Someone from the West Country, Devon or Cornwall
Jaunty – Master at Arms, Crusher, head of ship's police
Jock – Someone from Scotland
Jungle Juice – Something intoxicating, usually home brew

Killick – A leading hand
Kip – Sleep
KRs & AIs – King's Regulations and Admiralty Instructions
Kye – Cocoa, comes in solid block form, rock hard

Matelot – A sailor

Midshipman − An officer in training, also called Middy

Midships − Middle part of the ship

NAAFi − Navy, Army, Air Force Institution, equivalent roughtly to the American PX

Nelson's Blood − Pusser's rum

Nuthouse − The Admiralty

Oggin − The sea

OOD − Officer of the Day

Oppo − Shipmate, close friend

Paddy − Someone from Southern Ireland

Pay Bob − Paymaster

Pierhead Jump − Draft with very little warning, hurried departure from the jetty

Port − Left side of the ship when facing forward

Pusser − Being extremely formal and correct, derived from the old Navy's term Purser who was the paymaster and supply officer

Rattle − In trouble

Royals − The Royal Marines

Rubber − A loan

Rum Rat − Someone who will do almost anything for extra rum

Scouse − Someone from Liverpool

Scran − Food

Scran Bag − Kit left lying around is collected and put in the scran bag to be redeemed on payment of a fine, a bar of dhobeying soap

Screw − Ship's propeller

Seen Off − Like a Green Rub, having been cheated

Shower − A group or bunch of people, derogatory

Sippers & Gulpers − payment for a favour out of one's rum ration, this practice was illegal

Skate − Someone always in trouble, a ne'er do well

Smoke − London

Snorkers − Sausages

Sparkers − Wireless Telegraphist

Spliced − To get married or drunk

Splice the Main Brace − Order on a special occasion entitling everyone to an extra tot of rum

Sprog — New sailor

Squeaks, Rushes, and Duff — Types of Navy food eg. Bubble & Squeak is Bangers and Mash. Duffs are a solid pudding, (heavy)

Starboard — Right side of the ship when facing forward

Stern — Back end of the ship, the blunt end

Stone Frigate — Shore establishment

Strangling the Baron — Getting a lot of Harry Grippos

Taffy — Someone from Wales

Taking the Mickey — To make fun of someone, jokingly

Teddy Oggie — Cornish pastie

Ticklers — Navy tinned tobacco for making your own cigarettes

Tiddley — Smark appearance. No. 1 uniform was your Tiddley suit. Tailor made, not issue.

Tiddley Oggie — (also Tiddy) Someone from Devonport

Tiffy — Engine Room Articifer or any articifer.

Tin Fish — Torpedo

Turn to — Report for work, part of ship etc.

Uckers — Jack's version of the board game Ludo with dice and coloured counters

Winger (Wings) — Term originating from WW I referring to an older sailor looking after a younger one eg. being taken under someone's wing

XO — Executive Officer, like the Second in Command

Footnotes

1. Lund, Paul & Ludlam, Harry, *Out Sweeps, the Exploits of Minesweepers in World War Two*, London: New English Library, 1978, p. 24.
2. Poolman, Kenneth, *Illustrious*, London: New English Library, 1974, p. 34.
3. Cunningham, A.B.C., *A Sailor's Odyssey, the Autobiography of Admiral of the Fleet Viscount Cunningham of Hyndhope, KT GCB OM DSO*, London: Hutchinson & Co. Ltd., 1951, p. 263.
4. Newton, Don & Hampshire, A. Cecil, *Taranto*, London: New English Library, 1974, p. 162.
5. Poolman, Kenneth, *Illustrious*, London: New English Library, 1974, p. 60.
6. Ibid, pp. 59 – 60.
7. Cunningham, A.B.C., *A Sailor's Odyssey*, p. 244.
8. Ibid, p. 306.
9. Poolman, Kenneth, *Experiences of War, The British Sailor*, London: Arms & Armour Press, 1989, pp. 67 – 68.

Bibliography

Argyle, Christopher, *Chronology of World War II*, London: Marshall Cavendish, 1980.

Attard, Joseph, *The Battle of Malta*, Middlesex: Hamlyn Paperbacks, 1982.

Bailey, E.A.S., Editor, *Malta, Defiant and Triumphant Rolls of Honour 1940 – 1943*, Bridgwater: E.A.S. Bailey, 1992.

Chesneau, Roger, *Aircraft Carriers of the World, 1914 to the present*, Annapolis: Naval Institute Press, 1984.

Cunningham, A.B.C., *A Sailor's Odyssey, the Autobiography of Admiral of the Fleet Viscount Cunningham of Hyndhope, KT GCB OM DSO*, London: Hutchinson & Co. Ltd., 1951.

Fitzsimons, Bernard, Editor, *Weapons and Warfare*, New York: Purnell & Sons Ltd, 1967.

Fraccaroli, Aldo, *Italian Warships of World War II*, London: Ian Allan, 1968.

Glenton, Bill, *Mutiny in Force X*, London: Hodder & Stoughton, 1986.

Gunston, Bill, *Combat Aircraft*, London: Salamander Books Ltd., 1976.

Harrison, W., *Swordfish at War*, London: Ian Allan, 1987.

Johns, W. E. & Kelly, R. A., *No Surrender*, London: W. H. Allen, 1989.

Jolly, Rick, *Jackspeak, the Pusser's Rum Guide to Royal Navy Slanguage*, Torpoint: Palamando Publishing, 1989.

Lund, Paul & Ludlam, Harry, *Out Sweeps, the Exploits of Minesweepers in World War Two*, London: New English Library, 1978.

Lyn, Vera, *We'll Meet Again, A Personal and Social Memory of World War Two*, London: Sidgwick & Jackson, 1989.

Lyon, Hugh, *Encyclopedia of the World's Warships*, Salamander Books Ltd, 1985.

Newton, Don & Hampshire, A. Cecil, *Taranto*, London: New English Library, 1974.

Poolman, Kenneth, *Experiences of War, The British Sailor*, London: Arms and Armour Press, 1989.

Poolman, Kenneth, *Illustrious*, London: New English Library, 1974.

Poolman, Kenneth, *Kelly*, London: New English Library, 1974.

Popham, Hugh, *Sea Flight*, London: Futura Publications, 1974.

Preston, Antony, *Aircraft Carriers*, London: Bison Books Ltd, 1979.

Preston, Antony, *Great Warships*, London: Bison Books Ltd, 1986.

Preston, Antony, Editor, *History of the Royal Navy in the 20th Century*, London: Bison Books Ltd, 1987.

Robertson, Terence, *Escort Commander*, New York: Bantam Books, 1979.

Roscoe, Theodore, *Pig Boats*, New York: Bantam Books, 1982.

Smith, Peter C., *Battleship Royal Sovereign and Her Sister Ships*, Wellingborough: William Kimber, 1988.

Sturtivant, Ray, *Fleet Air Arm at War*, London: Ian Allen, 1982.

Children's T

By Douglas M. Borland, M.B., (

A COMMON constitutional type in childre
CALCAREA CARBONICA, but sometimes CALCAREA PHOSPHORICA
or CALCAREA SILICATA are more suitable to the individual case. This
leads to a consideration of PHOSPHORUS and SILICEA; it is useful
to know the outstanding characteristics of these remedies and those
that follow on.

In association with the SILICEA types consider also SANICULA and
AETHUSA. A little away from the strict CALCAREA type is the possibility of LYCOPODIUM, and following from that a further possibility
of CAUSTICUM.

Quite apart from the above, it is always wise to consider giving a
dose of TUBERCULINUM when treating children of the first group.

In the second group—BARYTA CARBONICA—the next drug to
consider is BORAX—the same type of child with similar indications.
This leads on to NATRUM MURIATICUM, which in turn raises the
possibility of SEPIA.

This leads on to drugs of "depression", and one of the gold salts
must then be considered, either AURUM METALLICUM or AURUM
MURIATICUM. When dealing with a sluggish mentality or sluggish
make-up there is always the possibility that CARBO VEGETABILIS may
be called for.

The third group—GRAPHITES—lead to the consideration of
CAPSICUM, and if dealing with any skin condition the possibility
that PSORINUM may be called for must be considered. Also, when
dealing with children, where there are definite skin indications
ANTIMONIUM CRUDUM should be thought of and, although it is not
really like the GRAPHITES picture, PETROLEUM should always be
remembered as a possibility.

In the fourth group—PULSATILLA—there are also a number of
possible drugs. After PULSATILLA the first possibility is KALI
SULPHURICUM, and as in every sulphur compound it is necessary to
consider whether the case could be a SULPHUR type.

When the mentality is very similar to that of PULSATILLA one has
to consider THUJA, and as soon as the PULSATILLA/THUJA group is
considered it leads on to SILICEA.

In turn, SILICEA always suggests the possibility of FLUORICUM
ACIDUM. If dealing with hot-blooded patients, think of BROMIUM

1

and IODUM. From IODUM with its emaciation and hunger pass to consideration as to whether ABROTANUM may be called for.

In the fifth and last group—the "nervy" drugs—ARSENICUM ALBUM heads the list with all its terrors. Terrors also suggest STRAMONIUM. Then comes the hypersensitive nervous system type and CHAMOMILLA comes to mind, and then CINA, which is a little more violent.

The strange digestive disturbances of CINA lead to consideration of MAGNESIA CARBONICA. Reverting to the strictly nervy type, one considers the possibility of IGNATIA, and with this nervous, restless, fidgety type there is always the possibility that ZINCUM may be called for.

The foregoing is a brief survey of the various groups and these are now considered in greater detail.

GROUP I

Calcarea carbonica

These children are typically soft, over-fat, fair, chilly, and lethargic. They often look surprisingly fit but, nevertheless, do not possess much energy either mental or physical. In early life they are often very over-weight, and although they appear very healthy when examined one finds soft fat rather than muscle.

There is a tendency to rickets, with enlarged epiphyses, big head, slow closure of fontanelles, and tendency to sweat. The children are chilly, yet they get very hot on the slightest exertion. They sweat at night, and very often will stick the feet outside the bed covers. This characteristic incidentally is not found *only* in relation to SULPHUR.

There are slightly older children of much the same type. They appear fairly healthy, look well-nourished, but are sluggish both mentally and physically. They are slow at school, slow at games, liable to sprain their ankles, have weak muscles, sweat on exertion, and constantly take fresh "colds".

They are liable to have enlarged tonsils, enlarged cervical glands, and rather big bellies. They lack stamina, are easily scared, and lack initiative. They are perfectly content to sit about and do little or nothing. Very often they are peculiarly sensitive, and can't bear to be laughed at.

They are clumsy in their movements and bad at games; this tends to push them back into themselves, so that instead of sticking at it

2

and becoming efficient they throw in their hands and give up the game altogether as they hate being scoffed at or laughed at.

They are just the same about work, very often having difficulty with one or other subject at school. They will not strive at this subject but just give in, and if they are not sure of themselves nothing will ever induce them to answer questions in class in case they are wrong and will be laughed at.

In early childhood these CALCAREA CARBONICA children nearly always tend to have a relative diarrhœa, and usually the stools are pale, apparently lacking bile pigment.

There are two or three outstanding odd characteristics which clinch the CALCAREA CARB. diagnosis. The one that is easiest to tack on to the sluggish mentality and sluggish physical make-up is that these children are much more comfortable when they are constipated and their bowels are inert.

If given an aperient it upsets them; if they have an attack of diarrhœa they are ill, but when their bowels are relatively sluggish they are comfortable.

The next thing that can be added to the sluggish make-up is an aggravation from any physical or mental exertion, or from any kind of rapid movement; these children suffer from car-sickness and train-sickness.

Another characteristic is a very definite dislike of too hot food. They are quite fond of ice-cream; have an aversion from meat and, occasionally, there is a definite craving for eggs—in any form.

There is one other indication for CALCAREA CARB. When the children are below par they become nervous and scared. They are perfectly happy so long as there is somebody about, and they sit peacefully or play; but when it gets dark they are scared to go to bed without a light in the room.

They develop acute nightmares and wake up in the night screaming. A very common type of the CALCAREA CARB. child's nightmare is seeing horrible faces in the dark.

Calcarea phosphorica

If instead of presenting this typical picture the child is beginning to lose some fat, does not flush up so easily, shows hypertrophy of adenoid tissue rather than enlargement of tonsils and cervical glands, has a more adenoid facies; in addition if the child is becoming a little more reserved, a little brighter at school, but with

3

a tendency to headache if overworked and a dislike of being interfered with, then the probability is that the child has passed from CALCAREA CARB. to CALCAREA PHOSPHORICA.

Further if the child is tending to become rather spotty, becoming thinner and beginning to suffer from growing pains, these are additional indications pointing to CALCAREA PHOS.

An important point in this connection is that in the CALCAREA PHOS. child the growing pains are definitely muscular. In a similar type of child, also with growing pains but not so touchy as the CALCAREA PHOS. child and locating the pains in bones, especially in the shin bones, the indication is for MANGANESIUM METALLICUM.

Thus it is apparent that minor differences may suggest fresh possibilities quite outside the CALCAREA group of drugs.

Phosphorus

The child is thinning down, tending to be definitely slight, even a little delicate; is much brighter mentally, more nervy, more excitable. In addition to being afraid in the dark is now sensitive to atmospheric disturbances, afraid of thunder; is anxious, sensitive, developing a definite dislike of being alone, less shy and more capable of expressing himself.

He may flush up on any excitement or after taking hot food, is losing his desire for eggs and is increasingly fond of meat and food with a definite taste, preferably a salty taste; he is still liable to night terrors. This presents the picture of PHOSPHORUS.

He still gets colds, but these do not affect the throat, they go further down with a likelihood of bronchitis supervening. He is very sensitive to sudden changes in temperature. This is an example of the way drugs grade into one another.

Silicea

Then there is another type of child who has fined down slightly; he is still chilly, very much thinner, has not grown nearly as much as the PHOSPHORUS child, is very much paler, and has a fine-textured skin. He has not the coarse curly hair normally associated with the CALCAREA type but rather finer hair, without the reddish glint of the PHOSPHORUS; it is becoming rather sandy.

This child is becoming much more touchy, more difficult, he resents interference and is more inclined to retire into his shell. He

4

is fairly bright mentally, very easily tired out physically; liable to sweat, particularly about the extremities or about the head and neck. Often he has developed a dislike of, or intolerance to milk, and the cervical glands may be enlarged. This is the picture of the typical SILICEA child.

Sanicula

But never think of SILICEA without considering the possibility of SANICULA, for the indications of these two remedies are almost identical. The SANICULA child is perhaps more irritable, and definitely more unstable mentally. Attacks of laughter and tears follow each other much more readily in the SANICULA child and he has much less staying power than the SILICEA type.

The SANICULA child never sticks long at anything; he is more obstinate and more difficult to control. There is likely to be a row if you interfere with the typical SANICULA child. But it is very difficult to distinguish between the SILICEA child and the SANICULA child, the physical symptoms are almost identical, and in most cases of this type, I have given SILICEA in the first instance, and only on failing to get a full response have I gone on to SANICULA.

Aethusa

One considers AETHUSA here because of the notorious susceptibility to milk of the AETHUSA type. Wherever there is a severe aggravation from milk in acute attacks, always consider the possibility that AETHUSA will control these attacks. It is the first drug to think of.

Also, whenever there is a milk aggravation consider the possibility of one of the milk remedies being indicated to control an acute condition, either LAC DEFLORATUM or LAC CANINUM.

Lycopodium

Reverting to the PHOSPHORUS type of child—that is the CALCAREA type that has thinned down into a PHOSPHORUS type. This, in turn, leads to the LYCOPODIUM type.

The child has grown a little, lost weight, become thin but instead of having the fine skin and the unstable circulation of the PHOSPHORUS child, it has become rather sallow. The tendency to sweat easily is disappearing and the skin is getting rather thicker.

These children appear to be very diffident, but it is not quite the shyness of SILICEA. They seem to lack assurance but give the

5

impression that basically they have a fairly good opinion of themselves.

They are liable to digestive upsets, and although they have good appetites and often eat more than the average, they are not putting on weight. The abdomen may be rather enlarged but there are no enlarged palpable mesenteric glands. Instead of the PHOSPHORUS desire for meaty and tasty things, these children are developing a definite desire for sweet things.

Instead of the CALCAREA desire for ice-cream, they prefer hot food. Very like the CALCAREA types they get headaches from over-work at school, and it is a dull type of headache. They are still chilly but much more sensitive to stuffiness than any of the types we have yet considered. This is the picture of the LYCOPODIUM type developing.

Causticum

Another drug which is not nearly sufficiently used in the treat-ment of children and which is a counterpart of LYCOPODIUM, is CAUSTICUM. These children are not unlike the LYCOPODIUM types but are a little more sallow.

The CAUSTICUM type of child is definitely more sensitive than LYCOPODIUM types. They are not sensitive to pain but are par-ticularly sensitive to any emotional disturbance. Often these children will cry because they think you are hurting another child. It is the idea of pain which affects them rather than the actual pain to themselves, and they often stand pain quite well, but cannot bear to see another child crying.

They have much the same sort of clumsiness as the CALCAREA children; are rather unhandy, and are liable to strain muscles, whereas the CALCAREA children sprain ankles. They are inclined to suffer from rheumatism and liable to get acute muscular rheumatism, particularly from exposure. These CAUSTICUM children often suffer from acute torticollis or an acute facial palsy after exposure to an icy wind.

Associated with this tendency to torticollis and facial palsy, the CAUSTICUM children get very definite growing pains which are usually accompanied by stiffness in or about the joints—a feeling as if their joints were tight. And linking up with the rheumatic tendency, the CAUSTICUM child when overworked or nervously distressed, is very likely to develop choreic symptoms, and the outstanding feature of the CAUSTICUM chorea is that the jerking persists during sleep.

The main distinguishing feature between the CAUSTICUM children and the LYCOPODIUM type is that CAUSTICUM children have a definite aversion from sweets whereas the LYCOPODIUM children desire them.

Two other points would confirm the CAUSTICUM diagnosis. The first is that the rheumatic troubles of the CAUSTICUM child are very much better in damp weather; and the second is that a CAUSTICUM child with any digestive upset tends to develop acute thirst after meals.

Two additional points which are sometimes useful—CAUSTICUM children often develop endless warts; they also have a very marked tendency to nocturnal enuresis.

Family History of Tuberculosis

Wherever there is a definite family history of tuberculosis, no matter which drug is indicated, the child will at some time be helped by a dose of TUBERCULINUM and my practice is to give one dose about once in twelve months. An article in an American journal recommended giving two doses of 1m, two of 10m, two of 50m, and two of Cm, on four successive days. It was maintained that this gave better results and can produce a practical immunity to tuberculosis in a child of tuberculous parents.

There is another point in which the treatment of children appears to differ from that of ordinary practice, and it applies particularly to the treatment of the CALCAREA CARBONICA type of child. Time can be lost by following the rule of never repeating the medicine so long as improvement is maintained.

Originally I would give one dose of CALC. CARB. 10m and, providing the child went ahead slowly but steadily with no lessening in its improvement, I could find no reason to repeat the medicine for six months or more.

But the average young child, free from acute illness, will tend to improve even if it has no medicine at all, and the constitutional drug ought to increase the rate of that improvement. I therefore started repeating CALC. CARB. at much more frequent intervals whenever the child was not jumping ahead, and in many of these CALC. CARB. cases improvement can be speeded up by more frequent repetition of the medicine.

It is quite a different matter in the case of an adult.

7

GROUP II

Baryta carbonica

The second group are all very much of the same type; they all apply more or less to the backward child, either a case of delayed development, or a definite mental defective. The outstanding drug in this group is BARYTA CARBONICA, which is more typical of the backward child than any other drug in our *Materia Medica*.

The characteristics of the BARYTA CARB. child are very definite; it is a dwarfish child, dwarfish mentally and physically. I have never seen a BARYTA CARB. child who was up to standard height, but they may be up to standard weight. The next glaring characteristic is that the BARYTA CARB. child is always an excessively shy child.

That shy characteristic covers quite a lot of the BARYTA CARB. child. It is nervous of strangers; scared of being left alone; very often it is terrified of going out of doors; a town-bred child going to the country is terrified in the open fields. They often get night terrors, without any clear idea of what the terror is; and they always have a fear of people.

Another characteristic linked with that fear of people is that the BARYTA CARB. children are always touchy; they do not like being interfered with; they are very easily irritated. The next thing is that throughout their lives they have been late in everything—late in speaking, late in walking, late in dentition, slow in gaining weight.

Another marked feature is an exaggeration of the normal child's forgetfulness. Every child is forgetful, every child is inattentive, but in the BARYTA CARB. child this is very much exaggerated. If they are playing they never stick to it for any length of time, they pick up a toy, play with it, and drop it; you may hold their attention for a minute or two, then they turn round and look at the nurse or mother or whoever happens to be there.

They pick up a thing from your desk and fumble with it for a minute or two, and the next moment they are playing with the handle of a drawer. It is that lack of concentration that is the outstanding characteristic.

As they get older the same report comes from school—the child is inattentive, never concentrates on a lesson, appears to learn something today and has completely forgotten it tomorrow. The mother would teach the child its alphabet a dozen times over, and ten minutes after it knew it, it would be allowed to go out and play and half an hour later it was all forgotten.

Another thing is that they are very easily tired out; any attempt at sustained effort exhausts them. When they are young they become cross and irritable, as they get older any sustained effort brings on

8

very troublesome headaches—usually a frontal headache with a feeling as if the forehead were bulging and sitting right down over the eyes, and it is an awful effort for them to keep the eyes open.

The next point about them—and it is pretty constant to all the BARYTA CARB. children—is that they are very liable to get colds, and their colds are characteristic. They always start as a sore throat, and most BARYTA CARB. children have hypertrophied tonsils.

To the hypertrophy of their tonsils can be linked the other glandular tissues; the BARYTA CARB. child very probably has enlarged cervical glands, possibly enlarged abdominal glands. With the enlarged abdominal glands is linked the fact that the child stands badly, there is often marked lordosis and a very prominent abdomen.

With the abdominal condition is the symptom that the BARYTA CARB. child is usually worse after eating—more inattentive, more irritable, more touchy, and very often more tired after eating.

The next thing about them—linked with the tonsillar hypertrophy —is that if they get enlarged tonsils and get cold they are very liable to develop a quinsy. Here is a tip that is worth remembering. To a typical BARYTA CARB. child with an acute tonsillitis it is wiser to give a dose of BARYTA MURIATICA rather than BARYTA CARB. during the acute phase; and very often they will need an intercurrent dose of PSORINUM after the BARYTA MUR. before reverting to BARYTA CARB.

It is quite easy to tack on the PSORINUM to the BARYTA CARB. because many of these children tend to get a crusty skin eruption on the head and crusty margins to the eyelids, they may have a definite blepharitis, and most BARYTA CARB. children are worse from washing—all of which are definite PSORINUM symptoms also.

They are very liable to get intensely irritable skin eruptions, often without much eruption but with intense irritation, and that again is liable to be worse after they have been bathed.

As would be expected with that type of child with low physique, they are chilly, and if they are exposed to cold their tonsils become affected. One other feature of the BARYTA CARB. children is a marked tendency to salivation; dribbling is a common characteristic of mentally defective children.

Above are the keynotes to the "mentally defective" group of drugs, and of these BARYTA CARB. is by far the most commonly indicated. Following that come the other drugs mentioned previously starting with BORAX.

Borax

The feature that makes one consider whether a child is a BARYTA CARB. or BORAX type is the manner in which the child is frightened.

9

They are both scared children and they are very often quite similar to look at, but whereas in the BARYTA CARB. child anything strange in its surroundings scares it, in the BORAX child it is any sudden noise in its vicinity which simply terrifies it.

The tendency to salivation and dribbling is equally marked in BORAX, but in the majority of BORAX children one is dealing with a definite stomatitis, and associated with the salivation there are white spots on the tongue, pearly spots round the margins of the tongue, spots on the lips and on the inside of the cheeks.

There is a very similar history in regard to night terrors in the BORAX child, but there is usually an exciting cause in these cases; the child has been doing too much during the day, or has been over-excited in the evening, and then it is almost sure to have a marked night terror.

With the BORAX child there is not the same degree of inability to learn. The child is simply idle. If he would give his heart to it he could learn, but he is just idle. These children never settle to anything, and even at play they do not persevere but get bored and change from one thing to another.

Another thing that distinguishes them from BARYTA CARB. types is that BORAX children are much more irritable, and their irritability does not end up in weeping as it very often does in BARYTA CARB., but it ends up in a violent passion—the child kicks and screams.

The next point which distinguishes the BORAX child from the BARYTA CARB. child is that the BARYTA CARB. child tends to get a generalised skin eruption, or a very definite crusty eruption on the scalp, but the BORAX child is much more likely to get herpetic eruptions—very often herpetic spots about the lips, or a generalised rash of small herpetic spots on the body.

BORAX cases are also more liable to get acute digestive upsets than BARYTA CARB. types which have the typical chronic constipation, the hard stool. BORAX is liable to sudden attacks of diarrhœa and vomiting. Another characteristic of BORAX which distinguishes it from BARYTA CARB. is the peculiar BORAX sensitiveness to fruit, with violent colic after eating fruit—colic followed by diarrhœa.

Associated with the tendency to inflammation of the mucous membranes, acute stomatitis etc., it is very common in BORAX children to find either enuresis or pain on micturition; pain on micturition is much more common, and very often it is without any definite urinary infection.

Another thing that distinguishes the BORAX and the BARYTA CARB. child when a little older is that the BARYTA CARB. child gets depressing frontal headache from over-study; whereas the BORAX child tends to become sick, and tends to get definite nausea from intense concentration.

Then there is the final clinching point in connection with the BORAX child, and that is the notorious BORAX aggravation from downward motion.

BARYTA CARB. children often get train-sick or car-sick; BORAX children will get train-sick and car-sick too, but BORAX children have a peculiar terror of downward motion, and it is that terror much more than the actual feeling of discomfort which is the characteristic of the BORAX children.

It occurs in numerous circumstances; the typical pointer is the child who screams every time it is laid down in bed if the nurse does not lower it very gently; but it is equally marked in older children who scream on going down in a lift. It is the peculiar terror, rather than the physical discomfort, which distinguishes BORAX from any other drug.

One useful practical tip is in connection with air-sickness. There are various drugs for train-sickness and sea-sickness but BORAX acts in the majority of cases of air-sickness, because it is the sudden dip which upsets most people, and particularly the terror of falling. Air-sickness has been completely overcome by three or four doses of BORAX before travelling by air.

BORAX is like BARYTA CARB. in being sensitive to cold, but it has much more sensitiveness to damp than BARYTA CARB.

BORAX is one of the sodium salts, and immediately one considers the sodium salts one thinks of the possibility of the others, and by far the most commonly indicated of these is NATRUM MURIATICUM.

Natrum muriaticum

In children the majority of NATRUM MUR. cases are rather under-sized and underweight. At first sight they are a little difficult to distinguish from the BARYTA CARB. child with its shyness, because the NATRUM MUR. child appears to have a very definite dislike of being handled; it has a very definite dislike of being interfered with and is liable to burst into tears, which is not unlike the shy terrified reaction of a BARYTA CARB. child.

But on closer investigation the reaction is quite different. It is not shyness in the NATRUM MUR., it is much more a resentment at being interfered with. The NATRUM MUR. child cries, but cries much more from rage than from terror. You can very often stop the NATRUM MUR. child's crying if you are sufficiently firm; but try to soothe it and it gets worse.

11

A NATRUM MUR. child will be nearly in convulsions with screaming when its mother tries to soothe it, whereas as soon as left alone it will settle down and sit in a corner and watch you. The BARYTA CARB. will sit in a corner and play with anything within reach—it has an entirely different mentality.

Another thing which distinguishes NATRUM MUR. from BARYTA CARB. is that though they both tend to be awkward in their movements, the BARYTA CARB. child is awkward because of inco-ordination, it is clumsy, but the NATRUM MUR. child knocks things over because it is in too big a hurry.

There will be a history of delayed development in the NATRUM MUR. child, particularly that the child was slow in learning to speak. It may also have been slow in starting to walk but that is not nearly so constant. Often the NATRUM MUR. child's speech is faulty, but it is much more a difficulty in articulation than a lack of mentality as in the BARYTA CARB. child.

The next characteristic of the NATRUM MUR. child is that it is probably small and underweight. In contrast to BARYTA CARB. where there are a mass of enlarged cervical glands, the typical NATRUM MUR. child may have very small shotty enlarged cervical glands in a thin neck. The BARYTA CARB. types have a chain of quite large glands running down the anterior border of the sterno mastoid; the NATRUM MUR. children have small shotty glands at the back of the neck and the neck itself is rather skinny.

The NATRUM MUR. child does not tend to run to the same degree of crusty skin eruptions as the BARYTA CARB. child. NATRUM MUR. cases get an eruption restricted to the margin of the hair, rather than spreading over the whole scalp.

There is not the same tendency to salivation in the NATRUM MUR. child and instead of the small patches found in a BORAX mouth, in NATRUM MUR. the tongue is sensitive and is red in places and white in places, not with the little white vesicles of BORAX types but with the irregular mapping which is associated with NATRUM MUR. either in children or in adults.

As the NATRUM MUR. children grow older, they develop school headaches; when under pressure, working too hard, attempting to concentrate too much, they get headaches. The headaches are almost identical with the BARYTA CARB. headaches; they are frontal headaches, with the same feeling of pressure down over the eyes, and they are brought on by intense effort—particularly mental effort.

The temperature reactions in NATRUM MUR. are definitely different from those of BARYTA CARB. In NATRUM MUR. often the child is chilly, sensitive to draughts, will shiver from a change of temperature, and will start sneezing from a change of temperature; but he is very sensitive to heat—stuffiness particularly—and to exposure to the sun, and is very liable to develop a sun headache.

The majority of these NATRUM MUR. children have a definite salt craving. It is most unexpected that children should have the excessive desire for salt recorded in the *Materia Medica*. But in practice one meets case after case in which there is a very definite salt craving in these children—they will steal salt as other children would steal sugar.

Another thing to look for in children needing NATRUM MUR. is a very marked tendency to develop hang-nails, splits up the side of the nails which are extremely sensitive, very painful, and very difficult to heal. It is a small point, but it is quite useful in practice.

A distinguishing point is the appearance of the skin. Typical BARYTA CARB. children usually have very little colour, they are sallow, rather earthy looking. BORAX children often have considerably more colour in the cheeks, the skin is a little more yellow, not quite so earthy looking and a shade more inelastic, thick and greasy.

NATRUM MUR. children probably are a little darker still, they flush a little more easily, they perspire a little more easily, and there is a slight increase of the greasy appearance.

Sepia

When considering skins the next possibility is SEPIA, which has the same kind of sallow greasy skin; and SEPIA is a drug which is far too much neglected in the treatment of children.

The outstanding feature of SEPIA children is their negative attitude to everything. They tend to be depressed, moody, indolent, disinclined for work, and not even interested in their play. If pushed they are liable to sulk or weep.

They are usually nervy children, scared of being alone, very often afraid of the dark, and yet they dislike being handled. Very often they have a definite dislike of going to parties, and there is a point which is sometimes confused with BARYTA CARB., a dislike of playing with other children.

It is the thing that later develops into the typical SEPIA dislike of meeting friends, and is often confused with the BARYTA CARB. dislike of people altogether, but mostly it is pure indolence in the SEPIA children, and once they get to a party they are perfectly happy.

The next point is that these SEPIA children, although so lazy and indolent, are definitely greedy, and SEPIA should always be considered for a definitely greedy child. Another thing common to

SEPIA children is that although they loathe to go to a party, when they get there and start dancing they wake up at once and are perfectly happy. It is astonishing the effect of dancing on SEPIA children. The heaviest, dullest child when dancing at a party will become an entirely different being, will suddenly come alive. It is a useful tip and the parents may give it when asked.

Another odd symptom which appears occasionally in children and is a definite SEPIA lead is that these slow-developing children very often acquire the habit of head-nodding. When faced with a head-nodding child always think of the possibility of SEPIA, do not dash off at once to one of the typical chorea drugs.

Various other points are fairly common in the SEPIA children. For instance, they are nearly always constipated, and associated with this is usually a tendency to enuresis. And one thing which is very constant in SEPIA children is that the enuresis takes place early in the night.

Usually if these SEPIA children are lifted about 10 p.m. they remain dry the rest of the night; it is in their first sleep that they lose control.

At a later age, in the sallow, dull, greedy, locked-up child, there is a history that she is developing fainting attacks, and these are induced by standing, or by taking up any fixed position in a close atmosphere—standing in school, standing in church, kneeling in church—the SEPIA child is very often liable to faint.

All these children—like all SEPIA patients—are sensitive to cold. Children are particularly sensitive to weather changes, and the typical SEPIA child will develop a cold from change in the weather apparently without any contact with infection.

Another useful lead towards SEPIA in children is that they are very often upset by milk. If a SEPIA child gets a digestive upset and is put on a milk diet he will certainly become constipated.

Associated with their sallow, greasy skin, SEPIA children tend to sweat profusely, and are liable to develop very itchy skins without much sign of an eruption and without much comfort from scratching.

Aurum metallicum

With this sallow, dispirited, sluggish type of child, with that depressed, negative attitude, one should always consider the possibility of gold, AURUM METALLICUM, or one of the gold salts. The typical AURUM child is always an undeveloped child. It is not so much a question of undersize and underweight as that it simply does not grow up.

The typical AURUM child of 5 years of age is probably about the level of a 3-year-old. The majority of cases needing AURUM are

14

boys, and in the majority of these cases there has been some failure of development—an undescended testicle, a very poorly-developed scrotum, something which indicated that the child was slow in developing even if developing satisfactorily. It is the type of symptom for which one might consider BARYTA CARB.

AURUM children always give the impression of being lifeless. They are always low spirited, rather miserable, lifeless, and they are absolutely lacking in go. They have no initiative at all and give the impression of finding everything a frightful effort.

The report from school is that they are backward and that they have very, very poor memories. One of the odd things about them is that, in spite of being dull, depressed, miserable, lifeless sort of creatures they do respond to contradiction; the child has no go in him and he makes some statement which is contradicted and he flies into an absolute rage; it is the one thing that stirs them up.

Another constant factor which is rather surprising in this type of child despite the impression of being sluggish, is that they have a weird hyperæsthesia to pain, they are terrified of it and extremely sensitive to it. And, in spite of their sluggishness, they are very sensitive to noise and have a very acute sense of taste and smell.

They are liable to very persistent, very troublesome catarrh. They have very definitely infected hypertrophied tonsils, practically always with a lot of offensive secretion in the tonsillar crypts. They get hypertrophied adenoids, again with very offensive nasal discharge; with this they get attacks of acute otitis with perforation of the drum, and very often a stinking, purulent ear discharge.

If they are forced to exert themselves they very easily get out of breath and may get suffocative attacks with acute difficulty in breathing, without any obvious physical cause.

Another odd characteristic of the AURUM children is that they are frightfully sensitive to any disappointment; they will grieve over it for days, quite out of all proportion to the normal child's reaction. And associated with that is the other typical AURUM symptom that the child sobs in his sleep without waking up, and apparently without having been distressed the night before.

Carbo vegetabilis

A drug which also has a very definitely sluggish condition and is sometimes a little like AURUM is CARBO VEGETABILIS, although the cause is entirely different.

CARBO VEG. children are definitely sluggish but it is more a physical than mental sluggishness and results from physical stagnation, not from any lack of brain capacity.

15

They are slow in thinking; they are dull mentally; they have a slow reaction time; and they are lacking in go of any kind. They are very easily discouraged, rather dispirited and miserable sort of children, and if they are pushed they become peevish, but it is a futile sort of peevishness without much bite in it.

Associated with the general mental sluggishness, there is always sluggishness of circulation. They are very often heavy, sallow complexioned children, and they have bluish extremities—bluish fingers, bluish toes, and the extremities are always cold.

The next thing about them is that if they are pressed at all at school, made to work, they are almost certain to develop a dull, occipital headache. They may get the same kind of headache from wearing a tight hat. With these dull, occipital headaches there is complete inability to work, to concentrate, almost to think.

Often the child has been pushed at school, is developing headaches, seems dead tired in the evening, and gets the most violent nightmares, so much so that the child is almost terrified to go to bed, particularly in the dark.

In these nightmares they see ghosts, faces, all sorts of terrifying spectres. These cold, sluggish children get very hot and sweaty at night, particularly the extremities, but it is mainly general, and the CARBO VEG. children usually have a sour-smelling sweat.

Another thing linked with the CARBO VEG. sluggishness of circulation is that they very easily get a pretty persistent epistaxis; very often these children have a severe epistaxis in the night.

Another symptom associated with the general sluggishness is constipation. They mostly have digestive difficulties and tend to have big bellies; they get a lot of flatulence. In spite of being constipated they very easily get attacks of diarrhœa—a very offensive, watery diarrhœa—and then they return to their constipated state again.

With these digestive difficulties they have marked likes and dislikes of food. They like sweet things—which often upset them—and they like to have their appetite stimulated with something tasty, so they like salt things. With their general sluggish digestion they are upset by fat things, rich food of any kind; very often they develop a definite aversion to fats, and frequently have a marked aversion to milk.

A fairly constant feature of all these CARBO VEG. children is that they are not primarily CARBO VEG. children; this condition has developed as the result of some preceding illness, sometimes it is a case of measles; sometimes an illness like bronchitis or pneumonia very often influenzal in origin, and it often dates from an attack of whooping cough.

GROUP III

Graphites

The third group is headed by GRAPHITES. This group is associated with children who have definite skin eruptions. Almost any of the other drugs already mentioned may be required for skin eruptions, for instance, CARBO VEG. children have a very obstinate eczema of the scalp, CALCAREA children have eczema of the scalp, CAUSTICUM children have a lot of skin eruptions.

There may also be a very obstinate eczema of the scalp with SEPIA indications. But the GRAPHITES group is the one to think of when a child has a definite skin history. There is a tendency when treating children with an irritan skin to give a dose of SULPHUR, and there have been many cases where that dose of SULPHUR has done harm and I am chary of starting with SULPHUR in these children with skin trouble.

The typical GRAPHITES child is fat and heavy. It is usually pale, always chilly, and nearly always constipated. In the majority of instances with obstinate constipation in a small child the abdomen is enlarged, a factor so constant that one does not stress it.

GRAPHITES children are always timid. They are rather miserable, and have a complete lack of assurance. The slightly older children hesitate over what they are going to reply to any questions put to them; the school report states that they are indefinite—there is the same hesitation here; and most of these GRAPHITES children are lazy; they have an aversion to work.

There is a queer contradiction in the GRAPHITES children. With the uncertainty and hesitation, laziness and general physical sluggishness, there is always an element of anxiety in the children. They always tend to look on the hopeless side of things; if they are going to a new school, they dread it. They are always looking for trouble.

The next thing about the GRAPHITES children is that, associated with their pallor, under any stress at all they flush up—they have a definitely unstable circulation. And under stress, when they are excited, with this flushing up there is a tendency to troublesome but not very profuse epistaxis, which comes on under excitement—that is the diagnostic point.

A constant feature of the GRAPHITES children, which at once distinguishes them from the CALCAREA children who look not unlike them, is that instead of the soft, sweaty CALCAREA skin, they have a harsh dry skin which tends to crack, particularly on exposure to cold. If these GRAPHITES children have been playing in water in cold weather they come in with their hands chapped and bleeding.

17

Associated with the dry harsh skin, are the GRAPHITES skin eruptions, and the type of eruption is constant no matter where it is. Cracked fingers which tend to bleed also ooze a sticky thick yellow serous discharge.

The same kind of condition arises in any of the folds in GRAPHITES types, the back of the ear, canthus of the eye, angles of the mouth, the groins, bends of the elbows, round the wrists, and particularly about the anus; in this site are found deep, painful fissures oozing a thin, sticky, yellowish discharge.

As the discharge dries it forms thick crusts which pile up as secretion of matter continues beneath; and the crusts come off to reveal the same kind of gluey yellowish discharge, very often streaked with blood.

In my experience children suffering from asthma who have a history of skin troubles are not helped by GRAPHITES. These cases of suppressed skin troubles which develop asthma are extremely difficult and I have found that GRAPHITES fails altogether. Many other remedies have been successful such as PSORINUM, ANTIMONIUM CRUDUM, NATRUM MUR., SULPHUR. THUJA has helped quite frequently, and with no other lead it would be wise to start with THUJA.

That can be linked to one or two other typical GRAPHITES symptoms in children. They are liable to get a very persistent purulent nasal discharge, a chronic otitis with a perforation of the drum, and again the same kind of yellowish excoriating discharge, with an irritating eczema of the external ear whenever the discharge runs over.

Associated with the purulent nasal discharge, many of these GRAPHITES children have marked hypertrophy of the tonsils, with offensive secretion in them, and as a result they often complain of difficulty in swallowing.

They often suffer with a chronic blepharitis and their lids are completely stuck in the morning with the same sort of gluey discharge; dried discharge adheres to the edges of the lids.

In spite of apparent fatness, they are flabby, and there is general muscular weakness. They are very easily exhausted; are sensitive to motion of any kind; and stand travelling very badly. There is a history of rheumatic pains, particularly affecting the neck and the lower extremities.

There is another GRAPHITES symptom which is sometimes useful in these flabby children—they are liable to attacks of abdominal cramp; this is not surprising in view of their constipated state. But in these GRAPHITES cramps the abdominal pains are relieved by giving the child hot milk to drink.

In the majority of cases, with the constipated stool they pass a quantity of mucus—stringy, adherent mucus. It links up with the type of discharge from the skin surfaces, although it is not commonly yellow.

Another useful symptom, which is common, is that these GRAPHITES children have big appetites; they are hungry children and are upset if they go long without food; they are better for eating. But in spite of their fatness and flabbiness, there is often a surprising and very marked aversion to sweets.

In typical GRAPHITES adolescents it is still more surprising, because there is the same flabby, fat, soft adolescent with, instead of the ordinary cracks behind the ear or cracks at the corners of the mouth, they have an acute acne. and one of the questions to ask is whether they eat many sweets, and if it is a GRAPHITES case the reply is that they cannot stand them at all, which is sometimes a very useful tip.

Another point about the appetite in the young children, is that they have a definite dislike of fish. Fish is a normal constituent of a young child's diet, and it is easy to find out if they dislike it. Most of these GRAPHITES children do have a very definite dislike of fish.

Where considering children with chronic otitis, chronic discharge with an old perforation, possibly with eczema of the external ear, another drug which must be considered is CAPSICUM.

Capsicum

The typical CAPSICUM child is again a fat, rather lazy, somewhat obstinate child who is very definitely clumsy in his movements—I have never seen a neat CAPSICUM child. Mostly they have rather reddish cheeks, but that is not constant; they may be pale and flush up much like the GRAPHITES child.

They tend to be very forgetful. They will be sent on an errand, and will come back without what they have been sent to get. It is partly lack of attention. They are always touchy, easily offended, easily irritated.

An odd feature in CAPSICUM children is a strange dislike of being away from home. I think it is partly their feeling that they are not appreciated, partly their touchiness, and partly laziness—they have to make an effort if they are away from home, they have to be more or less agreeable and at home they are very often quite unpleasant.

The CAPSICUM children are always rather dull; they are slow at learning in school, and their memories are poor.

These children tend to have local hyperæmias. In a typical CAPSICUM child with a mild earache the whole external ear is bright

19

crimson. A CAPSICUM child with rheumatism has usually one or other joint affected, with a localised blush over the affected area.

A CAPSICUM child with a cold gets very enlarged tonsils which are very hyperæmic—bright crimson—and the child complains of a burning heat in the mouth with intense thirst.

An odd symptom sometimes met with in these children with sore throats running a fairly high temperature, is that the child is very flushed, cross, sleepless and thirsty; wants cold drinks, and yet shivers after taking a cold drink. This has been seen repeatedly in a child who has a sore throat and is going on to definite mastoid symptoms.

Where there is mastoid involvement in a CAPSICUM case—and it is probably the most commonly indicated drug for mastoiditis—there is always a marked tenderness over the mastoid process, and a blush on the skin surface long before there is fully developed mastoiditis.

One of the nuisances of these mastoid cases is that they usually blow up at night, the child becomes extremely irritable, sleepless, worried, the mother can do nothing with it; it is as obstinate as a mule; she sends for you, and you have to examine it by artificial light and cannot see the blush.

Time and again I have seen these CAPSICUM children at night and could not make out the blush at all, but next morning in daylight it was perfectly obvious.

Associated with the tenderness over the mastoid area is the general hyperæsthesia of the CAPSICUM case; they are sensitive to noise, sensitive to touch, and they have a hyperæsthesia to taste.

In the majority of these children with acute illnesses there is some degree of urinary irritation. It may be an acute cystitis with acute burning pain, intense, irritable pain on passing urine, and it is always of the same burning character. But even without the acute cystitis, in the majority of acute illnesses, there is some urinary irritation, and it is always of a smarting nature.

In a child of this type, clumsy, rather red cheeked, rather sluggish, backward, with a chronic hoarseness and a history of having had acute sore throats—not quinsies, just acutely inflamed throats—very often with transitory attacks of earache, not going on to mastoid involvement, the majority of these cases will need CAPSICUM. The next of the skin drugs in children is PSORINUM.

Psorinum

PSORINUM children are fairly common. The majority tend to be thin rather than fat. They are always sickly children; have very

20

little stamina; are easily exhausted by any effort, physical or mental; very liable to become mentally confused under stress. They are rather dispirited, hopeless youngsters, and, like all children when they are out of sorts, they become peevish and irritable.

They are unhealthy looking; they look dirty and unwashed. A PSORINUM child is hardly ever without a pustule of some sort somewhere about the body. The skin in the child is very rough, and dry. In the adolescent PSORINUM case it is much more commonly greasy. But whether in the child or the adolescent, on exertion PSORINUM youngsters tend to sweat and they are always unhealthy, and smelly.

The skin condition of PSORINUM is not unlike the GRAPHITES skin. There is a tendency for fissures to develop about the hands and in the folds, but there is not the honey-like discharge of GRAPHITES. The discharge is watery or purulent, and it is always offensive.

In all PSORINUM skin conditions there is intense irritation. Many of these children suffer utter torture because they are intensely chilly, feel the cold very badly and are upset by it, but they have an intensely itchy skin and are driven nearly crazy by wearing woollen clothes.

With this dirty-looking grey, rough skin, PSORINUM children are upset by washing, which greatly increases the irritation of their skin.

Most PSORINUM children, in spite of their thinness, have abnormal appetites; one of the constants of PSORINUM children is that any lack of food brings on a violent headache, very often a definite sick headache.

In a typical PSORINUM child with a skin condition the skin irritation is intense, and the child scratches its face until it bleeds. Between the scratches is an unhealthy pustular eruption, very often associated with a generalised blepharitis.

In the acute condition it resembles the GRAPHITES type, but it is much more intense than GRAPHITES, often with the eyelids slightly everted looking almost like raw beef. The child scratches all over the body, and again there is the same purulent condition.

There is the same type of eruption on the scalp, and PSORINUM children are never at peace, always rubbing their heads against the pillow. There is also a yellow, purulent nasal discharge, excoriating the upper lip, and often a purulent foul-smelling otorrhœa.

This is the intensely irritant skin condition which only PSORINUM will cover, and for which one may be tempted to give all sorts of other things.

For hay fever, associated with the typical nasal discharge, PSORINUM is much the most commonly curative drug, given in the

21

interval. There is a very similar hyperæsthesia in the mucous membrane to that on the surface in PSORINUM children, and a dose in the spring will wipe out hay fever of long standing. It does not help in the acute condition, but a dose given in the spring, before the hay fever season starts, can stop hay fever altogether. PSORINUM has a spring aggravation.

There are two more common drugs to consider for skin eruptions. Firstly, ANTIMONIUM CRUDUM and then PETROLEUM, as the ANTIMONIUM CRUD. children with skin eruptions have the same marked aggravation from washing as the PSORINUM cases.

Antimonium Crudum

ANTIMONIUM CRUDUM children are very interesting. They are always fat, rather over-weight, usually pale, and they have a very marked tendency to redness round the eyes, and moist eruptions behind the ears.

Mentally they are interesting because they are such an apparent contradiction. They are irritable children, peevish, and they get more and more peevish the more attention they get—the kind of child that will cry if anyone looks at it and the more you attempt to soothe it the worse it gets.

The ANTIM. CRUD. child has night terrors, and is cross and irritable; and the more the mother attempts to nurse it the worse it becomes. Walking it up and down drives it nearly distracted.

Then, in contrast to that, they are very impressionable children, sensitive, easily upset emotionally, very liable to burst into tears from any emotional stress if their feelings are touched at all; and under stress they become pale and liable to faint.

ANTIM. CRUD. children with skin eruptions tend to get very large, crusty, smelly eruptions—the typical crusty impetigo seen on a child's face. More cases of impetigo in children clear on ANTIM. CRUD. than on any other drug in the *Materia Medica*. In adults also, nine out of ten cases of acute impetigo clear on ANTIM. CRUD.

All their skin eruptions are very much worse from the application of water in any form, and become very inflamed and painful from exposure to radiant heat.

ANTIM. CRUD. children are very clumsy, and very jerky in their movements and may have an actual chorea.

They suffer from warts on their fingers, either one or two small ones, or masses of warts which are usually flat and not very painful. Associated with the warty condition, most of these ANTIM. CRUD. children tend to have rather deformed nails—thickened and unhealthy looking.

22

Two other constant points about the ANTIM. CRUD. children. Firstly they are very liable to get digestive upsets from any acids, sour fruits, or sour drinks. Secondly they have a soft, flabby, coated tongue, usually with a white coating. It is like a MERCURIUS tongue with a white coating.

The outstanding points of ANTIM. CRUD. are not unlike PETROLEUM as far as the skin conditions are concerned.

Petroleum

But the majority of children with indications for PETROLEUM will be thin, rather than fat. Associated with the loss of weight in the typical PETROLEUM case the child has a very good appetite, and is very often hungry between meals.

PETROLEUM children are as irritable as the ANTIM. CRUD. children but from quite a different cause; they are much more quarrelsome, and easily take offence. The child is often quite bright mentally, but is lazy at school does not want to work and is inattentive and forgetful.

They are almost always sensitive to noise and scared by any sudden loud noise which they do not understand. They are very liable to be nervous of crowds. They are just as sensitive to cold as the ANTIM. CRUD. or PSORINUM children.

There are often signs of skin eruptions in the PETROLEUM children, and the commonest is an eruption at the back of the ears, deep cracks oozing a yellowish, watery fluid. Very often these cracks split and bleed.

But the same type of crack appears in any place in the PETROLEUM child particularly in any fold, at the corners of the mouth, at the angle of the nose, and very often there are similar cracks around the anus, in the groins, or in the axillæ; the fluid that oozes out forms thick crusts which are always very sensitive.

Almost all the PETROLEUM skin eruptions itch. They are more irritable during the day than the night, which is sometimes a help to distinguish them from SULPHUR eruptions.

PETROLEUM children are very liable to catch cold, and to have acute nasal obstruction, with an excoriating discharge, a tendency for the nose to get crusty, sensitive, bleeding, and very often crusts form on the upper lip and round about the sides of the nose.

With these nasal discharges there is also some deafness, with acute pain in the ear, and a sensation as if the Eustachian tube were blocked. They frequently have an otitis, with the same kind of watery, yellow discharge, and very marked redness of the external ear, an acute eczematous condition, with irritation and tendency to bleed.

Another link with the itching is very definitely itchy eyes. Often there is blepharitis with reddened margins, and cracks at the inner canthus, and an infection spreading down the lachrymal duct—they may even get an abscess in the lachrymal sac. Pus forms in the lachrymal duct and an excoriating discharge runs down the side of the nose, raw and bleeding, accompanied by acute conjunctivitis.

With the infective processes in the throat and nose these PETROLEUM children often have enlargement of the submaxillary lymph nodes.

Another thing very common to PETROLEUM children is a history of bladder irritation. It is often an enuresis, but much more commonly an acute irritation, it may be an acute cystitis, with the same sensation of rawness and smarting.

Another feature common to the PETROLEUM children is that after any exposure to cold they may develop acute abdominal colic and diarrhœa. And with the diarrhœa there is always a degree of inflammation about the anus and perineum, with a burning red raw eruption.

In cold weather the skin of their hands tends to crack, particularly on the finger tips, and these cracks are very sensitive, very painful to touch, with deep fissures which split open and bleed easily.

All these children have the typical PETROLEUM aggravation from motion, that is to say, they get train-sick and sea-sick. If the child is pressed it is very liable to develop a severe occipital headache. That occipital headache is rather rare from mental effort, and it is a little difficult to cover, but PETROLEUM sometimes meets the case.

In cases of sea-sickness where there is doubt between PETROLEUM and TABACUM, which is the other common drug for sea-sickness, there is almost always that occipital headache as well as the sea-sickness in PETROLEUM, and the TABACUM types do not have it at all.

Sea-sickness with occipital headache calls for PETROLEUM every time. In prophylactic treatment against sea-sickness it is very difficult to decide between TABACUM or PETROLEUM, but the occipital headache of PETROLEUM children indicates PETROLEUM.

There are various other drugs for skin conditions in children but these are much the commonest. There is the possibility of SULPHUR because it is almost automatic in skin affections, but it is better to take SULPHUR under the next group.

24

Pulsatilla

These are the "warm-blooded" drugs starting with PULSATILLA which is the most commonly indicated drug in children of this type.

PULSATILLA children are very typical. There are two main types. One is the very small, fine type, with a fine skin, fine hair, unstable circulation, liable to flush up from any emotion, very often going pale afterwards; definitely shy, sensitive; always affectionate very easy to handle, and always very responsive.

The other PULSATILLA type, is much fatter with definitely more colour, usually rather darker hair, a little more sluggish in reaction, a little more tendency to weep rather than to be bright and gay as the smaller, finer type, craving for attention without much response to it, always asking for a little more.

If you get one picture clear you are apt to forget the other. The factor common to both types is their temperature reaction, all PULSATILLA children are sensitive to heat, they flag in hot weather, lose their liveliness, lose their sparkle and energy.

They hang about, become either tearful or irritable, and are likely to get digestive upsets. But they are much more liable to be upset by a sudden change to cold in a hot spell—that is to say, they often get an attack of acute sickness or diarrhœa from being chilled in hot weather.

They tend to get cystitis, or to get earache. Sudden chilling during hot weather causes their troubles. Whilst generally they flag in hot weather, their acute conditions are much more liable to be brought on by chilling. In the same way they are upset by taking ice-cream in hot weather, this factor is quite as common as the ordinary PULSATILLA aggravation from too rich food.

Sometimes one misses a case because of the odd reactions in a feverish attack. The PULSATILLA children get acute colds in the head, acute coryza, and with this they are shivery, and very chilly. With the coryza, there is a certain amount of gastric catarrh, a feeling of nausea, and they may actually vomit.

But, in spite of their chilliness, their sense of blockage in the head is better in the open air and worse in a stuffy room. A PULSATILLA cold always has a bland discharge.

There is sometimes an apparent contradiction, they are very apt to get conjunctivitis, and in the PULSATILLA conjunctivitis the eyes are very sensitive to any cold draught, and water profusely in the open air. There is usually marked photophobia with itching of the eyelids, and PULSATILLA children are apt to get styes, affecting the lower rather than the upper lid.

A point that is sometimes a help in PULSATILLA earaches, which are very intense and usually brought on from exposure to cold, is a very violent pain, which spreads all over the side of the face, as well as into the throat.

If the condition has gone a little further, there is a feeling as of something bursting out of the ear, as if something were pressing right through the ear drum. Another thing is amelioration from cold—their earaches are better from cold applications.

PULSATILLA children are very often tired, edgy and sleepy during the day, and they become more lively as the day goes on, they are liable to get the PULSATILLA nervousness about sunset – the ordinary sunset aggravation of PULSATILLA.

They become very lively towards bedtime, are slow in going to sleep, and once asleep tend to get nightmares, night terrors, usually some kind of strife dreams—not necessarily being chased by the black dog of PULSATILLA—but always something worrying, terrifying. Most of these PULSATILLA children are afraid of the dark, afraid of being left alone, as one would expect in the shy, nervous type of child.

One thing that will almost always produce a night terror in these children is listening to ghost stories in the dark before going to bed; you can be sure that will give a PULSATILLA child a nightmare.

Another useful pointer is that these children are very liable to become giddy from looking up at anything high. The only other drug that I know in which this is so marked is ARGENTUM NITRICUM which has an aggravation from looking down, but it has also an aggravation from looking up, but this is very much more marked in PULSATILLA.

The PULSATILLA child often lies with the hands above the head and this is a useful pointer, although it is by no means constant.

Kali Sulphuricum

When considering the hot-blooded child of PULSATILLA type, the next thing to consider is whether it is PULSATILLA or KALI SULPHURICUM. Kent says that KALI SULPH. is merely an intensified PULSATILLA. I do not think it is.

The KALI SULPH. temperature reactions are identical with the PULSATILLA ones, the child is sensitive to heat and it flags in the hot weather, cannot stand stuffy atmospheres, is better in the open air, tends to stagnate if keeping still, and is better moving about. It has

26

an aggravation from rich food; and is liable to be upset by sudden changes of weather. But there is a distinct difference.

The KALI SULPH. child is much more flabby than the PULSATILLA child, it certainly does not approach the thin fine type of PULSATILLA although it approaches more to the sluggish heavier type of PULSATILLA. Its muscles are flabby, it is easily exhausted by muscular effort. It is more liable to sit about, and has a much more sluggish reaction generally.

There is more obstinacy in the KALI SULPH. type than in the typical PULSATILLA. The PULSATILLA child may be irritable, it may flare up in a temper but it is over; KALI SULPH. is much more liable to be obstinate.

Also the PULSATILLA children are shy, but the KALI SULPH. children tend much more to have a lack of confidence in themselves—it is not shyness. They are lazy, they dislike work and there is not the keenness and interest of the PULSATILLA children.

The KALI SULPH. children are not bright, they get tired out by mental exertion, whereas the PULSATILLA children are very often bright and sharp and do quite well at school.

There is a certain similarity in that they are both nervous, both afraid of the dark, they are very easily frightened, easily startled at strange noises, strange surroundings.

The typical KALI SULPH. child tends to be more sickly than the typical PULSATILLA child. The PULSATILLA child may not be strong, but the KALI SULPH. child tends to have less colour and if flushed it is much more a circumscribed flush on the cheeks rather than the variable circulation of the PULSATILLA.

Another thing that indicates KALI SULPH. rather than PULSATILLA is that nearly all KALI SULPH. children have a yellow-coated tongue, particularly the root of the tongue although the coating may spread right over.

Another point which helps is that there is a slight difference in the type of discharges. The typical PULSATILLA discharge is a thick, creamy, non-irritating discharge. The typical discharge in KALI SULPH. is a much more watery, more stringy, yellowish discharge.

As far as liability to actual acute illness is concerned, PULSATILLA is more often needed for acute gastric catarrh, acute gastritis, acute colic and diarrhœa; but if the gastritis has gone on to a jaundice in a PULSATILLA child the indications are more for KALI SULPH. than for PULSATILLA.

With a PULSATILLA type of child who has caught cold and developed bronchitis which has gone on to a broncho-pneumonia with

27

the ordinary PULSATILLA indications, that is to say, aggravated from stuffy room, relief from air, sense of suffocation, possibly a loss of voice, very dry mouth without much thirst, with a yellowish, watery sputum, and probably patches of consolidation at the left base—left base more commonly—the response is better from KALI SULPH. than from PULSATILLA.

With a PULSATILLA child who has whooping cough with a lot of rattling in the chest, and the ordinary PULSATILLA modalities, KALI SULPH. does more good than PULSATILLA.

That is perhaps what Kent means by saying KALI SULPH. is PULSATILLA intensified—in these acute conditions the symptoms are very similar and yet the more severe the condition the more definite are the indications for KALI SULPH.

It is sometimes useful to remember that the heavy PULSATILLA child is liable to go on to SULPHUR whilst the finer PULSATILLA child is much more liable to become chilly and go on to SILICEA or PHOSPHORUS.

I usually give PULSATILLA in low potency in chronic cases. They are mostly sensitive children, and where you are dealing with the sensitive type you do not want a high potency. When dealing with bovine types I go high, but in a sensitive type like PULSATILLA they blossom on a 30 potency. PHOSPHORUS is exactly the same, PHOSPHORUS children respond beautifully to lower potencies.

I have found very good results from ANTIMONIUM CRUDUM 12, repeated three times a day for two days, in impetigo. With CALC. CARB. or GRAPHITES I would give a high potency every time—a 200, or higher, as one is dealing with an insensitive type.

Sulphur

From the point of view of children, there are two definite SULPHUR types. Much the commonest is a fairly well-nourished, well-grown child, always with a definitely big head. They are usually fairly heavy in build and rather awkward and clumsy in their movements.

They are apt to have very coarse, strong hair, and always a fairly high colour. Their skin tends to be roughish, it will roughen in a cold wind, and they sweat easily. They tend to have rather red extremities, red hands and very often red feet. They always have very red lips, very often red ears, and they easily run to redness of the margins of the lids.

That is one of the exceptions to the coarse hair, because that type of SULPHUR child very often has poorly developed eyelashes; they have had repeated attacks of blepharitis, they have crusty eruptions about the eyelids which they have picked and scratched, and consequently the eyelashes tend to be undeveloped or poor.

The other SULPHUR type, which is usually thin, with a fairly big head but rather spindly legs, very often with a biggish abdomen, rather poorly developed chest, very often not so much colour, tending to be paler, with a definitely rougher skin.

This type has a drier, coarser skin, with a very marked tendency for the skin to split, to crack on exposure, and the child is rather more miserable generally. The child looks more seedy, has less vitality, is more easily tired, and always stands badly.

The heavier SULPHUR type have much more bite about them, they tend to be quarrelsome, impatient, rather critical, fault-finding, discontented, very often generally dissatisfied; are apt to feel they are not getting a fair deal, and often feel they are being underestimated.

They are lazy, but it is often very difficult to say whether it is real laziness or lack of stamina, because they do get tired out on exertion. They have a great dislike of interference, they think they know how to do a thing, they know what they want to do, and strongly resent their parents butting in, they think they would make a better show of it if they were left alone.

The thin SULPHUR type, are much more inclined to be miserable, low spirited. They have much less vitality, much less bite about them. There is the same sort of resentment of outside interference, though it shows itself differently. These thin SULPHUR children are liable to weep, and any attempt to comfort them is apt to annoy them, and they will turn on you.

These thin SULPHUR children have even less stamina than the fat ones, they are more easily exhausted and, like all SULPHUR patients, they cannot stand for any length of time. They stand badly in the ordinary instance, and if they are kept standing they go to pieces.

There is one outstanding characteristic of all SULPHUR patients, whether children or adults, and that is they have a large appetite—it does not matter whether they are fat or thin—and their appetite is well-defined in its likes and dislikes.

All SULPHUR patients have a desire for something with a definite taste; they like highly seasoned, spiced foods, and they have a very marked desire for sweets.

Occasionally a SULPHUR patient will crave salt, but it is not really a salt craving, it is much more something with a taste. Another point about SULPHUR children is that they have an almost perverted

29

desire for out-of-the-ordinary food, the unusual dish that the average child dislikes, the SULPHUR child will eat with relish.

Another constant feature in both children and adults is that they are always very sluggish after meals, they get heavy and sleepy, they want to lie about, and are irritable when disturbed.

One very useful pointer about SULPHUR children is that they are liable to get digestive upsets from milk. The small SULPHUR baby very often gets sickness, and may get diarrhœa and vomiting, from milk, and this marked milk aggravation is often overlooked.

The next thing that is constant to all SULPHUR patients is the skin irritation. Most SULPHUR patients have irritation of the skin somewhere, and it is characteristic. It is very much worse from warmth of any kind; warm room, warm bed, warm sun, warm clothing, all start up the SULPHUR irritation.

When the irritation is present they get definite comfort, and sometimes a peculiar sensation of pleasure, from scratching, and occasionally the scratching does relieve the irritation. It always tends to be much more troublesome at night, quite apart from being hot.

When they are about, active and occupied during the day the irritation does not worry them much, but when they are at rest in the evening or at night the irritation tends to become much worse, and much more worrying.

SULPHUR has every skin eruption known to the dermatologist. The point that distinguishes it as a SULPHUR eruption is the reaction to temperature, and the fact that it always irritates. It is an intense irritation that they cannot leave alone; they describe it in various ways—itching, feeling of animals crawling over the skin, sensation of stinging nettles, any description that fits an intense irritation of the skin.

In addition to the general surface irritability these children tend to get very marked irritation of all the orifices—nose, ears, mouth, urethra, anus—any orifice tends to be congested, red, hot and itchy.

In all acute or chronic conditions they tend to have a red-coated tongue, with a very red tip, and very often a red margin running along the sides, not unlike a RHUS TOX. tongue. Most of these SULPHUR patients have a dry mouth, a hot mouth, and they are thirsty. This applies more in acute conditions than in chronic.

Another point which is sometimes helpful in the SULPHUR type children. SULPHUR patients are always aggravated by heat, but one is apt to forget that SULPHUR patients have an unstable heat mechanism; they are very liable—certainly in feverish conditions—to waves of heat and also waves of chilliness.

Very often they get extremely hot, break out into a sweat and become shivery—very much the type of condition associated with MERCURIUS. Covered up they get hot and very uncomfortable; but when uncovered they feel a draught on the skin and are immediately chilly. But do not overlook SULPHUR because the child does not want to be uncovered all the time.

Another constant in the SULPHUR patient, no matter what the condition, whether it is a skin eruption, or a child with rheumatism, or a child with a tummy upset, no matter what condition, it is aggravated by bathing. And SULPHUR children nearly always look dirty.

Some children may at first sight appear to be not unlike CALCAREA children, that is to say, they are heavy, with big heads, are rather pale with a tendency to flush, have rather big bellies, and are clumsy; but they have not the CALCAREA chilliness, they are hot-blooded, and have a very marked tendency to the development of blackheads all across the forehead.

These children are nearly all SULPHUR cases. They have rather paler lips than the average SULPHUR child but, particularly with blackheads scattered over the forehead, always consider the possibility of the child being a SULPHUR type.

Another contradiction sometimes met with in SULPHUR children is that they have disturbed areas of heat; they have hot heads and cold hands, or hot hands and cold feet; or hot feet and cold heads—very often cold, damp heads—local disturbances of heat and cold as well as general disturbances of heat and cold. A child with cold feet does not automatically rule out SULPHUR because the child does not put its feet out of bed.

Typical of SULPHUR subjects is sluggishness. They are better for exertion; better when they are stimulated, and better when they are moving about. Some SULPHUR patients can be very lethargic, dull, uninteresting people but if they are stimulated in the proper kind of society they wake up; they are clever; and you would not recognize them as the same beings.

It is the same with SULPHUR children; badly handled they are dull, heavy, cross, irritable; and properly handled they can be bright, interesting, quite friendly, and very often clever. Some of the SULPHUR children have a most astonishing command of languages.

31

A fairly constant characteristic of all SULPHUR children is constipation. The majority of SULPHUR children suffer in some degree from constipation and very often it is quite severe. Associated with that is an enlarged abdomen, frequent enlargement of the liver, abnormal appetite, sleepiness after meals, and a very definite tendency to attacks of colic.

The above applies more to the heavier SULPHUR type, the thinner type is more liable to get attacks of ordinary SULPHUR modalities, that is to say, diarrhœa tending to come on early in the morning, any time after four a.m., and the stool is always offensive.

The other constant SULPHUR characteristic is an offensive odour. Discharges, eruptions, perspiration all are malodorous, and the SULPHUR child is very difficult to get clean and wholesome.

Another feature often met with in SULPHUR children is that they are often heavy and lethargic and sleepy during the day, and very sleepless at night; also they are liable to get most terrifying nightmares. These are not constant in character, but the child is always being frightened, very commonly being terrified of fire or something of that sort.

Another point which occasionally occurs in a SULPHUR child. It is quite lively in the evening, slow getting to sleep, gets off to sleep, and wakes up soon after in fits of laughter. It is an odd symptom, and always in SULPHUR children. Also they get a hungry period about 11 a.m., and all SULPHUR children are liable to be seedy, headachy, irritable and tired out if they have to wait for their meals.

Nearly all the actual acute diseases from which they suffer are associated with some skin irritation. SULPHUR is commonly indicated in acute styes with intense irritation of the lid margins, the lids are very hot and burning, aggravated by heat, and particularly aggravated by bathing—they smart and sting if an eye bath is used.

There are commonly indications for SULPHUR in chronic nasal discharges; in these children with a nasal discharge there is always the same SULPHUR offensiveness. The discharge is always excoriating, there is a redness about the nose, with intense irritation, the children tending to pick at it until it is raw and bleeding.

SULPHUR children often get chronic tonsillitis, a deeply injected throat, very swollen, feeling very hot, with very offensive breath. And most SULPHUR children with tonsillitis tend to get masses of glands in the neck—more than ordinary tonsillar gland enlargement and it tends to spread, and involve particularly the submaxillary glands. The tonsillitis is accompanied by irregular heat and cold, shivering attacks, sweaty attacks and thirst for cold water.

There are indications for SULPHUR in chronic conditions, chronic ear discharge, with the SULPHUR characteristics, the excoriating, offensive discharge, redness about the external ear, intense irritation; the aggravation of any pain from hot applications, particularly hot fomentations.

Chest conditions in SULPHUR children vary from a mild bronchitis to an acute pneumonia; and again certain features are constant. A tendency to waves of heat and sweat, very often occasional shivers, very often burning extremities, and a very definite heavy smell about the child.

There is one constant feature that runs through all SULPHUR chest conditions, it is a very marked sensitiveness to lack of oxygen—they cannot stand a stuffy atmosphere, they want plenty of air, and yet they are chilly in draughts. The disturbance is more commonly on the left side of the chest than on the right, but it is too slight a difference to be of much importance.

SULPHUR is one of the most commonly indicated drugs in jaundice of children—acute catarrhal jaundice—particularly with the marked intolerance that SULPHUR has to milk in its acute conditions, intense skin irritation, feeling of burning heat on the surface very often with attacks of colic, frequently with attacks of diarrhœa. A SULPHUR diarrhœa produces an excoriating discharge, redness and rawness about the buttocks, intense irritation, scratching.

The thin type of SULPHUR patient often suffers from acute rheumatic conditions with the usual characteristics—irregular sweats, feeling of heat, thirst, red tip of the tongue. The actual painful condition is worse from heat, it is rather more comfortable from cold, it is very much better from movement, although it is painful when starting to move; and there is liable to be a red blush of the affected joint. There may also be a history of the attack having been precipitated by bathing, either sea-bathing or swimming.

The desire for fat is very variable in children. It is very common in adults, most adult SULPHUR cases want fat with hot roast beef, for instance, but it is by no means so constant in children. Some do not like fat. If they do it is a help, but it is by no means constant. A number of adults also do not want it.

Butter does not come into the fat craving at all. The majority of PULSATILLA patients with a definite aversion to fat, like butter and like cream; but they dislike meat fat, and particularly hot fat. Many

33

PULSATILLA patients will eat fat cold but not hot. But most PUL-SATILLA patients will take butter, very often in large quantities.

The tendency to sweat is constant in the fatter type of SULPHUR; the thinner types usually have a dry harsh skin and do not tend to perspire.

Another thing which is sometimes a help about SULPHUR children is that they are extremely pleased with their possessions. The SULPHUR child's toys are the best that could be, and the SULPHUR child's family is the best ever. They also have an astonishing money sense; quite a small child has a very definite sense of values.

SULPHUR is not nearly so often indicated as it is used in urticaria. But it is very commonly indicated in urticaria in children, particularly if associated with digestive upsets. Children respond well to any potency, and most SULPHUR children respond very well to a 30 or 200.

Thuja

To continue with the PULSATILLA type of drugs, although the majority of these are hot-blooded drugs, there is one other that is always associated with PULSATILLA, and that is THUJA, although it is chilly in its reactions.

It is a little difficult to give a mental picture of the typical THUJA child because in the majority of outstanding cases there is an element of mental deficiency. In many THUJA children there has been some mental deficiency, some merely backward, some actually deficient.

In some there is an obvious pituitary dysfunction, and that tends to colour one's idea of THUJA. But there are THUJA children who are not mentally defective and who have not got a pituitary dysfunction, and that type of child is very like a PULSATILLA child in reaction.

The outstanding characteristic of the THUJA child is the fact that it is sensitive; sensitive to people. It is responsive to any kindness, it is conscientious in what it does, and it is easily upset emotionally. And there the first strong indication comes in: THUJA children have a peculiar sensitiveness to music, and this is one of the things commonly associated with mentally defective children.

Eighty per cent of the mentally defective children that I have treated have been abnormally sensitive to music. Much more sensitive than the average child; and even in the normal child with THUJA indications you get this emotional sensitiveness to music. They are affected by it; they may even weep from it. Associated with that emotional disturbance THUJA children have a sadness, a depression, very like the PULSATILLA depression.

34

The THUJA children, even the mentally defectives, are astonishingly conscientious. They are very often sensitive to motion, are very often car-sick. Another symptom is a strange contradiction often found in a perfectly lively, active child—they are apparently keenly interested, and yet have a strange hesitation in speaking, a difficulty in finding the words they want, or a difficulty in saying them.

Very often the difficulty in speaking gives the impression that the child is slow mentally, when it is not really slow, it is really seeking words. That may go on to a definite disinclination to talk; they are rather silent and appear to be rather heavy.

The majority of THUJA children are rather under than above average height, many are definitely small and rather finely built. THUJA applies equally well to either fair-haired or dark-haired types. A definite factor is that they appear to get wakened, the more active they are. If they are made to sit about they become dull, heavy, and depressed, but any activity brightens them up mentally.

Another common feature in many of these THUJA children is very faulty development of the teeth; with irregular dentition, and very early decay. The enamel of the teeth is definitely faulty in places.

THUJA children are sensitive to cold, although they are mostly better in the open air. They are very sensitive to damp, and liable to be much worse in the mornings.

Most THUJA children perspire on exertion, and even when they are not exerting themselves they mostly have a rather greasy skin which is more commonly noticed in the dark-haired type than in the fair. Some fair-haired THUJA children have a rather fine skin, and very often a downy growth on the skin, particularly on the back.

THUJA children do not stand up well to mental stress. They are liable to get a typical acute neuralgic headache under stress, from getting over-tired or over-excited, and the point about the neuralgic headache is that it very often picks out definite areas which are extremely painful and very often extremely sensitive.

These children tend to get chronic catarrhal headaches. They get thick, purulent, yellowish-green nasal discharge, possibly with crusts in the nose and bleeding. They are liable to chronic otitis media, and may develop a mastoiditis with very severe and localised pain, and tenderness over the mastoid region. If they are old enough they will tell you it feels as if something were being bored into the mastoid bone.

Another common feature of THUJA children is a poor digestion. The typical picture of the pituitary child with an almost pendulous

35

abdomen is an extreme example, and these children are extremely liable to develop a chronically irritated cæcum.

Often there is a full, boggy cæcum in the right iliac fossa, with a history of recurring attacks of diarrhœa; and the diarrhœa is fairly characteristic. It consists of pale, greasy, almost fatty stools, and these are always passed with a good deal of flatus; and the attacks are accompanied by a lot of gurgling in the abdomen.

Very often these children give a history of having crops of warts. The THUJA warts are soft, and bleed very easily on handling; if knocked the surface may break and bleed.

THUJA patients sweat on the uncovered parts. A girl of about twelve years of age was stripped to be examined, and the sweat poured off her when her clothes were removed. She was not sweating at all when covered. Occasionally that odd symptom of sweating when uncovering is found, but usually THUJA children are chilly and shivery when uncovered.

A particular case was of interest because there were rare bony deposits in the muscles in quite a young child, and she did very well on THUJA. The first pointer to the possibility of THUJA was that odd sweating when uncovered.

The other constant THUJA feature in children is their strange susceptibility to onions. They are very liable to gastric upsets, and an attack of diarrhœa from eating onions, cooked or raw. Another common symptom, although not met with in young children, may occur in the adolescent—they are liable to get acute digestive upsets from tea.

A history of vaccination is also a great help in deciding on THUJA.

Bromium

The next common warm-blooded drug is BROMIUM. It is one of the drugs which is very frequently missed. The common BROMIUM type of patient is usually over-fat, fair skinned, fair-haired, and the majority are friendly, cheerful, fairly happy types.

Then there are contradictions. The fairly cheerful, happy friendly type, are very easily put out, and if upset they very commonly flush up, and explain that they get a feeling of heat and tension in their heads.

They become nervous, anxious, very often frightened, in the evening, very much about the PULSATILLA time. They do not like to walk home in the dark and have the impression that somebody is following them, and they get scared—very much like the symptom of

36

PULSATILLA—they look not unlike PULSATILLA, and occasionally bouts of depression in the BROMIUM patient are not unlike PULSATILLA. But BROMIUM is a much more placid depression, much more a melancholy outlook than the acute tearfulness of the PULSATILLA.

The BROMIUM patient is a rather fat, fair type tending to run to crops of boils, either acne about the face or over the shoulders, and an adolescent needing BROMIUM always has some acne spots about.

There are further symptoms very like PULSATILLA. They are very sensitive to heat, uncomfortable in the sun and definitely uncomfortable in a hot room. They are better for motion and for exercise; and better in the open air.

By contrast the typical BROMIUM patient is very much better after food, whereas the typical PULSATILLA patient is heavy after a meal; and another contrast—in spite of the fact that they are better in the open air, they are sensitive to draughts.

The majority of the BROMIUM cases are of two types, one with chronic catarrh of the upper passages, the other the typical acute hay fevers.

Taking the catarrhal type first, the child with chronic hypertrophy of the tonsils, not the type who is liable to recurring quinsies, but one with an enlarged fibrotic tonsil, and often with a general enlargement of the submaxillary glands, which tend to be hard, and tend not to break down.

With the chronic tonsils they are liable to acute attacks of catarrhal extension to any of the sinuses, and in BROMIUM cases it is more commonly the frontal sinuses that are involved, rather than the antrums; with the involvement of the frontal sinuses the patients complain of intense pain, fullness, and a feeling of swelling at the root of the nose.

The nose feels choked up, and there is a thick, yellow, purulent discharge, and if any violent effort is made to clear the nose the discharge is liable to be bloodstained. Another point about that type is a thickened, rather inflamed, reddened upper lip.

Occasionally one of these children will get an attack of very intense croup, with a sensation of tickling in the larynx. The very violent croupy cough, goes on almost to suffocation, and is relieved by cold drinks. They may complain of a feeling of pressure, or constriction, of the throat, and the larynx in these cases is usually very sensitive to touch. There may also be the typical BROMIUM hoarse voice.

BROMIUM is useful for the fat, warm-blooded child, with rather hypertrophied tonsils, who gets an attack of hay fever coming on

37

usually about June; rather later in the BROMIUM child than in many of the others. Some start in the middle of May, but the BROMIUM cases do not usually start until June. The outstanding characteristic of the BROMIUM hay fever is an extreme hyperaesthesia of the mucous membranes and dust of any kind will set up an acute attack during the irritant period.

One small boy had a typical BROMIUM hay fever, and if he went into a room which was being dusted would start a violent attack right away, quite apart from any exposure to irritant out of doors. A few doses of BROMIUM completely stopped it.

These BROMIUM hay fever cases may get asthmatic attacks which are fairly typical. They get very sudden spasmodic attacks with a sensation of extreme constriction of the chest, and extreme difficulty in swallowing. Another point is that although their apparent hay fever does not entirely subside at the seaside their asthma entirely goes.

Another type in which BROMIUM is very useful is similar, the child is fat, tonsillar, sensitive to heat, with a definitely sluggish tendency and in addition there are generalised rheumatic pains, a type of muscular rheumatism. They are also very liable to cardiac affections, more likely a poorly acting cardiac muscle than a definite valvular lesion, but in some cases there is definite cardiac hyper-trophy in that type of child and they have improved very much indeed on BROMIUM.

The constant in all these cases is the feeling of constriction in the chest, feeling of tightness or constriction over the heart. Another constant is that feeling of constriction has developed when they have been facing any wind; there is also the sensitiveness to draughts which is particularly noticeable in BROMIUM heart cases.

Iodum

The majority of the IODUM children are dark-haired and rather dark-skinned, and intensely restless. They are very thin children, never still, always on the move, wandering about, fidgeting, restless; this is an outstanding feature of these cases.

On questioning, you will be told that these children are definitely irritable, and their irritability is characteristic. They are perfectly happy playing with other children and then suddenly, apparently for no reason, they break out into violence. Very often they are playing perfectly happily with a brother or sister and suddenly they pick up something and hit them.

It is that sudden, impulsive irritability that is the typical IODUM mental characteristic. Very often after such an attack of irritability, the child is extremely depressed, not weepy but just silent, depressed, rather losing interest in things.

These children usually have very large appetites; they are hungry for their meals, and they are hungry between meals. They become utterly exhausted if they go too long without a meal, and are very liable to get headaches from hunger. Although these children eat well they can never be fattened; they remain thin, and may actually be losing weight.

IODUM children are very sensitive to heat of any kind, hot rooms, hot sun, hot fire, hot baths; heat in any form aggravates the typical IODUM child.

These IODUM children often have a rather inactive skin. They get attacks of acute infection of the nose, with a tendency to spread into the frontal sinuses, and with such an attack there is an irritant, watery discharge, and a feeling of obstruction at the root of the nose. There is often actual swelling at the root of the nose, and it is tender on pressure.

Frequently with the coryza there is a very hot discharge, a tendency to sneeze, and with the discharge always very watery eyes. There may be a history of repeated attacks of that sort, followed by development of typical asthmatic breathing. With these thin children with a good appetite, with that sort of history, and with asthma which is definitely better in the open air, IODUM will usually meet the case.

These IODUM children with that kind of extending catarrhal infection very often get a degree of deafness which is usually associated with a chronic eustachian catarrh.

Another feature of IODUM children of that type with catarrhal infections, is an involvement of the larynx. They are very often hoarse, and have a painful larynx, which is tender on pressure. With the laryngitis they are apt to get acute croupy attacks which are extremely painful. One of the distinguishing points about these croupy attacks is that the child gets very hot, and has an intensely hot dry skin.

Very often in these croupy attacks the child is terrified. They could be mistaken for croup of ARSENICUM type; there is the same feeling of heat, the same burning in the larynx, the same kind of restlessness and anxiety, the child is very often terrified, and there is the same kind of choking feeling. But the ARSENICUM child is chilly whereas the IODUM child is hot and wants air. The ARSENICUM child will perspire slightly; the IODUM child will be dry and hot.

IODUM children are very liable to get all sorts of abdominal disturbances. Most of which are associated with very typical diarrhœic attacks, with very frothy, fatty, whitish stools, and may be associated with enlarged mesenteric glands; they may be associated with a general enlargement of the liver and spleen without any very definite blood change; or with definite pancreatic dysfunction, with the typical pancreatic fatty stool, and there may be glycosuria.

The IODUM children with a fair amount of colour, quite bright red cheeks, are very liable to get rheumatic symptoms. It is usually an acute rheumatism, with violent pains which are eased by moving, and are very much worse from heat. The pains are usually very sharp and stabbing in character, and there may be a pericarditis with very acute sharp pericardial pain.

One thing about the pericardial cases, is apparently a contradiction to the ordinary IODUM restlessness and relief from motion, the chest pains are aggravated by moving, the pains are brought on and are made more acute by movement.

It is very easy to confuse the rather dark skinned, flushed type of patient, rather depressed, with sharp, stabbing pains which are worse from motion, with a BRYONIA case. They are both worse from heat, but there is not the typical BRYONIA tongue in the IODUM patient, not the intense thirst as a rule. Most BRYONIA cases are more dull and heavy whilst the IODUM patients are more mentally alert. There is usually a complete aversion to food in the BRYONIA cases, and very often a suprising amount of hunger even in the acute IODUM conditions.

There is a certain similarity between the IODUM child and the BROMIUM child, but it is an entirely different type. The various symptoms are very much alike, but once the type of child is recognised it is not possible to confuse them. IODUM can easily be confused with SULPHUR but there is not the intense irritability of skin, the intense itching, in a similar type of SULPHUR.

One other feature of IODUM quite frequently met with in rheumatic cases, is a history of an acute diarrhœic attack immediately preceding the rheumatic attack.

Abrotanum

The clinical picture of the ABROTANUM small baby is characteristic of a congenital pyloric stenosis. The child is emaciated, with a dehydrated wrinkled skin which when pinched up, does not return to its normal state. It has an inordinate appetite, because it is vomiting all its food, and is hungry all the time. It has a comparatively big abdomen and spindly legs, it is always cross and peevish as it is being starved. It is usually chilly, is very often sensitive when handled, and it is tender to touch.

In these ABROTANUM babies there is not infrequently a delay in the healing of the umbilicus after the cord has dropped off—from lack of vitality and lack of nourishment. Several cases who either had a pyloric stenosis or spasm, recovered perfectly on ABROTANUM. Another had a pyloric stenosis, lost all symptoms for a period of four weeks after receiving ABROTANUM, but relapsed and was operated on, had a typical pyloric stenosis and completely recovered. Whether the others were really a spasm, or a true stenosis is not known, but three with a diagnosis of pyloric stenosis did recover with ABROTANUM.

An older type of ABROTANUM child is also a hungry child, with an inordinate appetite, and again it is a thin child. It always has a tendency to recurring attacks of diarrhœa, usually attacks of diarrhœa alternating with rheumatic pains, and always with a certain amount of inco-ordination, clumsiness, tremor, probably a certain amount of numbness in the hands, feet or legs.

The child cannot be trusted with any valuable china or it will knock it over or drop it; it is verging on a chorea. They are usually rather peevish and bad-tempered, and very often have a strangely cruel streak in their make-up. These children are definitely chilly; they are aggravated by cold, and by damp; and their rheumatic pains are liable to be very much worse at night than during the day.

Fluoricum Acidum

The last of the hot-blooded drugs mentioned earlier is FLUORICUM ACIDUM. The majority of FLUORICUM ACIDUM types, both children and adults, are fair haired and fair skinned. At first sight they are not unlike the SILICEA children. They are rather thin, underweight, usually fairly fine-boned, fine-skeletoned.

Not unlike the SILICEA types they have a yielding disposition, but none of the SILICEA irritability. They are very often extremely patient, and unlike most of the drugs in the *Materia Medica* they often have a strange enjoyment of life, and find it very pleasant indeed; quite simple things seem to give them an inordinate amount of pleasure. That is the normal peaceful state.

Mentally they are not unlike the SILICEA children in that they are very easily tired by mental concentration. They get headaches or brain fag at school, and are not exceptionally bright as far as book work is concerned.

A surprising feature of the FLUORICUM ACIDUM type of child, is that they are liable to get quite pointless and unreasoning hatreds of one or other individual in school. It is a weird difference from

41

the ordinary child's make-up which is striking. It applies to adults as well.

Unlike the SILICEA children, they are better from physical exertion. Playing games does them good, it wakes them up, they are better for it. The SILICEA child will be tired out by it. Like the SILICEA children, if they are kept standing for any length of time they get faint, headachy, and tired out. Again, unlike the SILICEA children, they usually have a good appetite, and get hungry between meals, with hunger headaches.

Quite a number of these FLUORICUM ACIDUM children need extra food at school in the middle of the morning or they finish the morning with a headache. They wake up hungry in the middle of the night unable to sleep unless they have something to eat, and in spite of the amount of food they eat they are still fairly thin. But many FLUORICUM ACIDUM children are not markedly thin or under-weight. Their type is small and fine but not definitely under-weight.

With their big appetites, they have a desire for highly-seasoned food, it does not matter very much what it is as long as it has a strong taste.

All the FLUORICUM ACIDUM patients are sensitive to heat; they are worse from hot rooms, from hot sun, from too many clothes and from too many blankets at night. A FLUORICUM ACIDUM child who comes home from school with a slight headache, rather a flushed face, feeling extremely hot, can very often get rid of the headaches by putting his head into a basin of cold water, or by bathing his face with cold water.

Another factor in FLUORICUM ACIDUM children is that they get a headache if at all constipated. These children also get the typical FLUORICUM ACID headache from being unable to get out of school to pass urine; again it is the same type of congestive headache.

Some of these FLUORICUM ACIDUM children have the fine hair associated with the SILICEA child, but with a tendency to patchy bald areas, without an definite skin disease. It is patchy areas of thinning of the hair rather than actual baldness.

Another teature associated with the FLUORICUM ACIDUM child is very faulty dentition, very poor enamel of the teeth, liability for the teeth to decay early, and very often abscesses at the roots of the teeth. FLUORICUM ACIDUM children rarely have a really sound dentition, and associated with that is the other important characteristic—unhealthy finger nails which are brittle, cracked and splintered.

Another feature is that they have red, sweaty palms to their hands and very offensive foot sweat, which tends to make the feet hot and

42

sore. Another pointer to a possible FLUORICUM ACIDUM patient, is a dry, red, fissured tongue.

The majority of these children have digestive upsets, or a tendency to a breakdown at school, or rheumatic conditions. The outstanding point about the digestive upsets is a tendency to attacks of diarrhœa; there is a liability to acute gastritis, and jaundice, and all these digestive upsets are very much aggravated by any hot drinks.

The typical FLUORICUM ACIDUM child with diarrhœa will get a violent attack after any hot drink, which is very often a useful pointer to the FLUORICUM ACIDUM case. In acute attacks they are liable to run a fairly high temperature, with a feeling of intense heat and complete intolerence of any bedclothes.

In their breakdowns at school, apart from headaches from concentration—the type of congestive headache which is better from cold bathing—one constant feature is that they make mistakes in writing. They transpose words, transpose letters, and the mistakes seem most senseless. The teachers complain it is pure inattention, and say the child could not make such mistakes if it were paying attention; but the child cannot help it.

Their rheumatic complaints have the ordinary FLUORICUM ACIDUM temperature aggravation, and the pains are very much worse when keeping still and better by moving about.

Another symptom of the FLUORICUM ACIDUM child who is tired out at school is a feeling of numbness in the arms or legs. An odd thing about this numbness is that it does not come on from pressure; even when the child is still the arms and legs are liable to become numb.

The diarrhœic attacks of FLUORICUM ACIDUM are always irritant diarrhœas; there is a good deal of peri-anal irritation, and possibly a number of painful peri-anal fissures.

FLUORICUM ACIDUM is really a hot-blooded SILICEA, with amelioration from motion, and with a cheerful outlook instead of the flat tired outlook of SILICEA types.

FLUORICUM ACIDUM and PULSATILLA patients are not easily confused for the PULSATILLA types are usually very much heavier in build, they have much less tension about them, are softer both mentally and physically. There is not the activity in PULSATILLA of the FLUORICUM ACIDUM case, they have a slower brain, are much more yielding, much less active. The PULSATILLA patient gets tired out with exertion, and the FLUORICUM ACIDUM patient is rather stimulated by it.

43

PULSATILLA is aggravated by exposure to cold water, gets chilled; the FLUORICUM ACIDUM types will bathe in cold water and it will wake them up. It is very much a question of degree; in one the patient is more taut, the other is gentle, yielding, depressed.

FLUORICUM ACIDUM will suddenly get irritable, much more violently irritable than PULSATILLA, will strike when the PULSATILLA would probably break out into wrath and then weep. FLUORICUM ACIDUM is very much more like PHOSPHORUS, much more intense mentally, more active, more alive than PULSATILLA.

GROUP V

Arsenicum Album

The last group of drugs includes all the outstandingly nervy children, and the key to the whole group is ARSENICUM ALBUM. ARSENICUM children are possibly the most attractive of the children. They are very highly strung, usually finely made, finely built, often with a very fine skin and fine hair; they are delicate-looking children.

They are always very nervy, very easily scared, very easily frightened, anything unusual will frighten them, they are afraid of being left alone in the house, afraid of going out alone, terrified of the dark, and they always have a very vivid imagination. They suffer from night terrors, and wake up in the middle of the night terrified, jump out of bed and wander through the house to find somebody to talk to.

It is always the feeling of some horrible occurrence hanging over her, very often she does not know what it is and is just terrified. When comforted and consoled, she will quieten down and go to sleep again, particularly if taken into the parent's bed and has somebody near.

They are usually of a variable colour and tend to be rather pale but flush on excitement. They are not sallow. It is a rather fine skin, and when flushed they often get hot heads, and cold hands and feet on excitement or over-exertion.

In spite of their delicate appearance these ARSENICUM children are always restless, always doing something, and not just sitting about looking at their fingers. They may take up a thing, do it for a while, then go on to something else, but they never spend their time doing nothing.

When they are nervy they go from their mother to their father, from their father to the nurse, then back to their mother. Each one gives them a certain amount of comfort but not for long, and they turn to someone else.

In spite of their restlessness and their activity, they get completely exhausted. They will be all right for a couple of hours, busy, happy, occupied, rather restless, and too mentally active, then suddenly become completely exhausted, grow pale, tired and lie down. Often they become depressed, and in a nervy, frightened state, feel they are going to be ill and want to have somebody near.

These children are inordinately tidy. A small girl will keep her dolls in a most astonishingly tidy condition. Even small boys, who normally break their toys and leave them lying about on the floor, if of ARSENICUM type, will put them away and be distressed, not because the toy is broken but because it is in a mess. They are upset if they spill jam over themselves and get into a mess, and their distress is out of all proportion to the cause.

Another very definite thing about them is that they are liable to catch cold, particularly from exposure to cold, and these colds are fairly typical. They usually start as an acute coryza, with watery, excoriating discharge, very violent attacks of sneezing and a tendency for the cold very rapidly to spread on to the chest.

In 24 hours the history of an acute coryza develops rapidly to bronchitis. With that extension the ARSENICUM child becomes hoarse between the development of the coryza and the onset of the definite bronchitis.

The other ARSENICUM types get a very similar mild coryza without any hoarseness at all, without any sign of bronchitis but they suddenly develop an acute asthmatic attack.

The asthmatic attack in ARSENICUM children is a very typical, very tight, dry, spasmodic asthma and it is always accompanied by acute terror. It is always terrifying for a child to get asthma, but ARSENICUM children are almost beside themselves with terror.

They are liable to get asthmatic attacks either early in the afternoon about 1 p.m. to 3 p.m. some time after lunch, or early in the morning, any time after midnight.

Another typical asthmatic characteristic is that as the attack subsides the dryness seems to disappear and the chest gets flooded with mucus with quantities of white, frothy sputum. When the attack is subsiding the dry whistle disappears and the chest gets moister. ARSENICUM will clear up the whole trouble.

ARSENICUM children are very sensitive to cold, and exposure to cold is certain to upset them. It either provokes an acute respiratory attack, or an acute digestive attack. These children get digestive upsets very easily; from exposure to cold, and also from over-indulgence in any watery fruits. Melons, strawberries, any of the

45

juicy fruits may give the ARSENICUM child an acute gastritis, usually with diarrhœa.

ARSENICUM children are extremely chilly, and in most of their chest and general conditions, they are thirsty with a desire for cold drinks, but when suffering from gastritis or gastroenteritis, the condition is aggravated by cold drinks.

The gastritis may be brought on by ice cream, and a mixture of fruit and ice cream is particularly dangerous for ARSENICUM children. During the acute stage of gastritis the pain is usually severe and is eased by warmth, either warm fluids or external heat applied to the abdomen. When a child likes warm drinks and is made easier by them, one should not ignore ARSENICUM.

Another point about these acute abdominal attacks is that the child is rather delicate and one that can go downhill extremely rapidly; an ARSENICUM child with an acute diarrhœa will become collapsed in a few hours.

With this collapse they are restless, worried, anxious, and liable to have constant small stools, little spurts of diarrhœa, and a marked aggravation of the exhaustion after each stool. The child appears absolutely grey, cold and sweaty. Nearly always in the ARSENICUM diarrhœa the stools are offensive.

In summer after over-indulgence in strawberries, etc., the children have been perfectly well the previous day and the next morning they are in a collapsed state after purging all night. It is remarkable how quickly the ARSENICUM children recover if given ARSENICUM.

In acute cases with violent onset ARSENICUM CM every fifteen minutes will clear up the trouble immediately. But ARSENICUM in low potency is not effective. The patients do not have enough vitality to respond to low potencies, and in extreme cases satisfactory results are unlikely from potencies of under 10m.

There is also a general hyperaesthesia in the ARSENICUM children. They are over-sensitive to everything, to smell, to touch, to noise, to excitement; smells will make them sick, noise will make them all jumpy and nervy, excitement will give them a nightmare.

They are highly strung children. If pushed at school they are liable to get chorea; and if they are not very gently, quietly handled they develop periodic headaches, recurring once in 7 or 14 days, violent sick headaches lasting anything up to from 24 to 48 hours, and they may last two or three days making the child completely prostrated.

It is always an intense congestive headache, with intolerance of noise, light, or disturbance of any kind. And this is one of the

46

ARSENICUM contradictions, with these congestive headaches they want their heads as cool as possible.

The child feels ill, its body may be cold, sweaty and damp; it has extreme nausea; it is restless and frightened, wants to be well covered—and yet wants its head cold, cold cloths, Eau de Cologne applications—anything to keep it cool.

ARSENICUM is less valuable in skin conditions than might be expected. It is more valuable in some of the chronic conditions than in the acute dermatites. The secondary syphilitic eruption is the kind of condition in which ARSENICUM is indicated.

Alternation of asthma and skin conditions is a very definite ARSENICUM indication; where asthma and diarrhœa alternate it is useful. A case of recurring headaches in which asthma developed, cleared on ARSENICUM. ARSENICUM very definitely has these alternations, but more frequently in adults than in children.

Chamomilla

The symptoms of CHAMOMILLA are almost indentical to those of ARSENICUM and yet they are entirely different drugs, and entirely different children. First there is hyperaesthesia, over-sensitiveness to noise, pain, people; there is exactly the same hyperaesthesia in CHAMOMILLA.

There is the restlessness of ARSENICUM, moving from one person to another, never still; and exactly the same in CHAMOMILLA, the child goes from one person to another and is never completely still, never at peace. And yet the two types are different.

In CHAMOMILLA there is extreme hyperaesthesia, the CHAMOMILLA pains are more intense probably than any other pains from which patients suffer; but the reaction is entirely different from that in ARSENICUM. CHAMOMILLA cases have an absolute frenzy of rage; they resent it; they resent having it; and they are furious that the doctor has not cleared it off at once. A CHAMOMILLA child is liable to strike out at you because it is hyperaesthetic.

There is intense restlessness in the CHAMOMILLA child, it goes from one person to another, and each time it is dissatisfied with the person it goes to, and as it leaves them it is quite liable to strike at them. It is quite different from the soothing that the ARSENICUM child gets from each one.

The CHAMOMILLA child who is over-sensitive to noise, does not get the nightmare the same night, the child is wrought up into a perfect frenzy, liable to scream and stamp when disturbed. It is quite a different reaction.

47

In the ARSENICUM case the child is restless, always moving about whilst the CHAMOMILLA child is better from motion, but particularly better from being carried about—it is passive motion. Jogging about an ARSENICUM child will probably terrify it.

Jog about a CHAMOMILLA child and it will probably stop screaming and begin to crow. You stop and it wants you to go on, and if you do not it will pull your hair. The reactions are entirely different although the symptoms in the *Materia Medica* are almost the same.

The CHAMOMILLA child is never still, it is never satisfied with anything it is doing. But it is not a question of passing from one occupation to another, it is a question of getting tired of one thing and throwing it away. It never puts away its toy in a cupboard, it just tosses it down, and picks up something else; if told to put the first toy in the cupboard it is liable to yell.

Another constant factor about the CHAMOMILLA children is that they get more excitable as the day goes on, more irritable, more difficult to manage, and they are liable to be particularly troublesome about 9 p.m. The CHAMOMILLA child often is quite impossible after it is put to bed until about midnight, then it appears to wear itself out and falls asleep.

All these children who get into a fury tend to get flushed, with red faces and hot heads, but the CHAMOMILLA child tends to get flushed on one side of the face, it is flushed generally but one side will be redder than the other.

CHAMOMILLA is almost universal for the teething child, but it is a mistake to give CHAMOMILLA to any teething child, the indications for it are quite definite. A teething child who needs CHAMOMILLA tends to get much more fractious at night and to have very swollen, inflamed, tender gums, and they tend to be one-sided with a marked flush on that side of the face.

The tender gums are made much worse by any application of heat and they are very much better from cold applications. They are much worse in a hot room, and the attack is liable to subside about midnight. It is worth noting that the toothache pains of CHAMOMILLA have entirely different modalities from the other pains.

CHAMOMILLA children are subject to attacks of acute colic, possibly because their parents give in to them; they see something they want and scream until they get it, and that evening they go down with acute abdominal colic—mostly the fault of the parents. These attacks of colic are accompanied by a lot of wind and are very much relieved by hot applications.

With these attacks of colic they are liable to get bouts of diarrhœa, with the typical green CHAMOMILLA diarrhœic stool. A CHAMOMILLA child with colic and diarrhœa gives the best illustration of CHAMOMILLA irritability; they scream the place down. It is painful, fairly acute colic, and the child makes it very clear that it is in pain.

Another contrast between CHAMOMILLA and ARSENICUM children, is that CHAMOMILLA children are usually hot-blooded. They have very hot heads, very often hot and sweaty, and they are liable to have burning hot feet which they push out of bed at night.

CHAMOMILLA children are ungoverned children, and they have mostly been allowed to get out of hand, but in addition the CHAMOMILLA child in a tantrum of temper can get into such a state that it gets blue in the face and starts convulsions from pure rage. So one has to be a little careful about the handling of the true CHAMOMILLA child.

One typical CHAMOMILLA child, about three years of age, when in a rage was liable to beat her head against the wall, merely because it distressed her mother.

One night about 10 p.m. after she had been quite impossible for the previous hour and her mother had left her to scream, she had gone into a convulsion. She was practically unconscious, dusky in the face, and twitching all over. So one has to be careful about the wholesome neglect of the CHAMOMILLA child.

Quite a number of CHAMOMILLA babies, teething and with acutely inflamed gums, develop convulsions, and this indicates an explosive nervous system in the CHAMOMILLA child which should be watched.

Teething children do well on a low potency. A few doses usually stop the disturbance, CHAMOMILLA 12 or 30, two hourly, in the average case, but in a violent attack repeat every half-hour until they quieten down.

CHAMOMILLA is also useful for acute otitis in children. It is an extremely painful condition, and in most cases the child does not want to be touched, and is intensely irritable, very often screaming with pain. If the trouble has been brought on from exposure to cold CHAMOMILLA is one of the greatest standbys in the small child, particularly if the one-sided flush is present.

CHAMOMILLA has cleared more acute otitis in small children than any other single drug. And it clears up without any puncture of the drum. But the child must have the CHAMOMILLA make-up as well as the otitis, or CHAMOMILLA will not work. The nervous system has to be all on the fret, and the child has to be irritable and touchy.

The PULSATILLA child develops otitis media from the same cause—exposure to cold—has the one-sided flush; but it is a PULSATILLA child, not a CHAMOMILLA one, and CHAMOMILLA will not do it any good. These are the two commonest drugs for acute otitis in children.

Cina

The next drug is CINA, which makes a very interesting comparison with CHAMOMILLA. Most people start with a dose of CHAMOMILLA and if it does not get results they give a dose of CINA. This is not a very scientific way of proceeding. It is better to know clearly what the CINA picture is like and where the difficulties arise.

The outstanding mental distinction between the CHAMOMILLA child and the CINA child is that in CINA there is a degree of obstinacy never met with in CHAMOMILLA. The CHAMOMILLA child is always unstable; the CINA child can be as obstinate as a mule. That is the main mental distinction.

In CHAMOMILLA there is the irregular flushing of one cheek and pallor of the other. The whole face may be red but more likely there is irregular distribution. In the CINA child much more commonly there is a circumscribed red patch on the cheeks, and very often a noticeable pallor about the mouth and nose.

The next distinguishing thing about them is that although both dislike being handled and resent interference, in CHAMOMILLA it is much more mental resentment whereas the CINA child is definitely tender to touch.

There is very often the same description of the two that they will scream when handled, but once the preliminary discomfort of handling is over the CINA children are quite peaceful, and they allow themselves to be carried about and it will quiet them down; whereas in CHAMOMILLA they want distraction all the time, and are always wanting to be doing something new.

The CINA child will want to be carried because the steady, passive motion soothes him.

Another point which distinguishes CINA from CHAMOMILLA. CINA children are very apt to vomit, as are the CHAMOMILLA types, but almost immediately after the CINA children have vomited they are hungry. Often the CINA children will cry for more food immediately after a meal, and the CINA child often suffers from nightmares, and night terrors if it has had a late meal.

Another distinguishing factor between CHAMOMILLA and CINA is their diarrhœic upsets. Both types have attacks of diarrhœa. The typical CHAMOMILLA green stool is absent in CINA. The typical CINA stool is a very white, watery stool.

A constant characteristic of the CINA child, both in its digestive upsets and in general, is its relief from pressure on the abdomen. If it has colic it will turn over on to its tummy, if carried about while it has colic it will turn over the nurse's arm so as to get pressure on its tummy. If it is restless at night, it turns over on to its abdomen and is at peace.

CINA children are always chilly and are sensitive to any draughts of air. These children are liable to irregular muscular twitchings, particularly after any excitement, and often in the muscles of the face.

In the slightly older children another mental characteristic of the CINA child is that they are frightfully touchy. They have a complete inability to see a joke of any kind, particularly if it refers to themselves.

CINA children all have a hyperaesthesia of the head, the head is sensitive to jarring, and they have a hyperaesthesia of the scalp. To soothe down a CINA child never stroke its hair. They have an inordinate habit of yawning, and keep yawning as if they would dislocate their jaws, and in some cases a definite history of acidosis links up with the tendency to yawn.

Two other points which indicate the possibility of a child needing CINA. One is that with their intestinal upsets they become very restless and liable to get meningeal irritation, with constant agitation of the head, rubbing it into the pillow. Even without definite meningitis they tend to develop a squint—an internal squint.

The other point is that all these CINA children appear to develop an irritation of the nose, it is red, itchy, and they pick at it—and that is quite apart from getting thread worms or anything of the kind. A yawning child picking its nose always indicates the possibility of its needing CINA.

Magnesia Carbonica

MAGNESIA CARBONICA and CINA are the two most commonly indicated drugs for diarrhœic attacks accompanied by peculiarly white stools. In addition MAGNESIA CARB. is an interesting drug in children.

The ordinary MAGNESIA CARB. child is a sensitive, nervous type and as a rule they come for treatment either as very young children or at about ten years of age.

The most outstanding feature of the MAGNESIA CARB. children is their lack of stamina. Some of them are quite well nourished but they all have very poor muscular power. In an ordinary healthy

51

child the muscles are quite firm, but the MAGNESIA CARB. child has soft, flabby muscles, and any physical exertion tires him out.

There is exactly the same sort of mental reaction. The older child at school gets mentally tired out and comes home with a severe neuralgic headache. The pains are violent, they may be in any part of the head, and tend to come on at night.

They are accompanied by very marked sleeplessness, the child cannot get to sleep at all, and a strange feature is that they are better if the child is up and moving about.

MAGNESIA CARB. children always have very definite likes and dislikes in food. They have a marked craving for meat, and anything with a meaty taste. And they have a complete aversion to vegetables of any kind. In small children there is an intolerance of milk; they get sour vomiting, and pasty, pale, undigested stools, which are usually white and soft and putty-like.

If the digestive disturbance goes further, there are watery stools which are usually excoriating. The type of child is very liable in an acute enteritis to develop an attack of bronchitis or definite broncho-pneumonia.

In their bronchial attacks the MAGNESIA CARB. children tend to get stringy sputum, which is very difficult to expel. It is not unlike the KALI BICH. sputum in appearance, but they have great difficulty in expectorating it at all.

MAGNESIA CARB. children tend to have a very dry skin. In small children it is particularly noticeable, they get a dry, almost scaly, skin, and a peculiar dry, almost coppery-coloured, scaly eruption of the scalp, almost as if it had been painted on to the scalp.

The adolescent MAGNESIA CARB. children are always dead-beat in the morning, even after a good night's sleep. It is an effort to get them off to school.

Another useful pointer to MAGNESIA CARB. children is that they are very easily startled by any unexpected touch, and in spite of this very inert type of skin, after taking any hot food or drink they flush up and sweat about the head and face.

These children are all sensitive to cold, and yet they are rather better in the open air. They are usually aggravated by changes in the weather.

Ignatia

The next of the nervy drugs is IGNATIA. It is unfortunate that IGNATIA has been distorted in the homœopathic text-books and has come to be looked on as the hysterical female. Using it in that way misses a great deal of the value which can be had from IGNATIA in other cases which are not hysterical females at all.

A child with a highly developed nervous system; a highly strung, sensitive, bright, precocious child, doing very well at school and being pushed—be it a boy or a girl—and the nervous system is getting over-taxed, will often present IGNATIA indications.

The first indication is that the child is beginning to develop headaches, a nervous, tired headache coming on at the end of the day, after a period of stress.

Then they begin to become slightly shaky—their writing is not so good as it was, their finer movements begin to suffer.

The next pointer is a rather strained expression, and this is a major keynote to IGNATIA in the non-hysterical type. It may be anything from a mere tension of the muscles to definite grimaces when the child is speaking, and it may go on from that to facial chorea, generalised chorea, difficulty in speaking, difficulty in articulation.

The child is becoming unduly excitable—either up in the air, or down in the dumps, and is incredibly hyperaesthetic to noise. If the child is attempting to do homework after school any noise nearly drives it crazy; it is liable to fly into a rage and then lapse into tears.

After any stress of that kind the child is quite incapable of working, its brain will not function, it cannot take anything in, cannot remember, and cannot think.

There are definite indications for IGNATIA in the peculiar modality of the headaches. The children come home from school with a congestive headache, which, strangely, is relieved by hot applications.

If their nerves begin to get frayed these children become scared. They may have been up against the stress of examinations, they lose their nerve altogether, and are in constant dread of something unpleasant going to happen, and they may become scared of doing anything on their own initiative—even scared of going out alone.

They get all kinds of digestive upsets, and the typical IGNATIA hysterical stomach develops, that is to say the child is upset by the simplest food but can digest the most indigestible meal.

Exactly the same kind of contrariness appears when the IGNATIA child gets a bad throat, an acute inflamed throat, and the only relief is from taking something solid, something to press on it, and the pressure relieves it for the time being.

53

These overstressed children get all sorts of disturbances. If they are in any confined place, particularly if there are a lot of people about, they get nervous, distressed, choky, and they are quite liable to faint. But it all keys in with the general picture of nervous stress.

As would be expected in a child of that type, who has been very bright, clever, successful, and is now rather going to bits, she is very apt to blame herself for it.

It is very often a child of poorer parents, who is doing quite well on scholarships, and now cannot do as well as she did. She starts to reproach herself, thinks that the failure is due to lack of effort on her own part, gets thoroughly depressed and almost melancholic.

Linked with the choreic tendency is a liability to get troublesome, irritating, spasmodic coughs, which come on at inconvenient times, and once started go on, and on, and on. That is one type of IGNATIA cough in the stressed child. The other type is a very definite, acute laryngitis, with a tendency to laryngeal spasm.

They are very liable to get rheumatic pains, and may even get acute rheumatism; and most of the rheumatic pains are better from definite firm pressure.

Zincum

The last of these drugs is ZINCUM and one adds it to IGNATIA because of the choreic tendency.

The typical ZINCUM child is very nervous, sensitive and excitable. They are easily distinguished from the IGNATIA children. The IGNATIA child, to begin with, is a very bright, quick reacting child, whereas the typical ZINCUM child has a slow reaction time.

When the IGNATIA children are tired out they may not be able to take things in, they have difficulty in learning, difficulty in remembering, but the ZINCUM children are slow of grasping what is said, slow in answering, and they are much more docile, less unstable than the IGNATIA children.

The ZINCUM child will come for treatment at about the same age, possibly a little older, and will present a history of delayed development. Delayed puberty very often gives the indication for the ZINCUM child.

The impression is that they are tired, mentally and physically—generally weary. And yet they are restless, twitchy, fidgety. When they are tired they get a very persistent, aching pain in the lower cervical region, very often with burning pains going right down the back.

Another feature of these ZINCUM children, particularly the very fidgety ones, is that they are liable to get cramp in bed at night, more often in the hamstring muscles than in the feet.

They are very sensitive to cold, and are always chilly. They get inflamed eyes from exposure to cold. These ZINCUM children have definite thickening of the margins of the lids, chronic blepharitis, and chronic conjunctivitis, and they develop intense photophobia.

They are acutely sensitive to noise, as sensitive as the IGNATIA children, but talking worries them excessively, and if the child is attempting to do any work and anyone is talking in the room it upsets them more than the noise of other children playing.

Also in adults, who are completely exhausted by people talking to them, it is very often a definite lead for ZINCUM.

Another strong indication for ZINCUM is a history of a well-marked, generalised skin eruption in early childhood, and a chorea developing about adolescence.

Many of these ZINCUM children develop an acute hunger about 11 a.m., and they simply bolt their food and their drink.

THE GROUPS